ADVANCE PRAISE

"In FAILURE RULES!, King distills the essence of truly learning from one's challenges and hardships and channeling that energy into making good happen."

—CHRISTIAN PICCIOLINI, ANTI-RACIST ACTIVIST
AND AUTHOR OF *BREAKING HATE*

"Everybody comes to a fork in the road. Maybe this book will help you continue your journey. Life isn't about how many times you hit the canvas; it's about how many times you get up and continue to fight."

—RICK RODRIGUEZ, MASTER BLENDER FOR CAO CIGARS

"Failure is a discipline unto itself; it must guide your decision-making even when you're being bold and taking risks. Just because you may encounter someone who has cheated their way up doesn't mean you should too. Fail upward instead. Integrity is far more appealing than deceitfulness."

—ANDREW WILKOW, HOST OF *WILKOW MAJORITY* ON SIRIUS XM

"The music my band (Agnostic Front) makes is in many ways powered by the valuable lessons of failure and hard times. The music then gives strength to thousands of people worldwide. This book has that same potential, so get into it."

—ROGER MIRET, SINGER FOR AGNOSTIC
FRONT AND AUTHOR OF *MY RIOT*

"If you want to make the most out of your failures and turn your life around, check out FAILURE RULES!"

—JOHN DIXON, AUTHOR OF *PHOENIX ISLAND* AND *DEVIL'S POCKET*, WINNER OF THE BRAM STOKER AWARD

"Fact is, failure became a friend of mine and I let it define me until I learned to leverage my failures as lessons! Read this badass book and learn to do the same because FAILURE RULES!"

—JOSHUA COBURN, MOTIVATIONAL SPEAKER, OWNER OF DISSIDENT CIGARS, AND AUTHOR OF *SHIT THAT NEEDS SAID*

This book is dedicated to all of the strong people in this world who have successfully negotiated failure to create good times.

COPYRIGHT © 2022 ANDREW THORP KING
All rights reserved.

FAILURE RULES!
The 5 Rules of Failure for Entrepreneurs, Creatives, and Authentics

ISBN   978-1-5445-3207-3 *Hardcover*
         978-1-5445-3206-6 *Paperback*
         978-1-5445-3208-0 *Ebook*
         978-1-5445-3204-2 *Audiobook*

CONTENTS

FOREWORD...11
INTRODUCTION...15
DEFINITION OF TERMS..23

FAILURE RULE #1: FAILURE PURIFIES
FAILURE, THE GREAT PURIFIER 35
FIRST, RECOGNIZE WHAT YOU AREN'T MADE FOR 41
PINK SLIP BLESSING...47
LEARN HOW TO STRATEGICALLY WORK FOR FREE (OR FOR LITTLE) 53
FIND YOUR CARL (GAME-CHANGING CONNECTOR)...61
BELIEVE IN THE POWER OF PIVOT POINTS 69
CATCH MOMENTUM, CULTIVATE FLOW STATES, AND PLAN WITH AN INTENT TO ITERATE 77
SEEK OUT THE IMMORTAL AND WRITE YOUR LEGACY EVERY DAY 85
KEEP YOUR ATTACHMENTS INTERNAL...95
ANTICIPATE FAILURE RULE #1 101

FAILURE RULE #2: NOTHING IS SAFE
MIND THE FIRE INSIDE..107
BORN TO LOSE, LIVE TO WIN...117
GLORIFYING SAFETY PRODUCES SHALLOWNESS 123
BEING COMFORTABLE IS OVERRATED...129
CHOOSE THE HARD WAY 137
LEVERAGE CHAOS AS AN IDEA ENGINE..147
WHEN UNLOVED, SING YOUR OWN LOVE SONGS...159
KNOW YOUR OPERATING SYSTEM AND OWN IT...167
MAKE REINVENTION YOUR UTMOST SKILL 173
ALWAYS BE BUILDING SOMETHING (ELSE) FOR YOURSELF.......................179
THE PORTFOLIO OF PURSUITS MINDSET 183
HOW CAN YOU GIVE THE WORLD WHAT FEW OTHERS CAN? 189
BE THE INERTIA 197
ABOVE ALL ELSE, FIND A WAY TO GIVE A DAMN 205
A SOUL ON FIRE IS A SOUL ALIVE 213
DON'T TETHER YOURSELF TO NOTIONS OF PERMANENCE 219
GET USED TO UNSAFE SPACES..225
GET BUSY LIVING...229
THE COSTS OF ALIGNING WITH YOUR CALLING JOURNEY ARE WORTH IT 233
DON'T OUTSOURCE YOUR STORY...239
ALWAYS REMEMBER FAILURE RULE #2 243

FAILURE RULE #3: MONEY IS SPIRITUAL
REJECT BOTH ENVY AND GREED 251
MONEY IS A THANK-YOU NOTE 257
TRANSACTIONS ARE SACRAMENTS 261
LOVE MEANING, NOT MONEY...265
LET DESIRE BE YOUR DRIVER..269
GUARD YOUR INNER SELF 275
LESSONS FROM A PUNK ROCK SON OF A PREACHER MAN....................................281
YOU GET WHAT YOU GIVE 285
UNDERSTAND FAILURE RULE #3...289

FAILURE RULE #4: BUILD YOUR THING ONE AND THING TWO DEPENDENCY (FAILURE PREVENTION)
THE THING ONE AND THING TWO DEPENDENCY 295
THING ONE 297
THE THING TWO ACCOMPLISHMENT ENABLED BY THE THING ONE ACTIVE MODEL...............................301
EMBRACE SACRIFICE AND BE CREATIVE AS YOU BUILD YOUR THING ONE ENABLER PURSUIT(S).. 305
SOMETIMES IT'S SIMPLE 309
THING TWO..313
CALLING ALIGNMENT AND THE DIVINITY OF PURPOSE 315
FROM THE ASHES OF FAILURE TO THE CLARITY OF CALLING................................319
THING TWO IS YOUR UNIQUE SOUL OUTPUT 325
SOMETIMES YOU NEED TO BURN THE CANDLE AT BOTH ENDS..........................329
THING TWO IS DEMOCRATIZED... 333
THING TWO ACHIEVEMENT 339
DON'T SKIP FAILURE RULE #4... 343

FAILURE RULE #5: YOU ARE NOT YOUR FAILURES (IMPRESSION MANAGEMENT)
DETACH FROM THE OPTICS OF FAILURE.. 349
REJECTION IS FUEL..357
READY, FIRE, AIM...363
KNOW WHEN TO BYPASS PERMISSION...369
BANKRUPTCY BLUES 375
WHEN YOU HIT A ROCK, LET IT PUSH YOU INTO A NEW STREAM 379
THE NECESSITY OF SHAME 385
LEARN TO ACCEPT TRAGIC MORAL CHOICE 393
LANDMINE..399
ACCEPT DIVISION IN FAILURE AND STAY GREAT 405
THE POWER OF FAILURE HUMOR 413
BE UNMISTAKABLY AUTHENTIC 421
EVERY DAY YOU CAN RE-SKETCH YOUR LIFE.. 425
DEVELOP BULLDOG TENACITY AND CREATE SOMETHING OUT OF NOTHING........................ 429
YOU ARE HOW YOU DECIDE TO RESPOND TO FAILURE.. 435
TATTOO FAILURE RULE #5 ON YOUR SOUL..441

CONCLUSION 445
THE FAILURE RULES! SOUNDTRACK.. 449
ACKNOWLEDGMENTS 475
ABOUT THE AUTHOR... 481

> *"Hard times create strong men, strong men create good times, good times create weak men, and weak men create hard times."*
>
> —G. MICHAEL HOPF, FROM THE NOVEL *THOSE WHO REMAIN*

FOREWORD

–JOHN JOSEPH, AUTHOR OF *THE PMA EFFECT*, MAY 2021

I graduated from the University of the Streets, New York City. There was a lot of failure in that curriculum. Those failures enforced their rules the hard way. And I learned them.

But it wasn't just my time learning at the University of the Streets that taught me how to battle hard times and serial failures. No, I was immersed in failure from birth. The failure of my father to respect my mother. His abuse and disrespect created a failing home life waiting for me at birth because I was conceived by rape. And then failure continued to entrap me as I was placed in a foster home with scumbags who treated my brother and me as subhuman meal tickets. I was ignored, unloved, and abused emotionally, physically, and sexually. There were no cute picture frames with my smiling face in it hanging up anywhere when I grew up. I was a ghost. Life had failed me from the get-go.

So, since life had failed me colossally, it stands to reason that my devious Enemy Mind would lead me to follow suit and cause me to fail myself. And guess what. It did. I let my Enemy Mind conquer me. I immersed myself into a life of violence, drug use, drug dealing, and every invitation into chaos that the streets would offer me. I've been locked up, homeless, and out of reach. When I sing the song "Hard Times" with my band the Cro-Mags, it ain't some hollow anthem about my girlfriend breaking up with me. My hard times almost got me killed more times than I could even possibly remember.

In reading *Failure Rules!: The 5 Rules of Failure for Entrepreneurs, Creatives, and Authentics,* you'll learn what I know: that hard times can make you. Hard times made me resilient and wise. They showed me the pits of depression and depravity and forced me to muster the will to defeat my Enemy Mind. My hard times taught me to distrust the material world and attach myself to the spirituality of inner life. My hard times motivated me to transform myself into a force for good in this world. Through Positive Mental Attitude (PMA), I've mastered my body through a plant-based diet and disciplined training. I'm fifty-eight years old at the time of this writing, and I still compete regularly in Iron Man competitions. My hard times inform my music with strength and meaning that listeners worldwide have found helpful for over thirty years. I still tour today with my band Bloodclot with no intention of slowing down. Through my writing, I try to inspire readers to conquer life's failures through fitness, nutrition, habits of discipline in all areas of life, and a reliance on keeping their PMA. I've written five books and am only getting started.

This is why I love the failure stories compiled by King in *Failure Rules!* The stories laid out here will give you strength to make your failures rule—like I did—even when you're stuck in the middle of the worst parts of them sucking. To do anything worthwhile and difficult, you have to expect failure. And you have to plan on how you're going to accept, use, and grow from it. The stories in *Failure Rules!* are a handbook for how to engage with your failures wisely. Each case study imparts unique wisdom that will help you in your journey. Whether it's an anecdote about retired Navy SEAL David Goggins, cupcake entrepreneur Gigi Butler, punk rocker Roger Miret, or King's own personal stories, this book will empower you to make your failures rule, especially if you're an entrepreneur, a creative, or someone struggling to live a more authentic life.

Learn how to redirect your life when you fail to conquer your Enemy Mind. Embrace that PMA and learn to love the pain of discipline so that you can push through your failures and prevent yourself from sliding back into the dark valleys of negativity.

Dig into *The 5 Rules of Failure*. Let hard times make you. Conquer your Enemy Mind. And keep that PMA as you discover how to make your failures rule!

johnjosephdiscipline.com

INTRODUCTION

LEARN THE F-WORD

"Make failure your teacher, not your undertaker."
—ZIG ZIGLAR, AUTHOR AND SALESMAN

I lied.

Actually, failure itself doesn't rule.

It sucks.

Failure can ruin lives. Ruin families. Destroy health. Obliterate self-esteem. And launch ripple effects tasted exponentially by those in its extended path.

Failure can plant an unbridled jostling within the heartbeat of your soul. A debilitating stirring that haunts your gut. An anarchic terror that paralyzes your mental capacities.

Failure can freeze your ability to digest food correctly, to make even the smallest of decisions, to exercise, to love, and to be loved.

Let's face it: failure really blows.

I didn't write this book to worship at the twisted altar of self-indulgent, willful failure. There is no lesson, no discovery, and no value in that.

But failure that is unintended, stridently fought against, creatively challenged, and humbly accepted when emerging inevitable, is valuable.

I wrote this book to speak to this type of failure. Failure happens to us all. It has different levels of visitation on each of us. When it comes, we need to revere it.

Before it arrives, we need to plan how we will greet it. In anticipation of it striking, we need to decide ahead of time how we will handle it.

We need to manage our fear of it with reason and strategy.

When it hits us, we will likely only be lowered to the level of our preparedness, not strengthened to rise to the intensity of its challenges. So it behooves us all to prepare for it.

We must never cower to the false gods of stability and security because we have been led to their altars by the affliction of the fear of failure.

And we must fortify our spirits to never let any failure define us. And to never let the impressions our failures may have on others define us.

To do this—to essentially be a failure prepper—it's helpful to study those who have conquered failure and analyze their journeys in advance of our own encounters with the F-word.

We can internalize unique strength by harnessing the lessons others have learned. Lessons that can teach us to either avoid failure or brace ourselves properly to collide into it, when unavoidable, with the *Divinity of Purpose* and meaning.

I say "we" because I include myself in the failure prepper group.

Just as you will discover that I am an enthusiast for entrepreneurialism, fintech (financial technology), fine cigars, good bourbons, hardcore punk rock, spy novels, traditional tattoos, and vigorous weightlifting, you will also come to understand why I am enthusiastic about the transformative value of failure. I am equally passionate for what the hardcore punk band Sheer Terror calls "Standing Up for Falling Down."

In his classic book A *Farewell to Arms*, the quintessential adventurer Ernest Hemingway noted that *"The world breaks everyone and afterward many are strong at the broken places. But those that will not break it kills."*

The world we live in carries a promise of failure to us at some point in our journey. It is inevitable.

Failure broke me repeatedly throughout my adult life. It broke me when I laid flat on my office floor—drunk before noon—on the day I conceded to proceed with filing for bankruptcy. It broke me when I finally peeled myself off of the floor only to then proceed to burn the rest of the afternoon at a strip club—ignoring my internal spiritual attachments in a desperate attempt to reach for some cheap external facsimile of comfort and love. I did this believing the lies of my failure moment—that I could not find real comfort or love elsewhere in the world, at home, or in my relationship with God.

When I had to pack up my family and move—with no job secured in our new destination state—because our home was on the precipice of being foreclosed on, failure broke me. It broke me several times as I had to pivot away from failing businesses. When I had to wait in line at the government building to apply for public assistance, failure broke me. It broke me when my son and I were estranged for many months, and I wasn't really sure if we'd ever find sustainable repair. And failure broke me when I honored my ex-wife's wishes to end our marriage of fourteen years.

I let these experiences appropriately break me so that they would not kill me. Because I did, I became immensely strong at the broken places.

This is why I wrote this book. To encourage you to thoughtfully let failure break you when you encounter it so that it not only does not kill you but makes you stronger than ever at the broken places—like a hydra that doubles its strength when it is harmed. When you learn to be a failure prepper, you will learn how to optimize each new failure that breaks you.

It was during one particularly introspective walk on the beach, which you'll learn about later, that I became convicted to take a deep dive into studying the world of failure. A core business relationship of mine had just failed. My marriage was circling the drain. And I was contending with a fresh batch of uncertainty. This is when ideas for this book began stewing within me.

This stew was violently, passionately, and urgently stirred by the sounds thundering through my earbuds on that beach walk—the sounds of the Cro-Mags and Motorhead. Specifically, the songs "Hard Times" and "Ace of Spades," respectively. Hardcore punk rock has always been a catalyst for driving change in me. You'll learn more about the punk genre of music as you keep reading. It is a theme throughout this book because of the honesty, grit, and wisdom I've harnessed from the genre's music and message.

That day on the beach, those songs invoked urgency and determination within me to commit to study, analyze, and collate my failure stories, my friends' failure stories, and my heroes' failure stories. Those studies revealed common threads, or rules, if you will. Those rules became **Failure Rules!** And the five you are about to learn are really just the beginning.

Along with listening to those two songs on that pivotal beach walk, two books also stuck out to truly fan the flames of momentum in the early writing of this manuscript. Those two books were James Altucher's *Choose Yourself* and Srinivas Rao's *The Art of Being Unmistakable*. *Choose Yourself* reinforced within me my power to rise up out of any failure—whether self-triggered or externally imposed. The *Art of Being Unmistakable* reminded me of the unique DNA of my creative Being and impressed upon me the vastness of distinct potential that lay within me—and all of us. Both books were critical kindling that nurtured the fires that burned to create *The 5 Rules of Failure*.

Embedded within the structure of this book, I've distilled five critical rules for engaging with and thinking about the F-word—most specifically, rules that apply specially to *entrepreneurs, creatives, and authentics*. I recount many of my own personal encounters with the F-word. Business failure. Relationship failure. Intersecting failures. Cascading failures. Like the ones you've already gotten a taste of in this introduction.

I chose to be raw and vulnerable about my failures because I believe that the strength that Hemingway wrote about originates from this space. You get strong at the broken places by looking at them, talking about them, and then putting yourself back together again in a renewed and improved way.

The 5 Rules of Failure is your field manual to help you look at your failures, discuss them with yourself, and guide you into putting yourself back together better on the other side of your failures.

To illustrate the value of *The 5 Rules of Failure*, I also look away from the mirror and peer outwardly to highlight the stories of people within my direct sphere of experience—friends, colleagues, business partners, acquaintances, cigar-smoking buddies—who have crashed and burned with blazing failure and have improvised, overcome, and adapted to emerge from those ashes with renewed and enhanced strength.

One step further, I gaze farther out into the stories of some public figures—historical and contemporary, famous and emerging—who have failed loudly along their mysterious *calling journeys*. Many of these hard-times heroes found their deep meaning by deliberately participating in the creation of positive, impactful, potentially immortal content.

I'll walk you through examples and case studies ranging from Nazi defeater Winston Churchill to punk rock icon Henry Rollins. From the biblical character of Job to failure comic Rodney Dangerfield. From legendary boxer Jack Johnson to political commentator Glenn Beck. From billionaire pantyhose maker Sara Blakely to country music star Toby Keith. From actor Dwayne "The Rock" Johnson to author J.K. Rowling. From podcaster Tim Pool to author Stephanie Land. From astrophysicist Neil deGrasse Tyson to former gang leader Elgin James, among others.

Paired with the numerous case studies you'll also find the peppering of notable quotes by subjects like rocker Lemmy Kilmister of Motorhead, stoic author Ryan Holiday, retired Navy SEAL Jocko Willink, tennis icon Billie Jean King, Rabbi Daniel Lapin, Beat author Jack Kerouac, former Democratic presidential candidate Andrew Yang, economist Adam Smith, hyper-entrepreneur Elon Musk, and ex-gunrunner and former mayor of Key West, Florida, Captain Tony Tarracino. Plus, many more.

These case studies highlight individuals who stepped outside of the circumstances of their failures and dissected, analyzed, and parsed out every bitter and sweet flavor of their failure experiences. They then utilized every instructive, fully nuanced lesson learned to shape their next step in a different way.

In most of these cases, it's clear that an adherence to the *internal spirit voice*—that mysterious voice within all of us that offers us guidance in our directional decisions—is what sets these people apart. This adherence creates strength that moves through failure in a distinct way.

They ignore the noise of normative, dreamless living. Instead, they decisively fuel the inner soul fire to drive their unique quest for living out their authentic path.

The experience and immediate, tangible results of failure suck.

It's the lessons we extract from the hard times of our failures that rule.

They have a way of forging new paths for us that flow into new realms of strength with a distinctly acquired wisdom.

Failure can carve within us the proper character traits needed to rightly handle future success: humility, empathy, discernment, and gratitude.

I did not write this book to attempt to seduce you with some iteration of the authority illusion. While I know failure well, I claim no authority on the subject as an expert. I generally do not trust anyone who claims to be an expert on something. True experts are loathe to identify as such—and their expertise is most marked by a humble acknowledgment that they are always in constant discovery of more expertise. So this is not a book loaded with clear, permanent-marker answers. No one has a patent on the secret sauce of the value of failure. Rather, this is a book of visceral observations, vulnerable recollections, introspective findings, and overarching themes—erasable, malleable, whiteboard stuff. Cherry-pick what is useful to you.

This book does not need to be consumed end to end sequentially. That can work, but feel free to merely take bites ad hoc as you see fit while skimming, should you be so inclined.

This is also not a book intended to moralize with an imposition of indisputable proverbs. Any lesson herein is one take, captured within one slice of contemplative time and codified for any who value it.

Ralph Waldo Emerson was right: "*A foolish consistency is the hobgoblin of little minds.*" With this truth operative, this book must be consistently contextualized, rescrutinized, reapplied with modification, and freshly imbibed with a chaser of newfound comprehension. As time goes on, I suspect that even I will read words written herein and decide I've evolved, changed, or enhanced my thinking on them.

In regard to the value within this text that proves to hold up over time and through applied critique, such value will be as much for my benefit and instruction as for the reader's—as I will need to refer to these rules and stories again and again, far into my future, to remind me who I am and how I need to remain oriented. My failures will surely extend to my own reasonable ability to consistently adhere to the very rules of failure I've identified.

So if you're new at getting knocked down and pushed around by failures as you step out as an entrepreneur, as a creative seeker of the truth, or as an individual living authentically, then open your ears to your *internal spirit voice*.

See beyond the optics and urgent pull of failure's immediate mess and pick at the good stuff left in the rubble.

Let hard times make you. Learn the F-word.

Because as you follow *The 5 Rules of Failure* and move forward into success, you'll find that after it sucks, **Failure Rules!**

DEFINITION OF TERMS

WHAT ARE YOU TALKING ABOUT?

As you immerse yourself in the stories that prove the merits of *The 5 Rules of Failure*, you may stumble across terms that feel like tripwires. The intent is certainly not to trip you—the valued reader—as you snack on these important failure stories.

No, the intent is to introduce you to new ways of thinking about the failures that touch your life and the choices you have as you encounter them. In this, there are many terms—*some invented, some more broadly known, and some directly borrowed from and attributable to others*—for which it behooves me to explain and define below in order to lubricate the comprehension of your reading.

1. **Failure.** The term *failure* is used within this text in the broadest possible manner, inclusive of the cumulative events of tragedy, struggle, and hard times that intertwine with the myriad realities of the human condition and inclusive both of avoidable failures that strike as a result of mistakes, misjudgments, and dereliction and unavoidable failures that visit us by virtue of uncontrollable circumstances, the actions of others, and the ramifications of larger, macro events in the seen and unseen worlds.

2. **Success.** The term success is used within this text as a measure of someone being in alignment with their *calling journey*. It does not correlate to a customary understanding of worldly success attached to the optics of stability, comfort, recognizable prestige, or mea-

surable financial wealth. The *success* referred to within the text may carry any or all of these qualities as a byproduct, but these qualities are not necessary for it to manifest. *Success* is only valued within this text as an indicator of someone fulfilling the promptings of their *internal spirit voice* and joining with the mysterious, tumultuous meaning of their *calling journey*. Therefore, it is possible that someone can be mired within the chaos of an extreme failure moment and simultaneously submerged within a profound *success* moment due to the ability for failure to pull someone succinctly into the current of their *calling journey*.

3. **Entrepreneur.** The term *entrepreneur* is used in this text to widely apply to a mindset rather than an achieved status of measurable ownership. Within the lessons of **The 5 Rules of Failure**, an entrepreneur is anyone who approaches their work life with an intentional sense of ownership, whether they founded, purchased, or simply work for an organization. The entrepreneur is one who seeks to impose their imprint on all their work and shape it into something that becomes a distinguished product of their unmistakable uniqueness.

4. **Entre-Employee.** *Entre-employee* is a term used by personal finance guru Dave Ramsey to describe one who approaches their work as a W-2 employee with the same sort of inventive mindset and ownership mentality that an entrepreneur with equity or a founder exhibits. The term is used in the same manner within this text.

5. **Solopreneur.** *Solopreneur* is used in this text to refer to one who runs a business who does not require and will not require any employees. In the digital age, this is often an online business that sustains itself through leveraging third-party vendors and strategic partners rather than direct employees. The *solopreneur* seeks a simplified business model that reduces the need for scaled human resource and physical office infrastructure. This business model is typically empowered by what Naval Ravikant calls the permissionless leverage of code and media. This type of leverage creates wealth without a heavy

reliance on labor and capital and allows one to make money while they sleep. *Solopreneur* is also the frequent entrepreneurial modality for artists monetizing their work.

6. **Creative** *(noun)*. The label of a *creative* is used within this text as a noun to refer to an artist in a very broad sense. A creative is anyone who feels compelled to create artistic output, with or without the intent to monetize, simply because their *internal spirit voice* urges them to do so. The artistic output of a creative can take numerous forms—writing, music, visual art, technical creation, business ideation, entrepreneurial invention, etc.

7. **Authentic** *(noun)*. The term *authentic* is used in this book's title and within its text as a noun that describes one who manifests their *Being* in the world in a way that is congruent with their true inner self. Striving to be an *authentic* is a goal that requires a spectrum perspective, as identifying the nature of your inner self is a moving target and attempting to manifest it accurately in the world is just as fluid and difficult. Hence, an *authentic* strives to be one with their inner self as much as is possible. An *authentic* will experience varying degrees of success on the authenticity spectrum depending on the fluid nature of variable circumstances.

8. **Internal Spirit Voice.** The term *internal spirit voice* is used prolifically throughout this text and is core to the understanding of **The 5 Rules of Failure**. The term is used to attempt to describe the elusive, ethereal voice within all of us that guides us through consequential decision points related to our *calling journey*. I believe we all have an *internal spirit voice* beckoning us to listen to its urgings in moments of high- and low-stakes decision-making. The nature and source of the *internal spirit voice* is something for everyone to attempt to trace. For me, I recognize it as an expression of the divine that is installed uniquely within each of us at our origination in the womb.

9. **Calling Journey.** The term *calling journey* is used as a key concept within the text. It refers to a calling of one's life that is plural,

multifaceted, and not dependent on a singular outcome, purpose, or manifestation. A *calling journey* refers to the totality of one's tapestry of purposes that are uniquely presented to everyone to appropriate, or not, based on how they utilize their free will and obey or ignore the promptings of their *internal spirit voice*.

10. **Divinity of Purpose.** The term *Divinity of Purpose* was coined by Jamey Jasta, the singer of the metal band Hatebreed, in the song that bears it as its title. The term is used in the song to describe the divinity found in the power of harnessing a sense of purpose to lift one out of dire circumstances, deep depression, and hopeless despair. The term is used similarly throughout the text here to refer to the power that harnessed purpose carries in helping you unite the voice of your *internal spirit voice* with your actions in pursuing congruence with your *calling journey*.

11. **Portfolio of Pursuits.** The term *Portfolio of Pursuits* is used liberally throughout the text to describe a mindset that seeks to diversify its sources of both income and fulfillment. One who carries a *Portfolio of Pursuits* mindset does so to ensure income redundancy to guard against an unsafe economic world and fulfillment redundancy to guard against the risk of future meaning deficits.

12. **Being.** The word *Being* is capitalized intentionally throughout the text. Psychoanalyst and author Dr. Jordan Peterson is known for capitalizing the word *Being* to connote the divine individuality inherent in each human Being. The term is used similarly within the stories that bolster the validity of **The 5 Rules of Failure**.

13. **VUCA (Volatility, Uncertainty, Complexity, Ambiguity).** The acronym VUCA is a widely used business term that describes market environments that are difficult to navigate because they are volatile, uncertain, complex, and ambiguous. A leader or investor can attempt to proactively hedge against each of these conditions. Within this text, however, the term VUCA is used to describe the individual work conditions and environment of a leader or individ-

ual contributor, not necessarily a market environment. While VUCA is typically seen as negative in a market environment, within the conditions of one's work environment, this text views those conditions as positive. A VUCA work environment is seen as positive because such conditions draw out the highest abilities of analysis, critical thinking, intense performance, and contributive value by one forced to work in it.

14. **Carl Moment.** I invented the term *Carl Moment* for specific use in this text. Its origins are described in the text by illustrating the profound impact meeting one influencer, breakthrough connector, or mentor can have on creating a strong pivot point in one's *calling journey* discovery. Carl was the name of one such connector in my own *calling journey* story.

15. **Wabi-Sabi.** The term *wabi-sabi* is an ancient Japanese term that originates from Buddhism and refers to the beauty of something that is imperfect and incomplete in nature. It stems from a worldview that acknowledges the imperfection of *Being* and of the natural world. David Lee Roth, rocker and ex-front man of Van Halen, describes the meaning of *wabi-sabi* as something that is perfect *"because it's a little fucked up."* The term is used most closely to Roth's definition within this text.

16. **Thing One.** The term *Thing One* is most associated with a character in *The Cat in the Hat* by Dr. Seuss. My use of the term in this text has nothing to do with Dr. Seuss's character. I use the term to describe a condition, pursuit, income source, business, or employment scenario that acts as a strategic key enabler to bring one closer to a higher-purposed North Star pursuit that most aligns them with the strongest fulfillment of their *calling journey*.

17. **Thing Two.** The term *Thing Two* is also most associated with a character in *The Cat in the Hat* by Dr. Seuss. My use of this term in the text also has nothing to do with Dr. Seuss's character. I use the term to describe a piece of one's *calling journey* that represents the

highest meaning, most unique manifestation, and most notable accomplishment (North Star). One can have more than one *Thing Two* within the totality of their *calling journey*.

18. **Safetyphile.** The term *safetyphile* is used in this text to describe someone who is irrationally attached to preserving safety within their personal and work life above all other motivators and values. The *safteyphile* loves safety more than meaning, purpose, maximized prosperity, and other people.

19. **Born To Lose, Live to Win.** The term *Born to Lose, Live to Win* is most commonly associated with the late rocker Lemmy Kilmister of the British band Motorhead, who used the phrase as part of the band's branding and ethos. Generally, it is expressed to describe one's disposition in the world in which the odds are stacked against them and losing is the most logically predicted outcome. Yet the individual decisively determines to act and live in a way that defies this disposition by seeking to win on their own terms despite the odds. The references to this mindset are used similarly within the text as an antidote to failure.

20. **Tragic Moral Choice.** This is a term that my father often spoke of to describe difficult decision points that bubble up in our lives in which there is no good option and no option that does not cause pain, harm, or tragedy. In these situations, the challenge is to rightly discern the option of least harm and decisively live in peace after pursuing that option. The term is used as such within this text.

21. **PMA (Positive Mental Attitude).** The acronym *PMA*, for me, is most notably associated with the song "Attitude" by the legendary Rastafarian hardcore punk band Bad Brains. Bad Brains adopted the concept from the literary works of American author Napoleon Hill, who wrote classic books, such as *Success Through a Positive Mental Attitude* and *Think and Grow Rich*. The term represents a deliberate approach to life that chooses a positive mental attitude, as much as possible, in all circumstances. The term is used in the same manner within the text.

22. **Failure Humor.** The term *failure humor* is used in this text to refer to cathartic, self-deprecating humor that makes light of life's failures and leverages comedy to highlight insights, strength, and lessons extracted from failure.

23. **Placism.** The term *placism* was invented by businessman and author Chris Gardner. It is used to describe bias and prejudice against those whose circumstances are temporarily negative, enshrouded in poverty, plagued with chaos, or otherwise situated at a socioeconomic disadvantage. *Placism* is often projected onto those who are struck with, working through, or recovering from failure. The text uses the term in the same manner that Chris Gardner does.

24. **Third Door.** The term *Third Door* was invented by author and motivational speaker Alex Banayan and is the title of his bestselling book. The term refers to the opportunity path that is achieved by creatively circumventing the widely accepted paths of the First Door (privileged access granted only to the connected) and the Second Door (the long line; the narrow, rarely accessed point of entry extended to the great unwashed masses). The *Third Door* is entered by plotting, scheming, and forging your own entrance into an opportunity. The text uses this term mostly as a verb to describe the act of creating a *Third Door* into an opportunity.

25. **TCB (Taking Care of Business).** As you may know, the acronym TCB is primarily attributable to Elvis Presley. Along with his backing band in the '70s being known as the TCB Band, Elvis himself personally held the concept of TCB dear to his soul as an identifying ethos of his life. Elvis wore various gold jewelry with the TCB emblem that included the signature lightning bolt to put the "flash" in *"Taking Care of Business in a Flash."* In **Failure Rules!** the acronym TCB is similarly used to mark a mentality that rises to the necessary hustles of an authentic entrepreneurial life in a flash. I have a TCB tattoo across my left wrist to remind me to harness this ethos as I work each day to further unite myself with my *calling journey* of mysterious meaning.

26. **Adjacent Possible.** The term *adjacent possible* is a key concept in Steven Johnson's book *Where Good Ideas Come From*. It is also a term widely invoked by entrepreneur and billionaire Sir Richard Branson. The core meaning of the term is that innovation and the evolution of invention, growth, and ideation starts with pushing to the edges of what is known today until you creep into what is possible tomorrow. In business and art, the *adjacent possible* is the notion that what you are creating or doing now is surrounded by all kinds of possible mutations that you can stretch into as you grow. These mutations are only visible as you lean into your business, your creative endeavor, or your exploratory ideation. The *adjacent possible* becomes visible and actionable as you progress along your *calling journey* and push yourself into new realms of interest and discovery. This is the spirit in which the term is used within this text.

FAILURE RULE #1
FAILURE PURIFIES

"The phoenix must burn to emerge."
—JANET FITCH, AUTHOR OF *WHITE OLEANDER*

PRINCIPLE: Failure burns off the areas of our lives that can gain from being reimagined, reconfigured, and reconstructed. Failure removes external entanglements that accumulate in our lives that mute our *internal spirit voice* so we can have an opportunity to hear it clearly and fall into the current of our *calling journey*. Failure strips us of inefficient foundations so we can create new ones that will serve us better as we move forward into the fullness of authentic living. Failure turns our attention inward by disassembling what is outward so we can restore the audacity, vision, and courage we need to actionably invoke our *Divinity of Purpose*. Failure purifies us so we can rise with renewed strength colored by the value of pain.

FAILURE, THE GREAT PURIFIER

"From the ashes, a fire shall be woken, a light from the shadows shall spring."
—J.R.R. TOLKIEN, AUTHOR OF *THE HOBBIT*
AND *THE LORD OF THE RINGS*

> **LESSON:** Failure purifies us, burns off the waste we have accumulated, and reveals the essence of our Being.

There are many strains of failure that can happen. They are not all avoidable. They are not all self-imposed. Some failure—the general experiential failure synonymous with the mere participation in the human condition—simply occurs to us or around us or enshrouds our circumstances without consulting our will and without ratification.

It is this type of failure—contained within **Failure Rule #1: *Failure Purifies***—that J.R.R. Tolkien, the father of high fantasy, knew well during his time serving with the British army in World War I. Most of his school friends had been killed in the war. Almost his entire battalion had been wiped out by the fighting. Had it not been for his own health problems and his subsequent periodic removals from the battlefield, Tolkien himself would have likely been killed. Tolkien's health issues, including a bout with trench fever, eventually found him weak, emaciated, and out of combat for good. During this time, he sought recovery and solace while staying at a cottage in the Little Haywood, Staffordshire, area of England.

It was in the ashes of his war-torn emaciation, nestled in the respite cottage of Staffordshire, that Tolkien's fire awoke, and light sprung from the shadows of the physical failures that war had imposed upon his Being. That fire was the action he took to begin writing *The Book of Lost Tales,* which was an attempt to create a mythology for England with its first installment titled *The Fall of Gondolin.* Tolkien never completed the project. Nonetheless, its incomplete drafting represented the imaginative awaking of the literary fire inside that was born in the ash-laden state left by the fire of war-imposed health failures. It was this purification by failure that created the circumstances in which Tolkien was able to ignite a new fire of meaningful output. This fire endured and would mutate and grow over the years into an unmistakable body of work to be studied for generations to come.

Tolkien's forced respite at the cottage in Little Haywood was a consequence of the general experiential failure synonymous with the mere participation in the human condition. Whether we like it or not, war is a symptom of deep-rooted failures in the human condition, and it has always punctuated life on earth. Sickness, like Tolkien's struggle with trench fever, is also a perennial force of failure attached to the human condition. The failure forces of war and sickness enshrouded Tolkien's life without his consent. And then those failure forces purified him.

Real failure is the great purifier. No matter what strain of failure befalls you, if it is real failure, it will strip you down to your true essence. In real failure, your old reliances, false assumptions, unworthy allegiances, and foolish attachments will disappear. Real failure will leave you empty enough to hear the quiet whisper of your *internal spirit voice* inside. Amid this emptiness, this voice will amplify into instructive audible clarity. It will urge you to take an unflinching assessment of the full depth of your own resourcefulness. **True, devastating, game-changing, full-blown failure will scorch the earth of your comfort. It will blaze through the garbage that entangles you with cleansing flames of truth.**

In 2013, my ex-wife and I began our divorce path by permanently separating. This was a fast-follow to a business divorce I had just gone through. It was when I found myself living alone in a hotel room with no office to report to by day and no family to come home to at night that the lights I needed to see sprung from the shadows.

It was in feeling the oppression of the shadow of war and being rendered medically unfit to further contend with its power, that J.R.R. Tolkien was able to see the lights spring from the shadows, revealing a new purpose for his life.

If you're walking through any strain of failure, take note of what extraneous rubbish is being torched off of you. You may realize that much of it needed to burn for you to move forward into your *calling journey*. As you persist through failure, keep your eyes wide open for new light to spring from the shadows. It is this new light—illuminated to prominence by the absence of the burned garbage lying in the ashes of your failure experience—that will guide you toward the next lighthouse along your calling voyage.

When you are at the burnt end of failure's purification, you can take true inventory of what remains and what has existed unseen all along. If you accept this purification with submission, you'll be able to take a true assessment of your applicable skills, useful compounded knowledge, aggregate physical and financial resources, and intangible spiritual and mental strengths. In the cleansed state of emptiness produced by failure's burning, you have an opportunity to finally see your Being clearly without the normal constraint biases colored by a high fidelity to security.

Real failure teaches you to find jewels disguised as dirty pebbles.

Real failure gives you eyes to see the unseen.

Real failure will teach you to isolate every line item of your financial, material, spiritual, and emotional life and make granular changes and adjustments that normal circumstances would never encourage you to do.

When you are stripped of all other encumbrances, you can discover the ability, courage, and audacity to transform the intangible, spiritual nature of ideas and animate them into real, material, robust realities.

These new realities are the fires that awaken from the ashes of failure. Your fire might be a unique business plan that blends cumulative lessons learned into a crystallized vision. The fire might rise from dormant and hidden skillsets now resurrected and repurposed toward wholly new and engaging opportunities. Your fire might ignite you to leverage underestimated relationships for brand-new partnerships and collaborations. Or, like Tolkien, your fire may nudge you to respond to long-muzzled creative impulses and follow them diligently for the first time.

After it sucks, one of the ways in which *Failure Rules!* is in how it can teach you the spirituality of ideas and imagination. Failure, if metabolized wisely, can help you master the art of converting dreams into material realities of reinvention.

Speak, craft, and push your intangible ideas into tangible existence.

Whether you're an entrepreneur, a creative, or a person pursuing an authentic life, to follow *The 5 Rules of Failure,* you need to learn to overcome paralysis when you see fences of material and circumstantial restriction erected along your path. It is in the abyss of failure that you can often best learn to harness your spiritual ability to build imaginative trampolines that catapult you over fences of doubt into the path of your mysterious, tumultuous *calling journey.*

This is where it all starts: in failure's ashes. This is where the rules begin: in the purification of failure's burn. This is where the fire awakens under the wings of the rising phoenix. This is where the lights emerging from the shadows make themselves known.

The phoenix must burn to emerge.

Learn **Failure Rule #1:** *Failure Purifies.*

Welcome to failure. Welcome to the great purifier.

FIRST, RECOGNIZE WHAT YOU AREN'T MADE FOR

"*I believe every human has a finite number of heartbeats. I don't intend to waste any of mine.*"

—NEIL ARMSTRONG, ASTRONAUT, AERONAUTICAL ENGINEER, AND FIRST MOFO TO EVER WALK ON THE MOON

> **LESSON:** Eliminate all of the clear "hell no" realities of your life to more precisely chase your "hell yes" pursuits.

Sometimes **Failure Rule #1: *Failure Purifies*** teaches you its truth by exposing you to the wrong way—a "hell no" path. It does this so you can be purified by that dead-end, red-light failure. Then you can better recognize the next right way to your *calling journey*—that solid "hell yes" green light.

I came home from my honeymoon in 1999 to a pink slip. I was newly married, very young, scared of adult life and about to naively start a marriage relationship with absolutely no financial foundation. I was stripped to my core. This new empty space forced me to look inward and upward to identify what was really inside. I was able to see clearly enough to choose what I found there instead of what might be lurking in my external peripheral view.

My wife at the time did not work, except very part time, cleaning houses for cash under the table. Luckily, our expenses were low. Even still, I found myself staring into the same abyss of uncertainty and confusion that I had been peering dead into since the day I graduated cum laude from college, not even knowing what the hell cum laude meant as I accepted my degree.

This abyss illuminated my ongoing struggle to answer the same old questions that many people ask themselves many times over the course of their existence:

What the hell am I going to do with my life?

Why the hell am I even here?

What is my calling?

What exactly is a calling, and what does that even mean?

Is a calling something I'm endowed with by God or just a manifestation of my own ever-changing human yearnings, dreams, and interpretations of my highest usefulness in the world?

At the time, all I knew for damn sure was what my calling wasn't: to be a bill collector. My *internal spirit* voice was shouting an emphatic "hell no!"

I instinctively knew my calling couldn't have been to collect on past due auto loans. It couldn't have been to accept being tethered to the phone, dialing and smiling on the outside and drowning and dying on the inside. It couldn't have been to coordinate with repo men to snatch debtors' cars from them while they were at work. It couldn't have been to sit in an office guarded by bulletproof glass designed to protect me from enraged debtors looking to exact revenge with a firearm on the cubicle monkey who made the call to order their repo. It couldn't possibly have been to sit in a cubicle wearing Dockers for the rest of my life, struggling to exercise my give-a-shit muscle and pretending to have even an iota of interest in sitting still, tucking in my shirt, and playing nice with low-level recurring tasks.

No, being a collections rat for Ford Credit and conforming to low-level office culture did not feel like a good foothold into my calling—whatever I thought it might look like at the time.

I would learn many years later, working in banking, the utility and practical value in the right cubicle job. If it carries meaning, trajectory, and the right mix of circumstances and strategic benefits, a cubicle job may be a key piece of a vibrant *calling journey*.

But back in 1999, none of those indicators existed. This cubicle job showed no signs of meaning, trajectory, or calling-enabling benefits. I was living a scene from the movie *Office Space* every day. Despite the practical fears it induced, I was happy inside when the proverbial Bobs came in and included me in their layoffs. The anesthetized cubicle automaton life was entirely anathema to everything I was.

My healthy rejection of this experience proved in time to be a useful catalyst. The cut leash of the pink slip helped ignite new fires inside within a few short months. Retired Navy SEAL and subject of the film *Lone Survivor* Marcus Luttrell commented on the *Joe Rogan Experience* podcast, *"The first forty years of your life you're just trying to figure out what you aren't."* He's right.

Sometimes the best place to start is to recognize what you aren't meant to do—anymore.

Then, leverage that revelation as a contrasting motivation to somehow move toward discovering what you are meant to do next to fall into your *calling journey*. Because that's what your calling is: a journey. It's not a singular future event, accomplishment, or status acquisition. It's a dynamic journey that, when followed, carries maximum meaning in its diverse experiences and impact. It achieves that meaning by aligning with the pulsating rhythms of your *internal spirit voice*. This is the voice that ever seeks to connect the integrity of your internal Being with the manifestation of your external Being.

This is all important because Neil Armstrong was right. Our time on earth is limited. We are all mortal—despite how much effort Silicon Valley billionaires invest in raging against the dying of the light in their exploration of immortality schemes.

We all have a finite number of heartbeats.

Neil Armstrong did not waste any of his heartbeats. He focused on the path of his *calling journey* and blinded himself to all distractions early on. His *internal spirit voice* beckoned him to a unique path of ascension and achievement foreign to me, and likely anyone who reads this. He served as a naval aviator. He worked as an engineer. He spent time as a test pilot. Then, his *calling journey* unfolded more into its fullness as he became an astronaut. In this, he performed the first successful docking of two vehicles in space. This wild, strangely linear *calling journey* culminated in Armstrong being the spacecraft commander for *Apollo 11*. On this, he commanded the first manned lunar landing mission ever. And then he walked on the moon.

My *calling journey* has not been linear, logically clear, or easy to interpret. My *calling journey* is not one that will likely ever garner me the unique spot in the history of humanity that Armstrong's has. Maybe yours will. I don't want to sell you short. And you certainly shouldn't sell yourself short either. However, for most of you reading this, I reckon it will likely take shape like a zigzag or a roller coaster. It will likely detour interestingly, frighteningly, and with dashes of enlightenment emerging incrementally, before the fullness of its impact and fulfillment unfolds with momentum.

As you struggle to hear your *internal spirit voice* guide you into alignment with your *calling journey*, remember Neil Armstrong. Remember you have a limited number of heartbeats. Do not allow yourself to accept for too long the numbing comfort that comes with stops at temporary way stations along your *calling journey* path. If, like me collecting on auto loans, you find yourself at a job or a circumstantial junction that you know is not in alignment with your *calling journey,* find your way out to the next step.

You may not know exactly where your *calling journey* is taking you. Sometimes it takes longer stretches of time before you find your "hell yes" pursuits. Armstrong knew his path with uncommon precision, and he pursued it with equally uncommon competency and focus. Don't be discouraged if you don't enjoy such clarity. Instead, be on guard. Recognize what you aren't made for—the "hell no" pursuits. Know that this is part of submitting to **Failure Rule #1:** *Failure Purifies.* Identify those jobs, relationships, circumstances, and trappings that emerge as cumbersome roadblocks along your mysterious, unraveling *calling journey* path. Then find a way to move out of them. Shed them as quickly as they are identified, if you safely can. Let them burn quickly into the ashes of experimental failure.

Remember **Failure Rule #1:** *Failure Purifies.* Rise up, out, and away from those empty stops like a purified phoenix. Do this by taking time to hear your *internal spirit voice* and letting it guide you.

Your heartbeats are finite and precious. Don't waste them.

PINK SLIP BLESSING

"Getting laid off was one of the worst things that ever happened to me. But it led to the best results."
—THOMAS SMALLWOOD, PROFESSIONAL TEN-PIN BOWLER AND THREE-TIME WINNER OF THE PBA TOUR

> **LESSON:** The benefits of failure's purification are not immediate or obvious; you need foresight and patience to recognize them.

Remember Failure Rule #1: *Failure Purifies.*

Sometimes it is the external force of a failing set of circumstances that purifies. When it hits, you must step back and remind yourself that purification is part of the process for all of failure's myriad modalities.

When I got the pink slip in 1999, I was relieved. I hated that job. I chose to do it only for utilitarian and financial reasons. Reasons that had temporary value but did nothing for the development of meaning in my work life. Prior to taking the job at Ford Credit, I had been seeking maximum meaning in my life. This took the form of competing in a bodybuilding competition while learning the integrity of hard blue-collar labor as I worked swing shifts at a steel plant. Then I moved on to singing in a hardcore punk band, writing for music magazines, and doing social work by helping juvenile delinquents integrate back into their communities after being released from lockup.

It was this last piece, helping at-risk kids, that got me into debt. The job didn't pay. Yet, I felt I needed to do it for as long as I could because I believed I was making meaningful impact in the lives of some of the kids. Also, my empathy muscle was growing daily through this experience, and I knew this would enhance my spiritual strength as I walked through life. I augmented my income with working as a bouncer at a local bar that featured live music. But it still left me short. As the relationship with my ex-wife continued to develop and we became engaged to be married, I knew I had to move on and deal with the debt that had crept into my life.

So I took the cubicle-monkey job, and starting on day one, I prayed, schemed, and dreamed about leaving the way station that was that job. I couldn't wait to get back on the highway of my *calling journey*. The pink slip and its burning power enabled me to get back on that road again.

It felt like spiritual suicide at the time. Every new day locked in the cubicle jail of meaningless monotony killed me just a little bit. I knew I had to get out of there as soon as I could before I succumbed to the full extinguishment of my spirit's fire.

Now, looking back, I know that it was a piece of my work history tapestry that was necessary and useful across time. Because, as you learned in the previous chapter, sometimes you need to first fully recognize, with the full width of your soul, what you aren't made for. Sometimes it is from this stripped-down, baseline position that you can best visualize the path of your *calling journey*.

When circumstances make your life choices for you, you need to allow that deposition to bring you into clarity. You need to lean in and find a way to instead choose your own circumstances as you claw your way forward.

Your calling isn't a singular destination. Your calling is your entire work-life journey and all that is woven within you throughout each pivotal inflection point. It's the cumulative byproduct of all that you have experienced, accumulated into your spirit, and internalized into your evolving self. Your calling is a living, breathing narrative that spins off of you throughout your entire work-life story.

Those who maximize the essence of their calling instinctively harbor an ever-critical consciousness that never accepts anything as a destination. Instead, they view every developing mutation as a new layer of their unfolding calling mystery.

Being periodically stripped of everything by the instructive scrape of failure can often be a crucial part of the journey of one's calling.

Professional ten-pin bowler Thomas Smallwood understands this.

Smallwood knew that his *calling journey* included professional bowling. As he worked to find alignment with this piece of his *calling journey*, he also knew he had to have a steady paycheck if he was ever going to get his now-wife Jennifer to marry him. So instead of working the lanes to knock down pins, he began working the lines of production at GM's Pontiac East Assembly plant. Like me at Ford Credit, Smallwood knew how to remain practical while also listening to his *internal spirit voice*.

With a wife and one young child, Smallwood got his pink-slip blessing from GM two days before Christmas. Of course, it didn't feel like a blessing at the time.

The purification of failure never feels like a blessing in the heat of its arrival.

Smallwood diligently pursued looking for another job over the following two months. But nothing was hitting. In parallel, he also continued to adhere to the whispering of his *internal spirit voice* calling him to the lanes. He scraped together $1,500 and attended the PBA (Professional Bowlers Association) tour trials. He finished third. This catapulted him to the top-eight echelons of bowlers who earned the PBA exemption for the 2009–2010 season. Shortly after this accomplishment, GM called him and offered him his job back. But Smallwood had already pulled out of that way station. He was already firmly back rolling on the highway of his *calling journey*. So he told them that he had to decline the job offer because he had become a professional bowler. He then advised them that he would be on ESPN that Sunday, should they care to watch. You can get a deeper flavor of Smallwood's journey by watching the CBS comedy *How We Roll* based on his story and featuring actor and comedian Pete Holmes playing Smallwood.

Sometimes what feels like the worst thing that has ever happened to you can lead to the best results.

When I lost the cubicle job, I was scared. It felt like a colossal kick in the balls after having just returned from my honeymoon. Yet the result was that I was more clearly able to act on the promptings of my *internal spirit voice*. With the obstruction of the job having been burned out of my life by the failure imposition of external circumstances, I could hear the promptings clearly. In listening to the *internal spirit voice*, I was forced to act on a desire I had been managing and teasing for quite some time. I wanted to start an independent record label. The blessed pink slip enabled the ignition of this dream.

Having graduated with an English degree and wanting to be involved somehow in the music industry, I had been writing for music magazines for pretty much nothing. It was a start. It allowed me to be involved in the music that held my deepest passion—underground punk rock and hardcore music. Pivoting from writing for music magazines to making a go at creating an independent record label was a natural next step. The pink-slip blessing gave me space to activate this bubbling, latent ambition. My ambition was finally freed from the circumstantial and psychological suppression of the heroin of mediocre stability—the entry-level office job.

I have a friend who made a series of ethical mistakes when he worked as a pharmacist. He endured the academic rigor to get his license. He jumped through all the hoops to make him successful in that field. But greed steered him into the chaos of due consequence, and he ended up serving five years in prison for some acts of bad judgment.

Many would crumble in the grips of a failure that carried such devastating consequences. But if you let it, failure is the great purifier. My friend embraced the purification of his failure. He allowed his rehabilitation to reshape him. He found a way to enable continuity of income to his family while he did his time. He followed the remaining narrow path of options that aligned him with his *calling journey*. Before he went to prison, he owned a singular cigar store that was just a side hustle. Once locked up, it became his only income source. After he was released from the joint, and as he moved through and out of the consequences of his failure, he then opened several other cigar stores. He adopted his management of them as his new full-time career.

I remember talking to his accountant about him once. His accountant had remarked how he had never seen anyone face such threatening circumstances and handle them with such humility and correction. He described my friend as one of the most inspiring clients he had ever had. My friend's deliberate failures of ethics issued him a pink slip for his career as a pharmacist. Yet in his recognition of the purification of failure, my friend converted that pink slip into a blessing. He now expresses gratitude every day because he gets to spend time with people enjoying the finer things in life instead of listening to sick people complain all day in long lines. We all have different *calling journeys*, and my friend aligned with his through the fiery purge of ethical failure.

When failure collides into you and you feel like it is the worst thing that ever happened to you, try to remember its purifying power. Find space to hear your *internal spirit voice* **remind you to pursue its bold promptings. Open yourself to hearing the** *internal spirit voice* **assure you that you have nothing to lose except future regret—the regret of never trying.**

When I took great risk to create my first record label in the midst of unemployment, it was the fear of future regret that gave me the strength to follow through. Learning to act to prevent future regret is the most valuable practice that I've mastered in my life. To this day, there is not one pursuit that has burned inside of me that I've not chased. Many failed. Some succeeded. Most did a healthy amount of both. But I've chased them all until full satiation was achieved. Then I moved to the next. This has produced the deepest satisfaction.

Find the blessing in failure's purification, and create space to hear your *internal spirit voice*. Eliminate future regret as you align your next steps into the mysterious tumult of your *calling journey*.

LEARN HOW TO STRATEGICALLY WORK FOR FREE (OR FOR LITTLE)

"In most every business, you learn by doing. The apprenticeship model is much more effective than the classroom for cultivating entrepreneurs."

—ANDREW YANG, ENTREPRENEUR, FORMER LAWYER, FOUNDER OF THE FORWARD PARTY, AND 2020 DEMOCRATIC PRESIDENTIAL CANDIDATE

> **LESSON:** Accumulating knowledge, gathering experience, and building relationships are more valuable than compensation when entering a new space.

When you have a vision for what you believe will fulfill you in the next step of your *calling journey,* immediate compensation is not your highest value. Finding that foothold into your space's larger ecosystem is your highest concern. Developing your depth of skill and honing the instincts of flow within your space is paramount. This often means you need to take thoughtful risks in how you enter your space. This often means you need to be creative, willing to lean in without pay, and willing to struggle to find that crack in the space's ecosystem that will let you in and get a grip onto some trajectory. As you do this, accept the imperfection of such an approach. Accept that it will necessarily include failure as part of its process. Embrace these failures with a full understanding of **Failure Rule #1:** *Failure Purifies.*

When I launched Thorp Records, I knew I had no idea what I was really doing. I knew I had to dive in and find some sort of foothold to give me an initial knowledge transfer. I needed a mentor or two, even if they were flawed and only moderately successful.

First, I found someone willing to give me some of his time and explain what he knew. He helped walk me through the mechanics of my initial few record releases. I began aggressively shadowing him. I bombarded him with questions. While on unemployment and looking for a full-time job, I'd drive to his office on my days off from delivering pizza for cash under the table. I'd spend the entire day working for free and learning anything I could. The smart moves and the failures. The disciplines and the derelictions. I begged him for other contacts to network with. I'd reach out to his rolodex and pull each thread of their collective stories. He gave me contract templates. I'd study, modify, and enhance them over time. That initial agreement template would evolve over the decades to blend into the right secret sauce for deals that worked for me, with various iterations for different engagements on over one hundred recording agreements. I learned the financials. I studied the marketing. I analyzed the branding and aesthetics.

Most of what I learned from my first mentor was bad advice that ultimately failed. But it was a great leap forward in the early footsteps of my stumbling entrepreneurial *calling journey*.

From there, I met many other worthy mentors in the independent music space. I studied and watched them. I had the privilege of working for some of them—getting a daily hands-on education accompanied by a humble salary. These jobs served to be invaluable apprenticeship-like experience for me. Whether it was running the wholesale department for the grindcore/metal label Relapse Records (Mastodon, Dillinger Escape Plan) or performing as the top salesperson for the indie distributor Lumberjack/Mordam Records (All-American Rejects, the Get Up Kids), I accepted working for little to internalize the lessons to be learned through paid apprenticeships in the independent music space.

I couldn't have built two record labels with an aggregate catalog of over 120 releases without these experiences.

But it was long before these experiences, back in the year 2000, when I released my first record. I vividly remember how excited I was to hold a finished compact disc in my hand. To pull a unit from the thirty-count factory box. The smell of the shrink wrap. The slick look of the artwork. The pride I felt seeing my logo on the product—knowing all the dreaming, risk, work, and creativity it took to get that first product to market.

I lost a lot of money on that record.

All the sweat equity, financial risk, and logged hours project managing all the moving pieces of launching the record label bore no income yet. I still needed to find a day job. The company had debt, but it also now had its first layer of recurring revenue. The education and feedback I gained by creatively wedging myself into the space was invaluable. Working for free in order to find an opening to build trajectory had produced a tangible result—a real product selling in the market. Utilizing a self-directed, informal apprenticeship model helped me form the loose initial framework for building my dream. The nominal success of this critical step one was highly rewarding. I knew that any monetary reward would take more time, more passion, and more tenacious unconventional learning.

It was the initial feelings of fear that came with the early failure of being underwater on the first record release that refined me and straightened my habits. It was the purification of that first failure that gave me shape and sight to know how to fashion my next evolving steps. **Failure Rule #1: *Failure Purifies*** was fully in effect.

The 2020 Democratic presidential candidate Andrew Yang learned the purification of failure and the necessity of encouraging the apprenticeship model of working for free, or little, early on in his *calling journey*.

After graduating from Columbia Law School, Yang did what many would've safely predicted—he began working for a corporate law firm. But this natural career ignition didn't last long or develop as expected. Yang quickly realized that this path would be a fast failure for him. It only took several months for Yang to realize that working at Davis Polk and Wardwell in New York City was not an atmosphere poised to fill his meaning bucket. It became quickly apparent that the corporate law firm gig was designed to reward its high performers with only an increased avalanche of stressful, indigestible billable hours and responsibility. The better he performed, the less free he was. The more value he gave, the less meaning he received. He described the experience as *"a pie-eating contest, and if you won, your prize was more pie."* Yang lasted only five months at the firm. He listened to his *internal spirit voice* that urged him *to go build something*.

This is where Yang's *calling journey* really got lit up and his understanding of the purification of failure began. His first venture—or effort to build something—launched and fizzled within a few short years. This first venture was called Stargiving. It was a website for celebrity-targeted philanthropic fundraising. It enjoyed some initial success but then ultimately became a casualty of the dot-com bubble somewhere around the close of year two.

But this failure didn't stop him. This failure was his teacher, not his undertaker. He failed fast and quickly moved on to other ventures. Leveraging lessons from the purification of failure, he got involved in a party-organizing venture while also serving as vice president of a healthcare startup. It was in the alchemy of these initial experiences in which Yang jettisoned the safety of the expected post-law school path and really solidified the underpinnings of his *calling journey*. These underpinnings were a love for building things and a fire in the belly to help aspiring entrepreneurs.

After leaving the healthcare startup, Yang then worked on a venture to help people prepare for tests. This venture was called Manhattan Prep. In this capacity, he personally taught the analyst classes at firms such as McKinsey, Goldman Sachs, and JP Morgan during the 2008 financial crisis. This company ultimately expanded to sixty-nine locations, was sold to Kaplan, Inc., and was the mechanism that made Yang a millionaire.

It was within this inflection point that Yang traversed from just being involved in building things to promoting that same ethos in others. Yang sought to multiply his passion for and focus on the entrepreneurial spirit by creating VFA (Venture for America) in 2011. Stemming from the core thesis of Yang's book, *Smart People Should Build Things*, VFA's mission was to disrupt the predictable path of top graduates being funneled into homogenized corporate jobs in a small, predictable list of big cities. Yang's plan was to instead recruit these top graduates to join a two-year fellowship to apprentice at promising startups that were more equally distributed throughout the country. By deliberately distributing talent proportionately across the entire country, VFA helped create the conditions for a more democratized entrepreneurial national footprint with built-in incentives. Yang's work with VFA eventually earned him recognition by President Obama as the Presidential Ambassador for Global Entrepreneurship.

If you're not sure how to secure initial traction into a space that provides no clear blueprint for entry, learn to work for free or for little. Learn to creatively penetrate hard-to-see cracks of entry into the space. Find a mentor at any level and build on that experience as you cultivate more mentors.

Expand your mentorship search to virtual mentors through following key thought leaders in your space—through books, podcasts, and other meaningful media. If the classroom isn't providing you with any practical clarity on how to take the next right step in your *calling journey*, find a way to safely ditch it and latch onto an apprenticeship path that evidences reasonable possibility for forward trajectory and immersion.

This is what author, entrepreneur, marketer, and purveyor of stoic thought Ryan Holiday did. Ryan ditched the classroom by dropping out of the University of California at age nineteen. He followed his *internal spirit voice*, rejected the cookie-cutter career path template, and went offroad to accelerate the fulfillment of his *calling journey*. After orchestrating marketing stunts for the controversial author Tucker Max, Ryan eventually found a strategic mentor by working for Robert Greene, author of *The 48 Laws of Power*. Under this paid, informal apprenticeship-like arrangement, Ryan learned far more than he would've languishing with untapped, brimming ambition in the university classroom. Under Greene's tutelage, Ryan blossomed as a thinker and a writer. He helped Greene work on his 2009 *New York Times* bestselling book, *The 50th Law*. He observed Greene's habits firsthand and absorbed his honed words of wisdom day in and day out.

Ryan consistently points back to his time working for and with Greene as invaluably formative and foundationally instructive in his career. It was from this core experiential framework of unconventional mentorship and apprenticeship that Ryan catalyzed a wonderful career in writing and marketing. Today, Ryan runs his own marketing firm, Brass Check, and has authored highly influential books, such as *Ego is the Enemy, The Obstacle is the Way, Stillness is the Key, Courage is Calling,* and *Perennial Seller.*

After going through the aforementioned business and marital divorces in quick succession, my entire orientation in the world drastically changed. Suddenly, I went from being a long-married self-employed entrepreneur to being a single person rebooting his career as an employee for an online commercial bank entrenched in the payments space. The purification that blazed through me from these relationship failures humbled me and positioned me to once again embrace the mindset of a wide-eyed, blank-slated mentee in a brand-new space.

Over the following five to seven years, I purposed to meticulously observe, mimic, and learn from my new mentor in the payments space. My mentor, who has been foremost a boss but also a trusted partner and friendly confidante, has been immensely influential in the construction of my ascension to competency in a brand-new space. After being a boss for so long myself, I had to disassemble all of my assumptions, habits, and preconceived notions about work. I had to embrace an apprentice-like posture to rebuild myself for this next phase of my *calling journey*. I was hardly working for free, or even for little, but I was working for a lot less initially than I was used to—and with a whole lot less impact, autonomy, and decision-making ability.

Over time, this all changed, and I gained all of this back to significantly surpass my previous roles in self-employment scenarios. This success happened because early on I knew that I was stepping into an amazing opportunity that would take a long time to mature and blossom. The learning curve would not be conquered quickly or simply. I had to learn, once again, to work strategically for less in order to embrace the trajectory of success that aligns with a view of the long game.

Listen to your *internal spirit* when it urges you to immerse yourself into an opportunity to work for free or for little when it shows evidentiary promise to move you forward in your *calling journey*.

If this means you need to walk out of the expected, prescribed corporate job that you are uncomfortably squirming in fresh out of college or grad school, like Andrew Yang, then do it. If this means you need to ditch the sterile, theoretical boredom of the university classroom, like Ryan Holiday did, then do it. If you are able to burrow into a space that aligns with your *calling journey* by uniquely securing a mentor or a meaningful apprenticeship opportunity and the cost is that you need to monster up and work for free or for little, then do it.

Swerve off the predictable highway and go offroad onto the unpaved roads of self-directed entrepreneurial exploration when your *internal spirit* demands that you do. Confront failure along the way, and let it purify you. Trust in the long game as you move into alignment with your *calling journey*—a *calling journey* underpinned with a raw, rugged individualism pregnant with wonder, meaning, and curious adventure.

Learn to strategically work for free or for little when an opportunity merits you do so. Else, wallow in the meaningless, mediocre safety of misalignment with your *calling journey*.

FIND YOUR CARL (GAME-CHANGING CONNECTOR)

"Networking that matters is helping people achieve their goals."
—SETH GODIN, AUTHOR AND FORMER DOT-COM BUSINESS EXECUTIVE

> **LESSON:** Be ever-open to unexpected game-changing connectors and mentors entering your path; seek them out as ladders in your *calling journey* climb.

When **Failure Rule #1:** *Failure Purifies* inserts itself into your path, its purification will cause you to dig deep to discover your *calling journey's* next step.

The afterglow I reveled in after bringing my first record to market didn't exist in a vacuum of joyful entrepreneurial fulfillment. No, it came accompanied by a heavy shadow that remained cast all around me by the unchanged reality of my deficient income. I was still contending with being unemployed from any substantial full-time work. I was contending with pizzas to deliver, a wife to support, and a baby to feed.

As I worked on refining my strategy for the next several record releases, informed by feedback from the first, the next Providential breadcrumb dropped.

I knew I needed to learn more about the music industry. I needed to add to my network in a way that had more impact or, as Seth Godin describes, in a way that mattered, that moved the needle. To achieve my goals, I needed mentors with more success, more credibility. My first mentor had taken me as far as he could. I needed to meet a game-changing connector to help attach me to the next step in my *calling journey*. I needed a breakthrough into the independent music space that would carry me into a more meaningful apprenticeship-like scenario.

I had been praying for that next step. That next sign. That next progression on my path. Then—out of nowhere—I was recalled back to my shitty, cubicle-monkey job at Ford Credit. With this, surface depression, panicked anger, and motivational urgency kicked into high gear. The recall was not a welcomed detour. It was a major grenade lobbed into my *calling journey* path. A monumental disruption. A colossal impediment.

I needed to consult my *internal spirit voice* on how to deal with the news.

So I kept dreaming. *Wilder.*

Praying. *Harder.*

Until it happened.

I then had what I now refer to as my *"Carl Moment."* Because everyone should have a Carl. Why shouldn't you have a Carl? *Who wouldn't like having a Carl?*

In the film *Envy*, starring Jack Black and Ben Stiller, Nick (Black's character) struck it rich with an invention that eliminated dog shit. He called it *Vapoorize*. It was a spray can that magically evaporated dog shit.

Tim (Stiller's character) was burning with envy, hence the film's title, over his best friend's entrepreneurial fortune. Nick, a wild-eyed dreamer, had now escaped the confining life at the sandpaper factory. Tim, having rejected an initial investment opportunity into the shit-killing venture, was still locked into the rigid conscientiousness of blind ladder climbing in a dead-end factory career.

But Nick's personality and values—loyalty, creativity, and kindness—were amplified by his wealth and success. The Poo Czar didn't want to isolate himself from his best friend because of this new economic chasm created between them. No, the Caca King instead wanted to graft his buddy into his bright new world of possibility and adventurous living.

So when Nick discovered that Tim had been canned from his factory job, he invited him into an equal partnership with no buy-in conditions. As Nick delivered his offer to Tim, he brought Tim equally into his new luxury lifestyle by offering up the services of his personal trainer:

> You've met Pete, right? My trainer. Don't feel funny around Pete. I got no secrets from Pete. Do I, Pete? I don't think so. So here's the deal: Buddy boy...you, you unemployed bum, you'll come kick ass with me. I want us to be partners. I want us to be equal again, man. Why not? I mean, for crying out loud, I've got a Pete. Why shouldn't you have a Pete? Who wouldn't like having a Pete?

Nick was acting as a game-changing connector, offering Tim an opportunity to step into a new phase of his *calling journey*. Offering to share Pete's services was a symbol of the larger offer he was extending. The offer had the potential to be a pivotal moment that might change the trajectory of Tim's *calling journey*.

Because who wouldn't like having a Pete?

Similarly, who wouldn't like having a Carl?

Finding a *"Carl,"* or experiencing a *"Carl Moment,"* is what happens when you meet a connector who creates a pivotal moment for you. That pivotal moment changes the trajectory of your *calling journey* and pushes you to a recognizably higher level.

Carl is a real dude. A great dude. I haven't spoken to him in several decades, and I only knew him for about a year. But meeting him was a transformative, game-changing event for my career that cracked the next step wide open in my *calling journey*.

I met Carl at the gym one night. I was pissed and tense from sitting in a cubicle for ten hours collecting on defaulted auto loans. All day I had been thinking about my burning desire to focus more acutely on building my new record label.

There I was. Pumping iron. Sweating. Thinking. Dreaming. Praying. Arguing with God. Pleading. Trying to figure out how to get the hell out of the job I was in.

And then I saw this dude in a Snapcase T-shirt. Snapcase was a hardcore punk band from Upstate New York. Strangely, years later I met the former drummer of the band, and he became a client of mine when I was doing financial planning in the Midwest.

Anyway, it was rare to see anyone wearing a T-shirt for a hardcore band, especially at a meathead gym in a Philly suburb. The hardcore punk scene is a small, tight-knit kind of niche tribe. I was never really into Snapcase but was stoked to see someone wearing their shirt randomly in the gym simply because it was a connection point to my hardcore punk roots.

I asked him about his shirt, and Carl and I became fast friends.

It turned out Carl was an attorney. He had quit his suit-and-tie job and moved to the Philly area from Colorado to work for Relapse Records. He was following his *internal spirit voice*. Relapse is a very extreme heavy metal/grindcore label that was in Lancaster, Pennsylvania, at the time. Back then, they had roughly thirty to forty employees.

Carl and I chatted about music and life over dumbbell curls. Carl explained that he was Relapse's VP. So he was number two on the org chart. Listening to his *internal spirit voice*, he took a pay cut and took his career offroad to do something he loved. Carl and I thought alike. Suddenly, it felt as if my wrestling with God might bear some fruit. I needed that next deeper foothold into the independent music space. It looked like Relapse Records could be it.

Within a week of continuing to endure the grueling cubicle life I had been recalled to, Carl finally responded to my follow-up emails. Within another few weeks, I landed a job at Relapse Records running their wholesale department.

Failure Rule #1: *Failure Purifies.* The failure of not finding a full-time job before unexpectedly being recalled to my loathed cubicle-monkey job purified me. It forced me to dig deep and wide in my search for a breakout connector to carry me into the next step in my *calling journey*. Without that event, I may not have agonized so deeply in prayer and creative ideation. I may not have thought to talk to the fellow meathead at the gym wearing the Snapcase shirt—with a strange feeling of intuition that maybe the conversation would lead to cracking open the door of my *calling journey's* next step.

Finding Carl set me free to my next step. I was on the front end of a paid education in the independent music business. Carl was the game-changing connector who created a pivotal moment. It was a moment that indisputably changed the entire trajectory of my *calling journey*.

Open your mind and your eyes to the possibility of stumbling into meeting an unusual and unexpected game-changing connector. Believe that this connector may help to radically push you into the next meaningful step of your *calling journey.*

Find your Carl.

Because who wouldn't like having a Carl?

Master blender for CAO Cigars Rick Rodriguez was purified by failure and found his Carl.

From an early age, Rick felt like he was born to lose. Rick's family immigrated to the US from Cuba. He was born and raised in Tampa, Florida. With a tumultuous home life and no father figure, Rick ran away in his early teens and lived with his girlfriend. Rick chose to embrace exile for a chance to find his way forward. While feeling like he was born to lose, he was intent to live to win. Maternalized by the relationship, his girlfriend at the time guided him through many of life's coming-of-age lessons. She even taught him how to shave.

As Rick's life continued, he took some treacherous turns into some bad decisions and risky associations. At one point, he somehow found himself babysitting a house full of cocaine for a nefarious associate. Within the mix of this incident, he also somehow experienced a Dick Cheney moment—he accidentally shot a friend in the ear. Guns, cocaine, and fear didn't blend well.

Rick knew his life needed a hard redirect if he was to avoid any more failures of bad decisions. Failure was in the process of purifying him, burning off impulses for bad decisions. But he still needed direction. He didn't quite know what the impetus would be to help him find a renewed path, but he had a feeling that tobacco had something to do with it. You see, cigars ran deep in Rick's family. Rick's grandparents were master rollers in Cuba before they left the island in 1954 to roll in factories in Florida. Yet the love of the leaf had skipped a generation. Rick's dad had never even smoked a cigar. But for Rick, when he first lit, puffed, and rotated at age twenty, he was hooked on the pleasurable magic of cigar smoking.

After a series of stumbling through jobs and false-start career paths, Rick found his way. That way, of course, was cigars. He took a job as a salesperson for General Cigars and rose to be their top performer for about three and half years. Rick's reputation within the company was so strong that the owner at the time, Ed Cullman Sr., took notice of Rick. This was the first step toward Rick finding his Carl. Because who wouldn't like having a Carl?

Cullman heralded Rick's passion for their products and asked Rick to apprentice under their current master blender, Benji Menendez. Benji was in the evening of his career. General Cigars needed a succession plan. Rick fit the bill.

Rick and Benji's connection was automatic. Rick quickly immersed himself into learning both the mastery crafts of tobacco blending and the larger wisdom that Benji had to impart. The gap left in Rick for never having a father figure suddenly began to be filled. Benji grew to not only be Rick's mentor but also the long-yearned-for father figure that he deeply needed. After a twisted journey of purifying failures, meeting Benji came to symbolize the pivotal game-changing connector that solidified Rick's folding into his *calling journey*. He had found his Carl.

Flourishing on the exhaust of Benji's accumulated wisdom and experience, Rick rose to be a distinct and influential master blender. His work has gone on to give thousands pleasure. He's brought cigar lovers amazing sticks in his CAO Flathead line, limited Amazon Basin releases, and many other great smokes.

As you work to interpret what your *internal spirit voice* is telling you, be on the lookout for game-changing connectors who may come into your life. Peer out at your potential network, and see if you can identify one that might matter. As you allow failure to naturally purify you along your *calling journey*, seek out candidates who might be willing and able to mentor you in an apprenticeship that will align you more quickly with the inertia of your *calling journey*.

Find your Carl.

BELIEVE IN THE POWER OF PIVOT POINTS

"*A pivot is a change in strategy without a change in vision.*"
—ERIC RIES, AUTHOR OF *THE LEAN STARTUP*

> **LESSON:** Pay attention to the groaning discomfort of stagnant mediocrity; let it push you into pivot points that join you with the next steps of your *calling journey*.

Sometimes **Failure Rule #1: *Failure Purifies*** shows up in our journeys in the form of a gnawing feeling of being unfulfilled—even as we are situated in external luxury and prestige. Recognizing the purifying power of that gnawing feeling can lead to powerful pivot points.

Truthfully, I really couldn't care less what you believe in. I hear people say all of the time that they believe that everything happens for a reason. It's a cliché and easy to claim. I don't think most people really believe that at all. Rather, they just say that to make themselves feel better when life does whatever the hell it wants to them. That said, I do believe that some things happen for a reason. Not many things, but some things. Big things. Consequential things. Undeniable things. Unexpected things, events, and pivotal moments. Stuff we couldn't manufacture, create, or force. You can call it fate, universal inertia, karma, whatever. I believe in God. So I call it God.

Meeting Carl at the gym that night was not only a game-changing connection that catapulted me into alignment with my *calling journey*, but it was also a powerful pivot-point moment that I believe happened for a reason. As the years go on, I am often reminded of how much of my work-life tapestry simply would not have unraveled the way it had if I had not met Carl that night. I did nothing traceable that could have manufactured meeting him, let alone orchestrated the course of events that unfolded as a result of meeting him. **Sometimes the unseen inertia that surrounds the contours of your life moves to shape circumstances and events in a way that nudges—and sometimes pushes—you into your** *calling journey*.

Meeting Carl was a pivot point created by such Providential unseen inertia. Since then, I have made it a practice to constantly pray for and try to prepare for pivotal, direction-changing introductions, opportunities, and key relationships.

While I recognize and believe in the power of pivot points sparked by the movement of unseen inertia, I also believe in the power of free will to help ignite such pivot-point moments. Outside of those unexpected things that can externally form around you to create pivotal moments, you also possess the power to lean into your *calling journey*. In times of high-stakes decisions, you can exert your will and, by audacious action, create powerful pivot points in your story. This type of pivot point happens simply through applying the agency of your individual free will to receptive circumstances. If you drift into a path that doesn't align with the whispering promptings of your *internal spirit voice* and then you reverse course and decide to begin to listen to it, the frequent result is that you can then boldly catalyze powerful pivot points. These self-effectuated pivot points end up distinctly coloring your *calling journey* story.

In the TV show *Better Call Saul*, the eccentric, morally flexible attorney Jimmy McGill, who later changes his name to Saul Goodman, made the bold decision to listen to the pounding sound of his *internal spirit voice*.

Jimmy, played by actor Bob Odenkirk, crawled his way from the mailroom of his brother's firm up to a job working in a prestigious firm, Davis and Main. At first, Jimmy seemed to take the new life in stride. He enjoyed the fringe-benefit trappings of a company car, a high-end apartment, an assistant, a swanky office, and nice bonuses. It seemed that he had landed. That the hard work had paid off. That he was finally enjoying the ripe, juicy fruit borne by years of arduous struggle.

Yet deep inside, Jimmy was disturbingly unsettled in this new life. On paper and from the outside looking in, it seemed perfect. Comfortable. Luxurious. Sophisticated. Prestigious. And full of future brightness. But Jimmy McGill was a lover of *wabi-sabi*. To Jimmy, something wasn't perfect unless it was a little fucked up. A little strange. And a little dangerous.

So Jimmy exercised the agency of his free will and deliberately sabotaged his bright new career in order to adhere to the monstrous wailing of his *internal spirit voice*. He still wanted to be an attorney, just not the kind that worked at a firm like Davis and Main.

Jimmy's pivot-point decision was a change in strategy around what type of lawyer he would be, not a change in his vision to become a lawyer. Jimmy knew he needed the freedom to be autonomous, to be absurdly colorful, to be wildly charismatic, and to pursue his own happiness without the safety of a larger entity strapping him into the seatbelt of corporate conformity. Jimmy needed to be Jimmy, and he couldn't do that at Davis and Main.

But Jimmy had cashed a fat bonus, which meant he couldn't quit, or he'd have to pay it back. This is where the brilliant emergence of Jimmy's true personality awoke into full blossom. He set out on a creative campaign to get let go in a way where they had no cause to fire him other than he was acting like a jackass. This way, he could keep his bonus. So act like a jackass he did. But in acting as a jackass, it became abundantly clear to the viewers that he was being his authentic self. It was an authentic self that would later constitute all he would become in his new legal persona as Saul Goodman.

Jimmy was inspired by seeing a large, gaudy, inflatable balloon guy advertising a local car dealership as he passed by it on the side of the road. It was this flash of inspiration that ignited Jimmy's career-suicide campaign. The inflatable balloon guy was wearing flashy, colorful clothing—including a bright-ass, wacky-patterned tie. Jimmy immediately went out and bought a whole wardrobe of suits and ties so colorful that even the most flamboyant of pimps might ask that he tone it down a bit. To the extreme dismay of his uber-professional colleagues, Jimmy began sporting a new choice suit and tie from his rainbow collection every single day at the office from that point forward. In one scene that culminated in his being let go, his boss—disgusted and fed up—noted that Jimmy's wardrobe gave him an optical migraine.

This was just the first weapon in his job-killing arsenal. He also employed various other guerrilla tactics to piss off his colleagues and the firm's leadership. He brought a juicer into the office to disrupt the quiet atmosphere with the loud blending sound. He took dumps daily in the office bathroom and deliberately did not flush. He then owned up to the task and justified his actions by claiming that he did it for the noble cause of water conservation. Somehow, he never learned the value of the saying, "If it's yellow, let it mellow; if it's brown, flush it down."

The final act of Jimmy's devious campaign of apparent self-sabotage involved bagpipes. No, he didn't simply blast the raucous Irish punk sounds of the Dropkick Murphys or Flogging Molly in his office to disturb his colleagues. Inspired by his boss, Clifford Main, who wound down the day with some light acoustic guitar playing as the office transitioned into after-office hours, Jimmy brought bagpipes to the office. Unlike Clifford Main and his acoustic guitar playing, Jimmy played the bagpipes loudly and unskillfully, smack dab in the middle of the workday. This was the final straw. Clifford Main finally gave Jimmy the well-deserved forced exit he had worked so hard to induce.

From the moment Jimmy caught wild inspiration by the inflatable balloon guy to the moment Clifford Main dropped the rope in the tug-of-war and let him go, Jimmy's powerful pivot point had been defined.

The events that took place between these two bookend moments forever shaped Jimmy's life. This pivot-point period injected meaning and purpose back into Jimmy's life. He may have forfeited comfort, wealth, and security and had to move back into the shitty back office of the strip mall nail salon, but he had fully reclaimed his authenticity and, by extension, his soul. While Jimmy's authenticity was indistinguishable from a questionable and penetrable morality, it moreover contained the benign elements of his charismatic lust for life, risk, and adventure that had been repressed within the corporate culture at Davis and Main.

Remember **Failure Rule #1: *Failure Purifies*.** Jimmy McGill was purified by his failure to conform to the culture of the swanky, high-end law firm. He was a misfit. Failure's purification stripped him down to his essence, allowing him to hear and follow his *internal spirit voice*—a voice that somehow spoke to him through an inflatable balloon guy. Listening to that voice forced Jimmy to embrace the depth of his authenticity as he boldly asserted his own agency to change his life.

New York Times bestselling author Robert Kurson was also purified by his failure to fit in at a high-end law firm.

Kurson was practicing real estate law as a Harvard-educated attorney. Yet nestled into the front-end blossoming of what the world would say was a promising career, Kurson felt off-kilter. Well before his actual career practicing law began, he recounted how he felt when taking his earliest footsteps onto Harvard's campus. Even then, Kurson knew something was not right. Like the fictional Jimmy McGill feeling immediately unsettled in his cushy job at the high-end law firm, Kurson recalls:

> Within thirty-six hours I knew I had made a horrendous mistake. I could tell even before classes started that this was not the place for me, that the people who would be happiest here were people who dotted every i and crossed every t and for whom order and carefulness ruled the day. But I stuck it out and became a lawyer and that's where the disaster really began.

Yet as Kurson waded into the onset of a career in real estate law, the external optics did not resemble a disaster at all. He flourished financially and had all the kinds of stuff he had dreamed of having—a BMW, a $3,000 bicycle, and a $2,000 stereo. But he was numb inside. He felt mediocre at best about how he performed his job despite the financial rewards that naturally flowed. Having never been one to take to drugs or alcohol in the past, he somehow found himself buying, in his words, *"as much junk as I could to numb the pain."* Deep inside he was unfulfilled.

Eventually Kurson decided he could no longer accept being unfulfilled. He instead acted with the power of his own agency and created a pivot-point moment that thrust him into the stream of his *calling journey*. He left his unfulfilling job at the law firm and dove into the scary, uncomfortable world of pursuing writing as a career. Like our pal Jimmy McGill, Kurson abandoned safety and luxury to join himself with the tumult and authenticity of his *calling journey*.

Kurson started over at the bottom, working as a data clerk at the *Chicago Sun-Times*. Like my paid education in the music industry at Relapse Records, enabled by my pivotal *Carl Moment*, Kurson found the crack to allow him a foothold in the space he wanted to grow into. But he was now grinding from scratch and completely bereft of all the comfort, trappings, and security of the life he knew in law. He had no blueprint for success. There was no linear, predictable path akin to the *Harvard Law School = High Paying Job = Security* chain of expectations. Devoid of a precise map to follow, Kurson had to rely on the vague direction of his *internal spirit voice's* compass.

Kurson interpreted the right directional next steps well from the compass he followed. He traversed from the *Chicago Sun-Times* to *Chicago Magazine* and then to *Esquire*, where he was a contributing editor for years. He continued to bugger on—one logical step to adjacent opportunity at a time, year by year—to build his writing career.

Inspired by the dynamic storytelling of his father, who would showcase his oratory skills on long road trips he took Robert on as a kid, Kurson went on to write multiple bestsellers. His first, *Shadow Divers*, animated the true story of two Americans who discovered a World War II German U-boat sunk sixty miles off the coast of New Jersey. He continued on with the bestselling works of *Crashing Through*, *Pirate Hunters,* and *Rocket Men*, which tells an adrenalized version of Apollo 8, mankind's first journey to the moon.

Don't overlook and ignore lack of fulfillment in your life. Let the failure of living an unfulfilled life purify you by driving you to home in on what your *internal spirit voice* is saying. Look for unexpected circumstances and opportunities that establish pivot points in your life and happen for a reason. Like when I met Carl.

If you need to change your strategy to actualize your vision, muster the courage to do it. Apply the agency of your free will with boldness to catalyze pivot points in your life that hook you more succinctly into your *calling journey*, like Jimmy McGill and Robert Kurson did.

Don't ignore the groaning discomfort caused by complacent safety achieved through mediocrity. Recognize that discomfort as **Failure Rule #1:** *Failure Purifies* imposes itself on you for your own good. Let that discomfort purify you and guide you into a powerful pivot point. One that flings you succinctly into the tumult of your authentic *calling journey*.

CATCH MOMENTUM, CULTIVATE FLOW STATES, AND PLAN WITH AN INTENT TO ITERATE

"There is a prevailing school of thought that something good must take time, sometimes years to create and hone. I have always felt that the books I have written fastest have been my best—because I caught an unstoppable momentum in the writing."

—MICHAEL CONNELLY, CRIME-THRILLER AUTHOR
OF *THE LINCOLN LAWYER* AND *BOSCH*

> **LESSON:** Deliberately create work conditions that allow you to fall into iterative flow states. This is more important than rigid plans or a blunt-force work ethic.

When failure strikes, sometimes all it takes to endure, conquer, and move forward through it—and bypass unnecessary delay—is to hyperfocus on at least one area of positive micro-momentum. If you are encountering an avalanche of failures in quick succession—*in your pursuit, your life, or even your failure recovery plan*—latch your stubborn fingers onto the saving cliff of identified positive momentum.

If you are at the front end of a startup endeavor and your burn rate is nearing the end of its runway, find the right trajectory levers that can extend that runway. Pull those levers, and fall into sustainable momentum. If you're carrying business debt that is weighing on your balance sheet while you wait for critical revenue ignition to materialize in your P&L, find the mechanisms of momentum that keep you moving, both financially and emotionally. If you're hustling toward the development of a skill on the side, keep working for free to develop that skill as long as you have meaningful momentum.

Momentum is the cure for the sting of failure. It is a tool to help you move forward rightly after Failure Rule #1: *Failure Purifies* **is done instilling its lesson in you. As failure purifies your pursuit's meaningless waste products, what's left can survive if momentum exists. Failure purifies by purging bad ideas so good ideas can gain and maintain growing momentum. Momentum and the flow states that sustain and increase momentum are the key to outrunning the initial brutality of failure's purification. As failure purifies, you need to mold it into your teacher or else risk it becoming your undertaker. If you do this, you can cultivate and harness sustainable momentum.**

Executive producer of the TV show *Bosch* and bestselling crime mystery thriller writer Michael Connelly credits momentum as the secret sauce of his writing approach. Connelly believes his best work was written fast because he *"caught an unstoppable momentum in the writing."* It is the *catching* of the momentum that you need to seize as failure gathers around your pursuit to purify what is not working. As you fight being time-poor in order to sustain momentum in your side hustle that you hope someday emerges as your primary pursuit and core income. As you struggle to ascend within an organization and are hungry to find one thread of differentiation that can elevate your visibility up the chain to the executive level. As you suck wind with the pummeling of initial costs when launching a startup—all the while scratching and clawing to pull and optimize every revenue opportunity to catch up and overcome. As you force yourself to muster up creativity late at night to pursue your art after working a long, taxing day at a day job that only meets the lower-rung requirements of the hierarchy of needs.

Flow state and iteration are key to shedding failure's purified waste and to holding on to the sustainable momentum of what's left. Peter Thiel, author of *Zero To One*, and one of the original members of the PayPal mafia, advises that *"having a bad plan is still always better than having no plan at all."* He is right. Face-tattoo-wearing heavyweight champion boxer Mike Tyson was also right when he proclaimed that *"everyone has a plan until they get punched in the mouth."* Because both Thiel and Tyson are right, you need to both have a plan and prepare to iterate.

I listened to Michael Connelly explain his writing approach once in a seminar he gave at a Thriller Fest conference in New York City. He explained that he relies only on a very loose plan around the direction of his main character, Harry Bosch, before he begins penning each new novelistic journey for the iconic badass detective. A loose plan might be a bad plan, but it's a plan. Since Connelly understands the predictable, repeatable magic of his own unique writing approach, he knows he must prepare to *catch momentum* and iterate to turn his loose, bad plan into an unmistakable literary product. He explains it this way:

> Not a lot is planned ahead. I usually have a few loose threads dangling from one book that I can then take to the next or even one further down the line. But I don't think a lot ahead. I think that by not planning [Harry's] future out I have a better chance of keeping him fresh and current and more reflective of the moment.

Plans are good, but the plans that often produce the freshest work are those that mutate as you iterate their implementation. My initial outline, or plan, for this book has only a very thin resemblance to the actual iterative execution of writing this book. The final product is even a more distant relative to the original plan. The iteration that brought dynamism to my writing of this manuscript was often achieved through flow states. In these iterative flow states, I *caught momentum*.

During the initial retreat into quarantine amid the 2020 COVID-19 pandemic, I likewise retreated by leaning heavily into the development of this manuscript. I would spend six to eight hours per day on the weekends writing. Edging a Howard Hughes-light approach, I would ignore all normal hygiene, connectivity with friends, and exercise while in the flow states I folded into. I would sit writing on my South Philly balcony in a robe, nothing else. Staring out at the Delaware river in between keystrokes, smoking cigar after cigar. Drinking coffee after coffee. Some of them Irish. Whatever it took to stay slipstreamed into the achieved flow state. Whatever it took to keep my mind nimble and my fingers tapping on the keyboard.

The flow states were partially induced by diverse musical input. This kept my mind fresh by the shocking switch-ups of sonic fuel. Like abruptly altering a workout or diet routine, the contrasting musical diversity kept me applying fresh diverse thought to the manuscript. I'd traverse from the thundering sounds of Motorhead to the folksy ballads of Bob Dylan. From the sleaze rock biker anthems of Junkyard to the island dreaminess of Jimmy Buffett. And from the twangy hillbilly outlaw country of Hank III to the Irish folk punk of The Pogues.

In these flow states, I found momentum. In this momentum, I found joy. In working for free on this manuscript—with reasonable hope that someday it would monetize by virtue of blessing others with its messages—I found satiating fulfillment.

Working for free—or for the belief in the probability of future monetization—while you have momentum will help you TCB and plow through the pain of failure's purification. Planning with an intent to iterate and capitalizing on conditions that facilitate flow states will lead you to your best work and to higher levels of mastery and excellence. This is how you confront **Failure Rule #1:** *Failure Purifies*.

Also, while in the initial months of the forced quarantine of the 2020 COVID-19 pandemic, I capitalized on the work-from-home advantage of flow-state retention. Without the constant, non-sequitur interruptions of an open-concept office environment, I found flow. This flow tremendously enhanced my passion for my work in banking. Within weeks my productivity increased by at least 2.5x. I could control my inputs. I was comfortable in my clothing, my leather office chair, and my home environment. I could smoke cigars while I worked, enhancing my cognitive focus. I no longer had to shrug off the momentum-stifling effects of a morning commute. I no longer had to contend with the feeling to leave the office for lunch to get a break from face-to-face interaction and organize my thoughts. I logged on earlier and logged off later. My lunch breaks were mostly taken while working. And when I did take a proper break, it was usually to exercise rigorously, which enhanced my flow for the rest of the day. The focus I found in the work-from-home flow states created new gains in my pursuit of mastery as an executive banker.

Learn to strategically work for free by catching momentum. Learn to cultivate conditions that facilitate the achievement of flow states. Draft your plans with an intent to iterate.

When I launched my first record label, I worked for free for a long time. I laser-focused on the meaningful momentum I was creating. I locked into nightly flow states and iterated my plan with nimble agility. It took four years before I could take a cent. I slept four hours a night for those four years. I'd start each day in the gym early before work. Then, I would work at my day job—my paid education in the independent music space—before coming home and spending time with my wife and kids. I'd have dinner with them, help bathe the young ones. Read them their bedtime stories. *Goodnight Moon*, *Cloudy with a Chance of Meatballs*, and whatever else.

After everyone was asleep, I'd fire up the computer from ten o'clock at night until two in the morning or so. In the stillness of the night, I would find my flow state. In the nocturnal silence, I would accelerate sustainable momentum and let failure purify me. Failure torched off of me mistake after mistake and failed record release after failed record release until I collided with success. I kept iterating my plans until success came more frequently and with sharper predictability. I did this every night for four years. It was nice to be in my twenties. I'm in my forties now; I need my sleep.

That one record label eventually split into two record labels that I still run with my cousin as a partner. We've released over 125 recordings and hold merchandise rights for about half the artists. We maintain rights and manage the portfolio now in the background of our full-time pursuits. This provides both of us a great deal of fulfillment and fun.

We treat the portfolio much like a 401(k), except with assets that are non-correlative to the market. We reinvest almost everything into new projects. Hopefully when we reach retirement age, the catalog will be large enough that the revenue will be multiples, and we'll be able to safely take strong residual passive income in perpetuity.

For a time, I attempted to operate the labels full time as a business instead of a managed portfolio of investments in music intellectual property (IP) rights. This lasted only a few years for multiple reasons. Multiple failures struck during this period. These failures purified my perspective. I focused on the areas of strength that could sustain momentum out of the failures. This is when we pivoted to the managed portfolio of IP rights model.

What has been preserved and built over time has now emerged as a long-term asset with staying power. This is a testimony to the early years of working diligently for free while hanging on to trajectory—back when profit and growth were not yet fully realized or certain.

The late, great, rock 'n' roll creative Ronald "Bon" Scott worked for free on developing his musical chops for many years before his *calling journey* aligned him to becoming AC/DC's front man.

Scott tumbled through a ton of jobs before his musical abilities gained the momentum needed to collide into a success stream. He worked as a farmhand, crayfisherman, weighing-machine mechanic, bartender, truck packer, and postman. Can you imagine getting your mail from the guy who went on to write "It's a Long Way to the Top (If You Want to Rock 'n' Roll)?"

Scott's way to the top was indeed long. Long before he was *"gettin' robbed, gettin' stoned, gettin' beat up and broken boned,"* he was grinding through day jobs with rock 'n' roll dreams floating in his head. At night, he would hustle to build his rock 'n' roll skills with no certainty of any paid future. It was always harder than it looked for Scott.

In 1973 Scott shoveled shit for a living at the Wallaroo fertilizer plant in Australia. After hard days of shoveling shit, Scott would distill his rock 'n' roll daydreaming into robust sessions of creative jamming with his band, the Mount Lofty Rangers, which was helmed by Peter Head from the band Headband. The Mount Lofty Rangers were developed for the purpose of connecting songwriters together to experiment. It was in this collaborative creative setting that Scott came into his own with his rock 'n' roll style. Peter Head taught Scott how to bridge chords and construct a song. Scott grew through this instruction and wrote songs such as "Bin Up In the Hills Too Long," a country-tinged rock song that was early evidence of Scott's trademark simple, sardonic, clever, tongue-in-cheek lyrical approach that the world would later receive from his iconic work with AC/DC.

Scott held down a shit-shoveling job to pay the bills while listening to his *internal spirit voice*. That voice urged him to pursue the actualization of his *calling journey* with rigor in the evenings. He worked diligently at developing his skills with the belief that he would someday monetize those skills. He sought mentors, like Peter Head, who apprenticed him into stronger mastery of his skills. He embraced a collaborative setting of experimental musicians whose plan was deliberately crafted to make room for unexpected iteration. In this environment, Scott caught momentum and capitalized on flow states. The stale drudgery of his serial day job failures was cured by Scott's hyper-focus on the areas of micro-momentum he had in his musical pursuits. Scott's momentum grew until he had his *Carl Moment*: meeting Vince Lovegrove. Lovegrove ran the management/booking agency for AC/DC. He hired Scott to help promote AC/DC. This eventually got Scott on the band's radar when they parted with the original singer, Dave Evans. After a series of events stemming from the game-changing connection made by Vince Lovegrove, Scott landed his gig as AC/DC's front man.

When your pursuit, your life, or even your failure recovery plan is being purged of multiple failures by purification, find the areas of micro-momentum you still have. Then hyper-focus on them. Like Michael Connelly's writing, home in and catch momentum to grow your quickened strength forward.

As you focus in on the areas of micro-momentum that you still have amid the attacks of failures, cultivate conditions conducive to flow states. This will help you turn your micro-momentum into sustainable macro-momentum. Like Bon Scott joining the experimental collaborative band the Mount Lofty Rangers, make a plan with an intent to iterate.

Cultivate the flow states that support momentum. Then catch momentum. And iterate your plan as you rebuild through failure's purification.

SEEK OUT THE IMMORTAL AND WRITE YOUR LEGACY EVERY DAY

"Please think about your legacy because you are writing it every day."
—GARY VAYNERCHUK, ENTREPRENEUR, AUTHOR, AND CO-FOUNDER OF EMPATHY WINES AND VAYNERX DIGITAL MARKETING

> **LESSON:** Diligently live your life each day with your legacy in mind; let the clearing of failure's purification be an opportunity to strategically rethink how you write the next chapter of your legacy's story.

As you rise reborn from each of your failures, you will be given a new opportunity to shape your legacy many times. With each new reinvention, you can take the pen and lay fresh new ink on the story of your life that will convert someday to your legacy. Plan now to think about this before **Failure Rule #1:** *Failure Purifies* sweeps into your life. Your legacy is too important to waste such fresh opportunities to write strategic plot shifts of your story.

I woke up the morning of this writing, October 4, 2020, to a phone call from my best friend. He called to deliver the tragic news that a mutual old friend had died in a car accident last night.

I have spent a good portion of the day digesting this news. My best friend and I hung out this afternoon, recalling all the great memories of our friend.

Amid our sorrow and bewilderment, we found laughter and joy in exalting the legacy of my friend's life. The immortal imprint he has left behind with those who knew and loved him. His sense of humor. His depth of curiosity. The level of extreme loyalty he exhibited his entire life to those he cared about. He did this in a sacrificial fashion. He was there unequivocally for his father, his sister, his longtime girlfriend and best friend, and his small group of close friends. He once endured a nine-hour drive with my ex-mother-in-law to help me with a six-hundred-mile move. Believe me, this act alone qualifies one for nothing short of sainthood.

My friend was a simple man. A blue-collar hero and a quiet patriot. He never married but still loved his longtime girlfriend and best friend deeply and faithfully. He held hard, diligent work as a high virtue. He battled vices, business issues, legal issues, and depression. Like many of us have. Yet he always found his way back to listening to his *internal spirit voice* that urged him to take faith in his abiding relationship with God, regardless of the circumstances that engulfed him. My last substantive conversation with him centered entirely around his spirituality and the way in which he was leaning into it.

Over the course of his life, my friend wrote his legacy every day in acts of service and love to those around him. May this writing serve to immortalize all that he was to all that he loved. May this be one piece of the legacy of Steven Campanaro that perhaps may continue on for years to come.

My friend Steve—or Sleeve, as we nicknamed him—doesn't have the opportunity anymore to continue writing his legacy each day.

You do.

Take Gary Vaynerchuk's advice and please think about it. Your loved ones and perhaps many others will benefit if you do.

Defense attorney and author of *Guilt by Accusation: The Challenge of*

Proving Innocence in the Age of #MeToo Alan Dershowitz has built a legacy of representing very controversial high-profile clients. Mike Tyson. Jim Bakker. Donald Trump. Julian Assange. Jeffrey Epstein.

No vile stack of accusations has scared Dershowitz away from giving his clients a robust impartial defense. Rape. Embezzlement. Impeachment. Sedition. Sex with minors.

And no vile accusations lodged against him personally have scared him away from defending himself and his legacy. In an interview on the Glenn Beck podcast, Dershowitz gave a rising defense of his position against his accuser, Virginia Roberts Giuffre. She accused him of sexually assaulting her as a minor under the control of sex trafficker Jeffery Epstein. Dershowitz has vehemently counter-accused that Giuffre was pressured to falsely accuse him by her counsel. In the interview, Dershowitz detailed the evidence in his favor and unequivocally predicted his eventual day of legal victory. He was eighty-two years old at the time of the interview. He explicitly spoke about the tainting effect the accusations were having on his legacy. He spoke with high confidence about how he would clear his good name and restore his legacy. At eighty-two, the thought of his legacy being erroneously destroyed roused him to the oratory flourish of a mighty young speaker.

Whether you believe Alan Dershowitz is innocent or not is immaterial here. Obviously, if he is guilty, his offense is reprehensible and would rightly do irreparable damage to his legacy. I detail his example only to highlight that he was driven to do whatever possible to preserve his legacy. Which, if he is innocent, is a noble fight. Either way, you ought to take your legacy as seriously as Dershowitz did his—because legacy is important.

Legacy is not important because you might care about preserving the spirit of your ego. Make no mistake: you *will* get pleasure and satisfaction in consciously thinking about and attempting to immortally codify your legacy, but that's *not* why you need to value it. **You need to value your legacy and your effort to try to document or pass it on, for the benefit**

of others. When you die, it won't matter to you—at least on this side of eternity. No, you'll be on the other side of eternity then. And then is when the benefit can residually live on for others—whether to a tight set of recipients within your family or to a wide swath of inheritors consuming what you leave behind through publicly available expressive output. Because a rightly cultivated and preserved legacy of value is a deliberate release of control—you are just a conduit funneling what lasting value you've gained from life to future beneficiaries. The value you pass on then becomes a force multiplier of wisdom, knowledge, and a well-lived example.

You have an opportunity right now to design a strategic offense to maximize the positive, immortal effect of your legacy. Dershowitz, in the evening of his years, is struggling to play defense. Play hard offense now while you can. Listen to Gary Vaynerchuk, and please think about your legacy now. Because you're writing it every day.

With death and legacy heavy on my mind at the time of this writing, I can't help but think about that day when the pallbearers will carry me to my grave. In that moment of earthly finality, none of the financial realizations of my pursuits will matter. There are no hearses with U-Hauls attached, as they say.

What will matter is what I helped bring into the world. Hopefully, the most acute hallmark of my contribution will live and carry on within the hearts, minds, and memories of my wife, children, family, and friends. I pray that despite my many flaws and imperfections, my actions and words throughout the years will yield a net positive imprint within those I love that I will one day leave behind.

Stepping beyond the direct relationship impact of family and friends, I then think about the other areas of my life that may color my legacy. What elements of my work on earth might live on to impact, inspire, challenge, and bless others for years or perhaps in perpetuity? These things will matter.

It will be the output elements of my *calling journey* that have immortality potential that might accomplish this. One element is the music I helped bring into the world through my record labels. Art that has held personal meaning to me and many other listeners worldwide. Songs of struggle, pain, and strife that give people strength to push forward and overcome through failure, tumult, and hard times. Music also accents and amplifies—with three chords and the truth—the sentiments of the good times.

We've released records by some of my favorite bands. Bands that most people don't give an aeronautical fornication about. But those who do care, cherish them—and their songs have become an unseen soundtrack to the story of their lives. These contributions that I actively participated in birthing into the world will outlast my life. The music that we help put out will outlive us and be available in perpetuity digitally, on vinyl and whatever formats and delivery preferences emerge in the future—for as long as freedom rules.

This is one key way in which true, deep satisfaction originates: being a part of the production or facilitation of potentially immortal content.

Back in 2014, within the scope of just a few months, many musicians in bands on my record labels passed away. Two singers and a guitarist spanned across both labels and two bands—Bulldog Courage and The Kings of Nuthin'.

All of these tragic deaths remind me of the potential immortality that art can contribute to the shaping of legacy.

I listen to both of these bands still today on the regular. Bulldog Courage memorialized anthemic hardcore punk choruses about friendship, standing one's ground, and long suffering through hardship. When their singer and guitarist died, the music and the message survived.

When the iconic greasy-haired, heavily tattooed, raspy-voiced swaggering front man of The Kings of Nuthin', Torr Skoog, passed away, his music and legacy did not. His songs still remain to bolster the outcasts, failures, and latecomers in this world with new courage in every wild intersecting rhythm between guitars, accordions, and washboards. And in every genre-clashing mashup of Little Richard-style rhythm and blues and Ramones-inspired poetic punk-rock chants.

The art that these bands produced stands alone and transcends the lives of the creators. The art itself becomes its own entity that provides pleasure long after the artists have passed. Beyond just being a reminder of its creators, the art itself affects me as a listener in such a way as to produce altogether new thoughts and emotions with continued listening.

This is the magic and power we have as humans to create and imprint our essence immortally. And technology has now enhanced the power, reach, and potential preservation of that magic.

We are often attracted to art—be it music, books, visual arts, film, audio, or other—when the content, delivery, and visceral contours of the art reveals an authentic story replete with not only the thrill of living but also the intrinsic agony of walking through the hard failure valleys of life. When **Failure Rule #1** is in play, failure often purifies us down to a state that compels us, in the end, to tell our failure story.

The failure stories we tell through our art have a chance of living on immortally. They have a chance to multiply the impact of our legacy for the betterment of many for years after we've passed.

Many of the case studies you will read about in this book center around people whose failure stories resulted in art that carries an immortal potential to cement their legacy. These individuals first traversed through their own unique hero journeys before endeavoring in their journeys as artists, determined to pass on every chapter of their story. Chapters full of catastrophes, regular failures, tiny bright spots, critical pivot points, and big redemptive successes. Failure that results in immortal art and content indeed rules!

Srinivas Rao's failures as a corporate misfit led to art with immortal potential—his *Unmistakable Creative* podcast and multiple books.

Johnny Cash's failure as a door-to-door salesman ("Hello, I'm Johnny Cash") led to prolific musical output that carries a wide immortal reach. This reach shows no signs of fading from generation to generation.

Stephanie Land's failure journey through poverty as a working single mom led to a bestselling book on the pain of the working poor.

Glenn Beck's dark period of suicidal tendencies and alcoholism led to the creation of a media empire that produces multiformat content that will live immortally, if freedom perseveres. Within the output of that empire, Beck's failure stories—and more importantly, the pivot points that carried him through—are on high-resolution display throughout.

Author Robert Kurson's failure to fit into corporate culture at a big New York law firm resulted in him gifting multiple bestselling books to the world.

Triathlete and Hare Krishna hardcore punk icon John Joseph (who wrote the foreword to this book), experienced addiction failures that resulted in the production of some of the rawest, most empowering and inspirational music and books the world has been blessed to receive.

Norman "Sailor Jerry" Collins's failure to conform to society's views on the art of tattooing ultimately helped him leave an iconic legacy. Sailor Jerry is the father of old-school tattooing. His immortal art has blessed the world with the essential simplicity and monolithic power of his tattoo flash designs, a successful line of spiced rum, and a boutique clothing line long after his passing.

Sailor Jerry's legacy of decisive nonconformity is cogently summed up in a marketing email titled "Outside the Lines" once blasted out by the Sailor Jerry Clothing company. Some of the copy read:

> People who are true to themselves may have scars, enemies and unpaid bills but they don't have regrets. The people we respect and admire have one thing in common. At some point in their lives, they turned away from the crowd and followed their own path. They ignore what's considered "normal" and instead live in pursuit of what makes them feel most alive. Here's to life outside the lines.

In his life, Norman "Sailor Jerry" Collins lived this. He definitely had scars. I'm sure he made enemies. And I'd bet that he had times contending with unpaid bills.

From the times he spent hopping freight trains across the country as a teenager—hand-poking tattoos on people along the way—to the years he spent hosting his own Libertarian talk radio show under the moniker "Old Ironsides," Sailor Jerry lived life with a nonconforming authenticity and left no regrets. He lived deliberately in a way that crafted a distinct legacy.

Very few people donned heavily tattooed skin in his day. Sailor Jerry wore his ink proudly, often sporting nothing but a white undershirt as he conducted tours of the Hawaiian islands on a large, three-masted schooner. To him it was all about art and passion. A passion he developed during his time in the Navy.

Sailor Jerry lived a life outside the lines. He was a prolific writer. He made his mark in music by playing saxophone in a dance band. He spoke his unvarnished opinion on his radio show. And most notably associated with his colored legacy, he shaped tattoo culture forever with his bold, unique, patriotic, and often irreverent designs.

I'm often inspired as I think of his spirit and tenacity when I glance at my own tattoos that originate from his flash designs. And those thoughts linger and expand when I savor sips of the fine rum that bears his name.

Sailor Jerry only lived to the age of sixty-two. But the life in his years and the legacy and imprint he left behind far outweigh the numeric count of his years on earth. Sailor Jerry wrote his legacy every day by aligning himself with his *internal spirit voice* and choosing to live a life authentically empowered by a unique *calling journey*. Because he did this, his namesake, art, words, and essence have been preserved and proliferated long after his earthly departure.

The immortalization of legacy can show up in odd and unexpected forms. I order a case of Marley Coffee "Lively Up Espresso Roast" Keurig K-cups every few weeks. Do you really think that Bob Marley had any idea that the multiplication of his namesake and legacy extension would ever reach to cleverly branded coffee products used in a hyper-convenient modern machine? I doubt it. But I do believe he was very conscious of writing his legacy every day in between hits of ganja, scribbling down lyrics, and crafting reggae masterpieces. Marley approached his music and message with an aim toward eternal themes and endless reach. His son, Ziggy, sums up his legacy this way:

> Proud about my father? What am I most proud of? I think I'm proud of the legacy he left, I think is what it is. He has left us so much.

As you struggle to hear your *internal spirit voice* **following each failure moment of your life, please think about your legacy when you contemplate the next shift in your story's plot. As you strategize how to best write your legacy each day through your deliberate actions of output and service, look for ways in which you could potentially immortalize your legacy through creating art. And if not through art, then through other meaningful mediums of legacy impact. For many, this is simply the benevolent traits, principles, and ideals that they may have seeded within their children's Beings that carry on to bless the world. Or it could be just documentation in any form that represents the essence of your life and the legacy you pass solely for your family to protect and preserve—for the ongoing benefit of future generations of the family tree.**

As failure purifies you, remember you only have a finite number of heartbeats to sustain you as you try to make a positive, lasting impact. Approach your legacy-building efforts with a strong offense *now* to strengthen you in case circumstances someday force you to defend it with all of your energy reserves.

Think of my friend Sleeve, of Alan Dershowitz, of Sailor Jerry, and of Bob Marley. Remember Gary Vaynerchuk's advice and think about your legacy. Think about it now so you can be deliberate in how you write your legacy's next chapter—with more insightful intention—on the empty pages left after each purifying failure you walk through. Never forget you are writing your legacy every day, whether you admit it or not. Write it with authenticity as you seek to immortalize it.

KEEP YOUR ATTACHMENTS INTERNAL

"The disease of our times is that we live on the surface. We're like the Platte River, a mile wide and an inch deep."

—STEVEN PRESSFIELD, AUTHOR OF *THE WAR OF ART*

> **LESSON:** Place your highest value on that which transcends the material things of life.

If you're unduly attached to the externals of your life, it will be difficult for you to hear your *internal spirit voice*. The more this voice is muted, the more difficult it is to connect with your unique *calling journey*. And the more profitless pain you will feel when **Failure Rule #1: *Failure Purifies*** announces itself in your life with all of its deconstructive force.

If you are ensconced too heavily into maintaining the financial, occupational, and status infrastructure you've built for yourself, you may find it hard to pull away and focus on what is happening with your inner life.

Buddha taught that uncontrolled craving leads to the grasping and clinging to external attachments. In this clinging, he taught, was the root of suffering. Jesus explained to the rich young ruler that if he really desired enlightenment, he needed to detach from his external material life and give away all of his belongings to the poor. In this, Jesus was making it clear that the key to balance and peace was rooting your attachments in what is internal.

So what exactly are internal attachments? Internal attachments are those values, macro and micro callings, spiritual instincts, and relationship centerpieces that transcend temporal circumstances, material fluidity, and the unavoidable emotional and physical pains that punctuate our lives. A devotion to a dying loved one that supersedes your commitment to your job. A calling that pulls you so strongly that you risk comfort to chase it into the unknown treachery of uncertainty and hardship. A nonconforming way of Being in the world that creates friction for you but that you must manifest to feel aligned with your internal self. An unflinching devotion to a belief in a higher power or a definitive reliance on a relationship with God.

Author Steven Pressfield always had a fidelity to his *internal spirit voice*. He followed that voice by taking on enabler jobs as a schoolteacher, a bartender, and an advertising copywriter. He followed that voice as he became homeless and was living out of the back of his car. Steven followed his *internal spirit voice* into the fluidity of changing circumstances by keeping his attachments consistently internal. **Failure Rule #1:** *Failure Purifies* was in effect for Steven as the external attachments of his life burned off so he could elevate the high value of his prioritized internal attachments.

For Steven, the key internal attachment was always the pull he felt to write. He prioritized his conviction to develop his writing skills above all external attachments that loosely held him at any given time. He did this because in listening to his *internal spirit voice*, he knew that the muse that chased him would never let up. He knew he needed to subordinate all surface attachments to his deep, internal attachment to actualizing meaning through his writing.

In an interview on the *James Altucher Show* podcast, Steven described how he had left multiple jobs and lost a marriage due to his fidelity to his calling to become a writer. He recalled that he would work for various advertising agencies to save up money to fund time to write his next book. He would leave each job around every four years. Steven recounted how, on many occasions, he would face temptation to stay at these jobs. His bosses would offer him comforts of mediocrity that might allure most people to stay—higher salaries, fancier offices, more perks, all the predictable strings. Steven would doubt himself, wondering if he was as crazy as everyone thought he was for quitting a stable job to go burn his savings to write a book. But he always doubted his doubts in the end and followed his *internal spirit voice*. He jettisoned external attachments and remained attached to his internal calling to be a writer. When Steven resisted his employers' pleas to stay, each time he made a deliberate decision to leave the framework of an ordinary life and cross the threshold into the realm of an extraordinary life.

Steven detailed key portions of his journey into an extraordinary life in his book *The War of Art*. In that book, he reveals anecdotes of his interlude with homelessness and living out of the back of his car. It was in that key transition period that Steven fully eschewed his external attachments and pressed forward into the grip of his internal attachments. This ultimately led to him becoming a bestselling author and writing multiple screenplays. It also led him to seeing his book *The Legend of Bagger Vance*—centered around a man battling his demons through the medium of golf and leveraging themes from the Bhagavad Gita (Hindu scripture)—become a film starring Matt Damon and Will Smith.

In the Star Wars story, Luke Skywalker is found initially living within the shallow safety of an ordinary life. Yet as he helps his aunt and uncle tend to the harvest at their farm on Tatooine, his *internal spirit voice* is urging him to break out into an extraordinary life of adventure. That voice gets louder and becomes audible through the conduit of Obi-Wan Kenobi. Obi-Wan encourages young Luke to leave his aunt and uncle and travel with him to Alderaan. Like many people, Luke still ignored this calling and chose to cling to the safety of his life out of fear, obligation, and a comfort bias. But if one clings to their life, they will lose it. And Luke almost lost his—until the *Divinity of Purpose* entered and dismantled the safe externals of his life. In the vein of the story of Job, Luke discovers that his home is destroyed and his aunt and uncle are killed. With his external attachments tragically purged, Luke embraces his calling and crosses the threshold into the life extraordinary. He transforms from a Being chained to externals into a Being whose faith is centered internally. And as a result, he dives into a wondrous life full of heroism and meaning.

I know there are many people who do not engage with art, work, business, or any area of life with a prism of depth that seeks to maximize attachments to the internal. I know that many people are entirely content and satisfied with parading through life seeking the path of least resistance, the path of most pleasure, and the path of highest safety.

For many people, their objective in life is to seek comfort, security, and avert failure at all costs. The adventurous call to an extraordinary life does not pull them. I get that. Sometimes I wish I was like that. But, like Steven Pressfield, I have a very different frequency flowing within me.

Sometime after graduating college, I decided to pursue a job that I viewed at the time as emblematic of an ordinary life. After quitting student teaching English to seventh graders—because the ordinary framework of the job I was training for was incompatible with my soul—I took my English degree without the teaching certification and went to work as a union steelworker. At that point, I walked away from a known and largely predictable path and decisively stepped into the unknown. I had no idea how a job at a steel plant might fit into my larger *calling journey* at the time, but I knew it was my next step into it. I left the template of an ordinary life and stepped into the onset of an extraordinary life.

Working in a steel plant, in and of itself, sounds not only like an ordinary life to most, but a downright monotonous and painfully boring ordinary life. Yet for me, the season of my life spent working at the steel plant was filled with extraordinary lessons about people, hard work, and the beauty of the oft unseen working poor. But after a year or so, I knew I had gained all I needed to gain from that experience. I knew that chapter had to close. I had grown slightly tired of the grit and grind of factory life. I thought I'd try something soft. Something comfortable. Something *nice*. Something *ordinary*.

So I got an entry level job in a mutual funds wholesale firm. My brother worked in that space and referred me. This was a nice gesture by him, and I wish I had been more worthy of his help. I had really wanted to give it a try. I thought that I needed the normalcy of an office job at that inflection point, but I was wrong.

Before I even finished training, my *internal spirit voice* was urging me to leave. It was urging me to once again embrace financial discomfort to chase more accessible meaning. So I detached from the external attachment to the new job and quit within a week or so. I didn't yet know where I would go, but I knew I had to leave.

Once I crossed that threshold and wandered into the realm of the extraordinary, I found my footing serving at-risk kids. I became a counselor to juvenile delinquents who were reintegrating into the community after being released from lockup. In this, I aligned with my *calling journey*, held fast to my attachments to the internal, and extracted all the meaning I was meant to receive for that next season in my life.

As you struggle to stay aligned with your *calling journey*, be patient with yourself if you detour into rest stops of an ordinary life. If you find yourself at these stops, just don't stay there longer than you should. Your *internal spirit voice* will tell you how long you're supposed to be there.

Keeping faith to your internal attachments may mean leaving a stable career with a six-figure salary so you can leverage savings and retrain for a lower-paying career path that carries more meaning. Like Steven Pressfield walking away from advertising jobs every four years so he could leverage his savings, write a book, and more fully align himself with his *calling journey*.

Only you can know what a fidelity to your internal attachments means to you. Only you can know what your risk tolerance is. Only you can judge the depth of clarity you need to have in your moments of critical decision-making. However these variables shake out for you, just make sure you find your way back to the extraordinary realm—somehow, some way, and at some point. Make sure you find a way to always rejoin yourself with the fulfillment of your *calling journey*.

Let the failure of being unduly attached to life's externals purify you so you can regain an attachment to the internal. Do not mourn inappropriately when your external attachments deteriorate. Instead, seize the opportunities in that freedom by embracing the extraordinary newness of being grounded in internal attachments.

ANTICIPATE FAILURE RULE #1

FAILURE PURIFIES

As you forge forward into your *calling journey's* mysterious contours as an *entrepreneur, creative, or authentic*, remember **Failure Rule #1: Failure Purifies**. Anticipate failure's purifying power, and be prepared to harness it amid the pain and confusion of your failure moments. Remember that failure *will* burn off the areas of your life that can gain from being reimagined, reconfigured, and reconstructed. Prepare yourself to submit to the purifying power of failure that will strip you of your faulty foundations and give you the glorious opportunity to rebuild them with deeper strength and sharper strategy.

As you anticipate failure's coming purification, remember J.R.R. Tolkien's interlude with exile at the cottage in Little Haywood. Think about how the lights that emerged from the shadows of Tolkien's failure state—caused by war and sickness—came to illuminate for him the creative literary fire within that beckoned him to oxygenate its flame. Plan to clearly recognize what you aren't made for—your "hell no" paths—so you can align with your *internal spirit voice* and chase your unequivocal "hell yes" pursuits, like Neil Armstrong did, knowing that your heartbeats are finite and precious.

Ready yourself for the reality that the purification of failure never feels like a blessing in the heat of its arrival. That comes later, like it did for professional tenpin bowler Thomas Smallwood. Similarly, you must ready yourself to seek out opportunities to work for free or for little as you stumble through the learning curve failures of entering a new space.

You must press on and focus on building your experience, knowledge, and relationship stacks with formal or informal apprenticeship and mentorship scenarios as much as can be accomplished. Like Andrew Yang would advise.

As failure continues to purify you on your journey, be ever-seeking for those key game-changing connectors that might totally transform your trajectory into a closer alignment with your *calling journey's* next big steps. As you seek, remember the significance that CAO Cigars' master blender Rick Rodriguez experienced when he met his game-changing mentor, Benji Menendez.

As you anticipate the purification of failure during your *calling journey* marathon, be constantly attentive to the inner discomfort and groaning that ails you when mediocrity and stagnancy set in. Think of the audacious, authentic ways that fictional lawyer Jimmy McGill responded to such groaning in the TV show *Better Call Saul*. If you choose to act audaciously in response to your groaning, obeying your *internal spirit voice*, prepare also to have a plan with an intent to iterate as you travel away from your discomfort. Remember the power of momentum in this, as thriller writer Michael Connelly reminds us. It is the power of momentum that will be the key for you to outrun the brutality of failure's purification.

Be cognizant that as **Failure Rule #1: *Failure Purifies*** imposes itself on your story, you should consider how you might share your story to imprint your legacy for the instructive benefit of others through some form of art output. Think of the reach of legendary tattooist Norman "Sailor Jerry" Collins's legacy carried by his authentic tattoo flash designs, his writings, his libertarian radio show, his music, the clothing line, and the spiced rum that proudly bears his name decades after his death.

And always hold most tight your internal attachments as you brace for, and endure, failure's purification. Do not live on the surface. Live deep more than wide. Don't be tethered to the grip of external attachments.

Instead, eschew external attachment. Let failure purify you, and fall into the tumult of an extraordinary life. Like author Steven Pressfield did when he quit his job and ended up living out of his car before emerging as a bestselling author.

The phoenix has to burn before it emerges. Many times, you must also burn by the torch of the great purifier—failure—before you can emerge into the glorious joining with your mysterious, tumultuous *calling journey* of meaning. Plan on this. Anticipate this with eagerness. Because **Failure Rule #1:** *Failure Purifies* is the best sign of the coming of each bright new beginning.

FAILURE RULE #2
NOTHING IS SAFE

"The world is changing. Markets have crashed. Jobs have disappeared. Industries have been disrupted and are being remade before our eyes. Everything we aspired to for 'security,' everything we thought was 'safe,' no longer is: College. Employment. Retirement. Government. It's all crumbling down."

—JAMES ALTUCHER, INVESTOR, CHESS PLAYER, PODCASTER, COMEDIAN, SERIAL FAILURE, AND AUTHOR OF *CHOOSE YOURSELF*

> **PRINCIPLE:** The world is inherently unsafe. Jobs, industries, economies, relationships, and physical health are all inherently unsafe. Therefore, meaning, fulfillment, survival, and prosperity can be found in holding tight to internal attachments and holding loose to that which is attached to the unsafe external world. Nonattachment to this unsafe world enables nimble reinvention. It allows a path toward being content in all circumstances. It produces the freedom for one to *live to win* in an unsafe world—in spite of having been *born to lose*.

MIND THE FIRE INSIDE

FOLLOW PURSUITS WORTHY OF YOUR LIFE

"I think there's a fire burning in every one of us to make a dent in the universe. But, it gets extinguished by the mediocre visions of those who defend the status quo encouraging us to be practical and realistic...I did what was practical. I made every decision based on its external value. And eventually the fire went out."

—SRINIVAS RAO, PODCASTER, AUTHOR OF *THE ART OF BEING UNMISTAKABLE*

LESSON: Build sustainable conditions to mind your fire inside.

Because nothing is safe anyway, it behooves you to follow pursuits worthy of your life. This means that you need to keep the fire inside burning. Otherwise, you fall into the trap of basing your life on external decisions. When you do this, your fire burns out. When you allow your fire inside to burn out, you will feel the dull comforting lie of external safety. And you will also suffer the deep penetrating emptiness of a fireless life.

In the end, you will come to realize that the illusion of external safety and permanent stability is a crushed myth. Because **Failure Rule #2** holds true, an undue fidelity to a belief in safety is anathema to an alert soul's modus operandi.

So as you mind the fire inside, take your eyes off the distraction signs that promote safety first and instead enjoy the edgy, bumpy exhilaration found in the gravel road of rugged authentic living. Chase pursuits worthy of your life as you embrace a measured detachment from material dependence and worship. Don't let the meat hooks of safety, material comfort, and the allure of a pain-free life detour you from making inextinguishable the fiery pursuits worthy of your life.

Fire doesn't just happen on its own. It needs support. It needs to be minded by conducive conditions. Take it from Smokey Bear:

> Fire occurs whenever combustible fuel in the presence of oxygen at an extremely high temperature becomes gas. Flames are the visual indicator of the heated gas. Fire can also occur from lower-temperature sources. Over time, combustible materials, such as smoldering embers can reach their ignition temperature.

Fire. We all know Smokey Bear is right on the science of fire. Fire is essential to the physical lives we lead. We need it for warmth, for cooking food, and for energy production, and my cigar doesn't do me much good without it either.

Srinivas Rao, in his book *The Art of Being Unmistakable*, describes a sort of metaphysical, spiritual fire in all of us. It's a fire that burns for a life authentic. It's a fire that burns to elevate the highest use of our most unique talents and gifts. This intangible fire inside works very similarly to the science of physical, tangible fire. If you don't nourish the conditions necessary to keep this fire inside going, you will slide into numbness, mediocrity, and disenchantment. In order to follow pursuits worthy of your life, you need to mind your fire inside. Because a soul on fire is a soul alive.

Combustible fuel. The fire inside that burns to unite with the path of your mysterious *calling journey* needs combustible fuel to keep burning. That fuel is created by the consistent engagement with the next perceivable steps of your *calling journey*.

What do you need to do right now to keep your fire inside going? What is that combustible fuel for you?

If you are an entrepreneur contending with declining revenue, you may need to find your fuel in the adjacent possible. What is right next to what you're doing now that draws from, expands upon, and will be additive in a meaningful way to your product or service offering? Find and develop that adjacent possible, and turn it into combustible fuel to help you mind the sustainability of your fire inside.

Are you struggling with a meaning deficit while stuck in a well-paying corporate job? Then, in the form of some strategic side hustle or shadow career, you need to engage with your *calling journey's* next steps. This will help you to create the necessary combustible fuel to keep your fire inside burning. Take that class you've been considering. Reach out to that potential mentor you admire and see what wisdom they may have to share with you. Put pen to paper on your business idea, and take the first affordable step into making it a reality. Whatever those next actionable steps are in your *calling journey,* you need to engage with them. You need to create the combustible fuel necessary to keep the fire inside burning.

As you engage in the next meaningful, affordable step in your *calling journey,* on your way to pursuing something worthy of your life, know that failure will come. Because nothing is safe, pursuing something worthy of your life is also not safe. Sometimes such pursuits are inherently less safe by their very nature. So, as you proceed, find the most minimum viable steps. Make sure that if the steps you choose should fail, you can absorb those failures without calamity.

Know that failure is part of the formula to success, not an indication of unresolvable defeat. Actions and failures travel together. To make them good traveling partners, you must maintain healthy friction between these two companions when they intersect. This is critical to ensure that your failures produce actionable feedback for correction. Actionable feedback is necessary to best lead you closer to success in each subsequent next step.

If you can do this while relying on a backdrop of stability—even if it is a backdrop ultimately not worthy of the fullness of your life and calling—you will be far better off and prepared to reach the eventual actualization of pursuits worthy of your life.

Oxygen. If engaging in the next steps of your *calling journey* is the combustible fuel that keeps your fire going, then what is your oxygen? *Your oxygen is your spirit.* Your spirit needs to be fortified, inspired, informed, and flexible in order to be applied effectively to your efforts. You can't create combustible fuel with your efforts unless you first have a properly nurtured spirit. This means that you must find instruction and inspiration in mentors, both virtual and in-person. Find those who can help color your ideas and decisions. Develop a diverse portfolio of mentors to call upon. Read full-length books. If nonfiction, explore the stories of great people who have trod the paths of authenticity and meaning that you seek. If fiction, extrapolate the hero's journey lessons from the protagonists you follow. When you watch films and television, look for applicable story lines and nuggets of insight that help you understand the dynamic of your own *calling journey.* Build an arsenal of reliable, inspirational, and pragmatic inputs to properly nurture your spirit. You will need this as oxygen to breathe into your combustible fuel as you struggle to keep your fire inside burning.

High-Temperature Heat Conditions. Smokey Bear points to different heat sources that sustain fire, high and low. For the fire inside, high-temperature heat conditions produce the technicolor pivot points that radically push us deeper into the flow of our *calling journeys.* When those rare moments occur, you need to appreciate the rarity of such moments. These rare moments cause the fire inside to burst into actionable flames that catapult you firmly into an entirely new phase of your *calling journey.*

Like when a new product you release wildly outperforms even your high watermark projections, taking your business—and by extension your *calling journey*—to an entirely unforeseen new level. Like the day you sign your first client to a long-term contract as a new gig economy worker or as a self-practitioner. Like when you finish that first manuscript you've been working on for years in the cracks of your life. Like, for me, when in one day I received a material promotion in my executive banking career, signed a deal with a *New York Times* bestselling co-author to collaborate on a novel, and signed the Celtic punk band Flatfoot 56 to my record label Sailor's Grave Records—a band I always loved and had been talking to for years (and who played my wedding complete with kilts and bagpipes). These are all examples of rare moments of high-temperature heat conditions that populate our *calling journey's* highlight reel over time. They are important but rare. Appreciate them when they occur, and use them for motivation in the trenches of everyday low-temperature heat conditions.

Low-Temperature Heat Conditions. To sustain the fire inside, you need more than just the rare high-temperature heat conditions of perfect culminating circumstances to keep a meaningful fire inside going.

Often, it's the consistent burn of well-managed low-temperature heat conditions that keeps us safely moving along our *calling journey* with a meaningful fire inside. The low-temperature conditions don't result in us feeling the thrill of the high temperature fire burning inside us. Instead, the gains made amid the low-temperature heat conditions are what move us toward the moments of high-temperature rarities.

It's in the late-night minding of your side-hustle business when the last thing you want to do is log on to your laptop and push the needle. But you do it anyway, to keep the firing inside going. Because you hope someday that your side hustle evolves into your core income.

It's in the early Saturday morning hours when you crack the books for the class that you're taking on the side to mind your shadow-career ambitions. It's the last thing you want to do after working all week at your day job, but you do it anyway. Because you know your temporary lack of enthusiasm doesn't reflect your long-term interest and vision. So, you keep the fire inside burning.

It's the five hundred words you bang out late at night on your slow-cooking manuscript. You're exhausted, but you do it anyway. Because you know that even when you feel like shit, you can still produce good writing.

Muster the discipline to manufacture low-temperature heat conditions to mind your fire inside. Else, the monotony of life will threaten to extinguish your flame.

Remember **Failure Rule #2:** *Nothing Is Safe.*

If you fail to create combustible fuel by engaging in the next steps of your *calling journey*, you will not actualize the pursuits worthy of your life. If you fail to nourish your spirit, you will not have the sustainable oxygen needed to keep your fire going. If you fail to maintain discipline in everyday low-temperature heat conditions by engaging in the next steps of your *calling journey*, then your fire will extinguish. You need to do this even when those steps are tedious and you are tired. Otherwise, you will miss the opportunity to follow the pursuits worthy of your life.

When author Srinivas Rao was working at corporate jobs trying to live up to the external societal expectations that he had bought into, his fire inside burned out. In this experience, he became painfully aware that the fire inside was the only thing—intangible, elusive, and metaphysical as it may be—that would ever help him find alignment with his *calling journey*. He knew that if he didn't find a way to reignite that fire inside, he would never find a way out of the meaningless career stumbling he had fallen into. He knew the fire inside was the one thing that would help push him into pursuits worthy of his life.

Srini endured terrible bosses. He experienced deep depression. He exhibited physical symptoms of his depressed state—like irritable bowel syndrome. This all stemmed from the near-catastrophic meaning deficit he was battling.

After much introspection, Srini finally made the decision to walk away from the stumbling meaninglessness of his corporate job-hopping career path. He chose instead to leverage the spiritual lessons he learned from surfing to craft his own unmistakable life. This led him ultimately into a path in which he helped tell the stories of those who also crafted unmistakable lives. With a deliberate decision to radically change his life and reignite the fire inside, Srini joined himself with pursuits worthy of his life. He went on to author several books and to host the *Unmistakable Creative* podcast, among many other endeavors.

Are you joining yourself with pursuits worthy of your life? If you're not, how will you ignite the fire inside to allow yourself to do so?

These are the questions that the cupcake goddess Gigi Butler once asked herself.

Gigi relentlessly pursued stardom as a country music singer in her twenties and into her early thirties. This, to Gigi, was a pursuit well worthy of her life. And she stuck with this chase for many years after having moved to Nashville.

Yet, as she grew weary in the chase, she saw less evidence of a trajectory leading her to the actualization of the pursuit. This subtle whispering of her *internal spirit voice* began growing louder as she struggled each day running her own cleaning business. The cleaning business was an enabler business that supported her as she chased the country singer dream (see **Failure Rule #4:** ***Build Your Thing One and Thing Two Dependency***).

Gigi's entrepreneurial fire inside was ignited early in life. When she was just a young girl of seven, she sold eggs to her neighbors out of her little red wagon. When she was only fifteen, she took control of her work life and bought her own cleaning supplies. She used those supplies to start her own cleaning business within her rural California community. Gigi had always kept the fire inside burning. Early on, she learned how to create combustible fuel through her engagement with each tiny, affordable next step in her *calling journey*.

As you know, fire doesn't just happen. It needs a mix of certain conditions to ignite and maintain. One of those conditions is the presence of oxygen. The oxygen for the fire inside is a well-nourished spirit. Gigi's spirit was bolstered and sustained by a deep abiding faith in God, a commitment to a strong work ethic, and an indefatigable belief that her *calling journey* was leading her toward a culminating high-temperature moment.

Gigi bypassed the college path early on for her pursuit of country music stardom. This pursuit was always undergirded by self-directed entrepreneurial efforts, most prominently her cleaning business. Gigi always had a *Portfolio of Pursuits* mindset while embracing the **Thing One and Thing Two Dependency** model (see **Failure Rule** #4). She built her cleaning business in Nashville by leveraging the friendly customer service skills that she mastered while waiting tables at Red Lobster as a *Third Door* into building a clientele. Through this, she met and befriended many affluent and well-known people who became her clients. Some of these clients were big-time country artists like Taylor Swift and Leanne Rimes.

Gigi's whole life has been full of a consistent, steady engagement with the minding of the low-temperature fire inside. She never stopped believing that it would eventually build to a high-temperature, pivot-point-inducing flame.

One day she was cleaning a toilet for one of her clients and her cell phone shivered with an incoming call from her brother. He was hanging out in New York City and stopped into a fancy cupcake shop. He knew his sister loved baking and that she made some banging cupcakes. He also well knew and understood her entrepreneurial spirit. He told her that the red velvet cupcake he was eating at this popular shop wasn't that great. He told her that hers was way better. And then he told her she should open up her own cupcake shop.

Gigi stood looking in her client's bathroom mirror after the call pondering the idea. She pondered for a long time, staring into the mirror. She looked at the dirty, ragged cleaning clothes she was wearing. *Why not?* she thought.

Gigi knew **Failure Rule #2** well in that moment: *Nothing Is Safe*. Her dream to become a country singer was not safe. She finally accepted that it had failed. All she had left was a successful cleaning business that she knew was not a pursuit fully worthy of her life. She also knew that she had learned from all of her failures. Most importantly, she was determined to not give up chasing a pursuit worthy of her life. Even though it would not be safe.

Much has transpired since that moment in the client's bathroom where Gigi obeyed her *internal spirit voice*. With a new idea hatched in large part by her brother's encouragement, she leveraged her talent, her limited resources, her faith, and the support of her family as she opened her first cupcake shop in Nashville.

But failure struck quick, hard, and frequently in her effort to launch the cupcake shop. She was rejected by four banks for loan requests. Much like me when I launched my first record label, she defaulted to the only option she had—she maxed out her credit cards. Gigi did this to the tune of $100,000.

Gigi felt the weight of **Failure Rule #2** when, on her shop's opening day, she found herself with only thirty-three dollars left in her checking account and stacks of large, unpaid payables sitting on her desk.

But Gigi consistently applied the oxygen of her spirit and leaned on her faith to help her navigate the way through. She continued utilizing the *Thing One and Thing Two Dependency Model* (**Failure Rule #4**) and kept working her cleaning jobs while running the cupcake store. She minded her low-temperature fire inside by engaging diligently in each next affordable step in her *calling journey*. She did this step by step until she was in the black. Then she opened more stores and franchised her brand.

By 2013, Gigi's cupcake stores boasted over one hundred locations, could be found across twenty-four states, and had generated over $43 million in annual sales.

Along with running her cupcake empire, Gigi is now also a well-sought-after public speaker. She has written a book about her journey called *The Secret Ingredient: Recipes for Success in Business and Life*.

When Gigi is asked about what kept her going through each failure and hardship—what maintained the oxygen of her nurtured spirit—it is her faith that she credits the most. She explains it this way:

> When I tell my story to people, I always stop myself at this spot because I don't want to shove my religion down anyone's throat. We're all free to believe in our own way. But I mention it because He was an important part of my story. He was. He took a broken-down country singer and helped her to make a beautiful life.

As you strive to chase pursuits worthy of your life, remember Gigi. Think of her on the opening day of her cupcake store when she was $100,000 in debt and had thirty-three dollars in her checking account, a large stack of unpaid bills, and no real marketing plan to dig her out.

Think of Smokey Bear, Srinivas Rao, and Gigi Butler and accept **Failure Rule #2: *Nothing Is Safe***. In this acceptance, press on anyway by minding your fire inside, one engagement at a time, with your *calling journey's* next steps. Do this until you collide into pursuits worthy of your life.

BORN TO LOSE, LIVE TO WIN

"Life's not safe. Your work's not safe. When you leave the house, it isn't safe. That's why you have to enjoy the moment."
—LEMMY KILMISTER, THE LATE, GREAT SINGER FOR MOTORHEAD

> **LESSON:** When you feel the weight of having been born to lose, defiantly choose to instead live every day with the intent to win.

He may not be the prettiest face to put behind a message, but despite the two grotesque moles that pretty much owned his face, the late, great rocker Lemmy Kilmister of the British rock 'n' roll band Motorhead knew the truth of **Failure Rule #2:** *Nothing Is Safe.*

Lemmy's real name was Ian. While he could never verify the origin, many have traced his nickname to his school days. It was said that he was nicknamed Lemmy because he would often say, "Lemme (lend me) a quid 'til Friday," it was alleged, to borrow money to keep his slot-machine habit going. Lemmy was always a gambler.

Starting in his early school days of taking payday loans to support his gambling, taking up smoking at age eleven, and prioritizing rock 'n' roll and women in his teens, Lemmy never lived safe. Lemmy maintained a life on the edge right up until his death at age seventy. His consummate appetite for alcohol, amphetamines, and rock 'n' roll barely dissipated right up until his dying day.

I have a memorial tattoo with Lemmy's portrait on my leg. It is accompanied with lettering touting Lemmy's trademark catchphrase—Born to Lose, Live to Win. The phrase is embedded on his tombstone in the past tense, Born to Lose, Lived to Win.

I didn't get the Lemmy tattoo because I am an advocate of alcohol abuse, amphetamine use, or other wildly dangerous behavior that anyone in the world other than Lemmy could not withstand for very long. No, I got it because consistent with his Libertarian leanings, Lemmy saw the world as inherently unsafe. He saw himself as predisposed to failure and losing. And he took on the ultimate challenge of defying the dangers of an unsafe world and overcoming the limitations of a predisposition to failure. He followed his internal spirit voice that called him to conquer failure and leave an indelible imprint on rock 'n' roll culture. He did this by defeating his failure tendencies, carrying the burden of his unsafe addictions, and living to win anyway.

Through all the failures I've traversed across my life, many times I've had a nagging feeling that I was utterly born to lose. I've often felt a day late and a dollar short. It is in these moments that I reflect on the unchanging imperfection of the human condition, the unsafe nature of walking through life, and the glorious adventure of getting up every day and choosing to live to win anyway.

So when I feel overwhelmed and am reminded that I was born to lose, I intentionally channel my inner Lemmy, and I choose to live to win anyway. And while I do my best to channel Lemmy as much as possible, I still sometimes find myself overwhelmingly struck with the fragility of this unsafe life.

A few nights ago, I woke up at two thirty and did not fall back to sleep until six thirty. There was literally no specific issue in my life causing my mind to cave into sleepless worry. My life has literally never been better than it is right now, as I type this, at this very season of my journey. Yet it was this specific realization, and my sense of disbelief of how good I have it right now, that ushered in a frightening bout of foreboding joy.

In this writhing, tense, state of foreboding joy, the calmness of rational gratitude did not slow my racing mind. It did not rid me of the anxiety I was uncharacteristically experiencing. Post-traumatic stress disorder (PTSD) from past life shitstorms, cascading crises, and unending strings of failures overtook my spirit at the most deep and profound level. In my mind, I cataloged all the things that had gone wrong in my life and traced how many of them could possibly go wrong again. I war-gamed all sorts of tragedies, calamities, and misfortunes that might yet still come my way. Job loss, income stream eliminations, lawsuits, health threats, investment degradation, harm that could affect my children, fear of issues in my marriage—pretty much everything imaginable except an electromagnetic pulse (EMP) bomb exploding over my home. Of course, there was no evidence of any imminence or probability of any of these things. Intellectually, I knew that I had already hedged against most of these risks through strategies I've employed in the iterative building process of my life. A building process acutely informed by lessons from the past.

Yet here I was wide awake in the middle of the night unable to enjoy any rest. I lay restless, unable to internalize the beauty of the gratitude I intellectually acknowledged. Because nothing is safe, our deliberate efforts to *"enjoy the moment,"* as Lemmy advised, are also not safe.

It is your challenge to work through the moments that you slide into the anxiety of an unsafe world. You must feel every ounce of the terror this anxiety produces. Then you need to remind yourself of the rational actions you've taken to mitigate the risks in your life, or plan to finally enact them. Lastly, you must move swiftly back into a joy-driven engagement with every precious moment you are given. You must always find a way back to living to win.

In the post-9/11 age, the world should be acutely aware of the reality that nothing is safe. After the terrorist attack on the Ariana Grande concert in Manchester, UK, in 2017, Motorhead's show scheduled the following day was canceled. The decision was made by police and organizers. In an interview with *Loudwire*, Lemmy was asked if the event changed anything for him and if he would feel comfortable playing after the attack. He told the interviewer that he didn't care and would've gone on stage the day after if the police and organizers would've let him. He echoed the often-used logic that if he stopped, the terrorists would win. To this, he added, *"Fuck those people. They don't like rock 'n' roll, and I don't like them."* The interviewer, appearing to expect a different answer, then continued her line of questioning by asking the same thing differently. She asked Lemmy if he felt vulnerable. Lemmy responded:

> We've always been vulnerable. You know, every day you go out of the house, you could end up under a bus. Or somebody could be hitting you over the head for your money. Nothing is safe. Everybody seems to be obsessed with safety. Well, nothing is safe, okay? Nothing. Make the most of it while you're safe now. You might not be tomorrow, baby.

Many of us think differently about safety and its rightful place in our lives. When my wife and I would sit on our South Philly balcony, hordes of helmet-less sports bike enthusiasts would drive by doing wheelies while making a raucous scene on Columbus Boulevard. I absolutely loved it. It was one of my favorite things to see during my time living there. I was jealous that I wasn't part of the action. My wife, however, was offended and annoyed at the disturbance they made and appalled at the danger they put themselves in. I would disagree with her opinion but respect the reality that we all view safety differently. It is not that she was wrong or I was right. It is that we all have agency to cultivate our own individual risk tolerance matrices. And the risk tolerance matrices of the sport bike enthusiasts bore absolutely no resemblance to hers, while it sat adjacent to mine.

As an entrepreneur who intentionally contends with danger, uncertainty, and risk regularly, you have to remember that nothing is safe. *Nothing.* Life is defined by the reasonable risks you take. You have to enjoy every moment of your ride—or, as Lemmy said it, *"make the most of it while you're safe now."* Learn to do this no matter how high the stakes or how tense the stress.

As you travel the unsafe gravel roads of your *calling journey*, learn to enjoy the moments along the way. Because doing *is* becoming, learn to appreciate the process of becoming. Learn to love each version of yourself on your way to your North Star *Thing Two* dream (See **Failure Rule #4**).

In the first episode of the fourth season of the TV show *Billions* (written by Brian Koppelman), alpha male hedge fund shop owner Bobby Axelrod (played by Damian Lewis) sports a Motorhead T-shirt for a reason. In the show, Bobby Axelrod embodies the spirit of aggressive, reward-focused, intelligent risk-taking. Axelrod operates with an implicit acceptance of myriad possible eventualities. Bobby clearly values winning as his highest goal. However, his winning often devolves his character's journey into an immoral cautionary tale. Yet Bobby also highly values the thrill granted to him by the very action of pursuit itself. He is addicted to this feeling of being truly alive, which, in the rare times scruples are actually in play for him, is meaningful and admirable.

In the scene in which Axelrod is sporting a Motorhead T-shirt, the driving, iconic sounds of Motorhead's classic song "Ace of Spades" thunders as he goes about the battles of his day defending his self-made empire. The classic song urges that:

"If you like to gamble, I tell you I'm your man
You win some, you lose some, it's all the same to me
The pleasure is to play, makes no difference what you say
I don't share your greed, the only card I need is the Ace of Spades"

Axelrod channels Motorhead because, like Lemmy, he knows that you win some and lose some. He also knows that as an entrepreneur, the real pleasure is to play. And in the playing, nothing is safe.

Nothing.

Now, from a broader philosophical standpoint, I suspect we may all know this. We all know that we don't really know how long we will live. We don't know how or when we will die. And we all know that on any given day a million unexpected or unforeseen things could happen. Only the delusional would be arrogant enough to think that they could prudently control, or prevent, all of the millions of potentially unpredictable variables that shape the timing and nature of our various fates.

While we all likely know and understand this, it doesn't really do us much good to obsessively think about all the horrible things that could happen to us on any given day, either in business or in life.

Keeping prudence and risk awareness subordinated in their proper places, you need to recognize your journey as unsafe while you prepare to enjoy each moment as you choose to live to win. Reasonably prepare to mitigate the known risks in your life but stop pretending life is safe and expecting it to be so. Because nothing is safe, you must subordinate your concerns of safety and prioritize chasing what aligns with your *internal spirit voice*.

As you chase the pursuits worthy of your life, don't overlook the pleasure and joy nestled within every nook and cranny of a life authentic. Joy is there to find amid the chaos. Joy is discoverable within the dark shadow of safety's absence.

Don't let exaggerated feelings of failure's terror prevent you from taking the ride you were created to enjoy. Don't let that inhibition prevent you from savoring the joys that exist in intentionally *living to win* even as you wake up many days feeling as if you were *born to lose*.

GLORIFYING SAFETY PRODUCES SHALLOWNESS

"If your world is just about safety, then your world is too small."
—DR ROB LONG, FOUNDER OF HUMAN DYMENSIONS

LESSON: Don't inappropriately glorify or outsource safety in your life.

Good ol' Teddy Roosevelt said, *"Never yet was worthy adventure worthily carried through by the man who put his personal safety first."* Roosevelt didn't need me to write this book to know the truth of **Failure Rule #2: Nothing Is Safe.**

Yet you should still be conscious of the role of safety in everything you do. Just because nothing is truly safe doesn't mean you can't decide how best to make your paths as safe as possible. You should always value safety and measure it responsibly against the weight of other competing values as you properly place it in its due role. But what you ought not do is to unreasonably venerate safety above all else, all the time, or because a posing authority urges you to.

Putting safety first at all times and in all circumstances is impossible. Even if you were to quarantine yourself indefinitely, risk still exists inside your body and mind and all around you, wherever you are, no matter how you live, because you exist in an inherently unsafe and imperfect world. A world in which sickness, inevitable death, and unexpected harm have never been eliminated.

If, within the agency of your own personal risk assessment, you decide to place safety first in a given circumstance, you are then acting within the framework of freedom and individual choice. This is appropriate, individually curated, and a matter of your own personal judgment. It's unwise to run on an icy driveway or put your hand on a hot stove. Yet we all have, and we should be able to keep the freedom to be unwise.

However, whenever an external authority claims they have constructed rules, policy, and protocol as a means of putting your safety first, know that such expressions of benevolence are nothing but deleterious platitudes at best, and bald-faced lies at worst. Whether it is the Parents Music Resource Center (PMRC), which pushed for censorship under the banner of safety in the nineties, or the big tech tyrants trying to normalize cancel culture under the same banner in the new millennium, platitudes of safety-above-all always come from a source seeking control, censorship, and conformity. Whether it is the Patriot Act of the early 2000s or the War on Drugs of the eighties, policies largely built on the imposition of uniform safety are always at odds with the fundamental nature of intrinsic individual liberty and choice.

If you choose to elevate safety first under any circumstance in your life, do it because you are personally convicted it is the best path for you. Never bow to external imposition of elevated safety prioritization—be it from politicians, corporate leaders, or your well-meaning parents.

Dr. Rob Long's company Human Dymensions consults with organizations on how they ought to rightfully view decision-making in the workplace around the topic of risk. As an executive banker, I always have risk top of mind. Yet the safety concerns related to managing risk do not always outrank other concerns, objectives, and goals. Dr. Rob Long's consulting business is built around helping clients evaluate when safety ought to be first, and when it ought to fall down lower in the ranking. As you read in the anchor quote, he often warns that if your world is just about safety, then your world is too small.

As malevolent German bombs rained down on Britain in World War II, the British people immediately embraced a safety-first mentality to rightly create space to absorb the realities of war. They hunkered down and went underground. The bombing was incessant and horrible. The Brits remained underground for weeks. Yet after a while, they grew bored of the restrictive confinement of living with a safety-first mentality. The bombing never relented, but they began coming out from hiding anyway. They made adjustments and learned how to subordinate safety to a lower position than first, while still trying to mind their lives as safely as was possible. Schools reopened. Businesses reopened. Like many around the world have done through the COVID-19 pandemic of 2020, the Brits found balance, adapted their lives, and kept buggering on. Putting safety first simply made their lives unbearably too small living in bunkers. They had to break out.

Mike Rowe titled one of the episodes of his show *Dirty Jobs* on the Discovery channel "Safety Third." The episode was titled as such to arouse curiosity and to counter the assumption that safety must always be placed first. Rowe's point was not that safety should never be first or that somehow it ought always to be arbitrarily third but that fundamentally **Failure Rule #2** is universally true: ***Nothing Is Safe.***

In an interview on CNN, Rowe explained the anecdotal impetus for the episode. He was working on a crab boat out in the oceanic divide between two of the largest landmasses on Earth (Eurasia and the Americas)—the Bering Sea. He was working thirty feet up looking down at turbulent waters and a boat deck that appeared like the top of one's shoe when peering down. In that moment, Rowe's innocuous sense of reliance on the boat captain's provision of safety was in question. He felt very frightened. He went down to the wheelhouse to see if the boat captain had plans to halt the work until conditions became safer. He asked his boat captain about OSHA and was told that the priority was the ocean, not OSHA. Stunned, Rowe then listened to the boat captain lay upon him the unvarnished truth of the job. The boat captain said:

> I'm captain of this crab boat. My job is not to get you home alive. My job is to get you home rich. You wanna stay safe, that's on you. Be careful out there.

With that message, Rowe's long position of outsourcing his safety to some perceived authority was shattered. He took a moment before returning to the dangerous work and made sure that he applied every conceivable safety precaution he could. He knew—for maybe the first time—that safety was not valued first by anyone in charge. He knew that it was entirely up to him to evaluate his own safety and take measures into his own hands to ensure whatever safety could be accomplished. He deeply realized that safety was a matter of personal judgment and responsibility, and no one could guarantee it for you. He realized that just because he was in compliance, didn't mean he was out of danger. He now fully understood **Failure Rule #2:** *Nothing Is Safe.*

Don't let authorities bully you into a forced opinion as to where you need to place the value of safety in your life. Don't rely on authorities to keep you safe. Develop, through sober reflection and analysis, your own individual risk tolerances for the activities of your life. And then appropriately plan to mitigate risk as necessary to the level you've placed safety within each activity of your life. Remember, as the crab boat captain advised, that if you want to be safe, it's on you.

This means that you must be the judge of the role of risk and safety as you step out as an entrepreneur. This means that living an authentic life in alignment with your own uniqueness is more important than the safety of collective conformity. This means that your commitment to your work as a creative must never be subordinated to the safety imposition of a censorship-heavy cancel culture.

The prepper movement may rightfully be accused of taking safety and precaution to the extreme. It might be thought that preppers may sometimes fail to enjoy the moment. This has often made them the subject of mockery and critique. And, to a degree, fair enough.

Yet I don't view those who prepare for the worst but hope for the best as safetyphiles if they continue to live their lives with robustness after solidifying their preparations. I see the root of their commitment as a desire to protect against their acknowledgment of their own fragility. I see their preparations as resulting from a sound understanding of the insecurity of the world. They know nothing is safe, so they feel compelled to make safe whatever they imagine will enable that. And then they live their lives feeling freer as a result—with safety handled and subjugated to its rightful place down the priority ladder.

I am more intrigued by those who are numbed by a sense of false comfort produced by a lifetime of outsourcing safety to external authorities. Those trapped in this bubble sometimes seem to take absolutely no thought about the fragility of their life. They do not ponder the fragility of their physical mortality. They act boastfully in their circumstantial assuredness. They assume perpetual continuity in their financial certainty. And they have no realistic concerns about their employment longevity. They expect the government, FEMA, their boss, or other authority figures to have already figured out and planned for all their contingency needs. They actually feel everything is safe. For those in this bubble, an uninterrupted life of stability can blind them to the reality that nothing is safe. In this bubble, spiritual depth fails to take root and shallowness prevails.

Those cloistered in such uninterrupted financial, occupational, and physical certainty may easily miss the rich wisdom, insight, and character blessings that mark a life marred by instability, affliction, unraveling failure, and forced reinvention. Those who have experienced little hardship, little upheaval, and little occupational instability may easily miss out on experiencing the valuable level of self-awareness that can be wrought from walking through life's failure spaces. Those with little exposure to such volatilities risk the atrophy of their resilience and reinvention muscles.

As a result, safetyphiles fail to acquire the adaptivity skills that force one to necessarily take the deepest dive into internal strength, spiritual reliance, and acute pragmatic analysis. Those bereft of this ability risk suffering a shallowness of the soul that can be produced by the deadly softening of safety abundance.

Nothing is truly safe, so don't outsource your sense of safety to others. Evaluate your own risks, and mitigate them as you see fit to effectuate degrees of safety where you reasonably can.

Remember the words of the crab boat captain: *if you want to be safe, it's on you*. Find depth in your life by taking reasonable risks coupled with reasonably applied mitigants. Avoid the shallow life. Don't keep your world small. Avoid being a safetyphile. Don't inappropriately glorify safety. Because **Failure Rule #2:** *Nothing Is Safe* stands firm.

BEING COMFORTABLE IS OVERRATED

"Being an entrepreneur is like eating glass and staring into the abyss of death."
—ELON MUSK, FOUNDER OF TESLA AND SPACE-X

LESSON: At the end of your life, you will appreciate the reasonable risks you took more than the safe comforts you protected.

Being an *entrepreneur or a creative or living an authentic life* often implicitly carries with it a higher degree of risk and discomfort than other modes of Being. You may find this path as unpleasant and uncomfortable as eating glass. You may struggle with many moments that feel like you're staring into the abyss of death—when comfort is whispering in your ear to embrace it. In these moments, you must often reject comfort's call. Because its benefits are overrated.

And because **Failure Rule #2:** *Nothing Is Safe* applies to everything. Even to being comfortable.

In the film *Trouble with the Curve,* Clint Eastwood plays Gus Lobel, an aging, cantankerous old-school baseball scout for the Atlanta Braves. Personally, Gus is contending with failing eyesight. Professionally, he is contending with an industry that has turned to rely more on *Moneyball*-style statistical analysis for recruiting rather than the instincts of a seasoned, slightly mean old man. New executive blood threatens to lay Gus and his scouting philosophy out to pasture. But Gus will hear none of it. With the assistance of his boss and ally, Peter (played by John Goodman), Gus sets out to lend proof of concept to his claim that instinct and experience could still win the day in scouting strategies over the new-school statistical analysis approach. Along the way, a young executive, along with the rest of the Atlanta Braves' leadership team, tries to persuade Gus to just retire. They highlight the benefits of comfort that Gus would enjoy if he just gave in to their pressure. He is told in one scene, *"Well, you can take an early retirement, collect disability. With the pension we offer, you should be comfortable."*

But Gus Lobel didn't base his life or his decisions on what made him comfortable or safe. He was a man of grit, a man of white-knuckle work ethic, and a man who wanted to make an impact more than make a cushy life for himself. His decisions were dictated by his *internal spirit voice*, not the allure of immediate trappings. His response to the offer was decisive: *"Save it. Being comfortable is overrated."*

As the film unfolds, Gus presses on against the grain by lobbying for a young, unknown pitcher named Rigoberto to be drafted. With a portion of predictability, the pitcher proves to have the talent that Gus claimed to have detected. Gus wins the philosophical and professional battle against the haughty young executive out to fire him. Gus knew that meaning, impact, and adhering to the instinct of one's *internal spirit voice* was more important than caving to the nudgings of those calling for resignation and comfort.

The temptation to value security higher than it appropriately merits can be seductive with the lure of a big payday. A sense of safety is attractive and can command a large pull on one's decision-making. The promise of safety and comfort is a tough one to reject at all, let alone quickly and decisively like the character of Gus Lobel did.

Gus Lobel knew well **Failure Rule #2: *Nothing Is Safe***. He knew that the comfortable safety of just taking his pension would not meet his needs for meaning in his life, and thus wasn't really safe at all. For Gus, meaning—and all it would bring to his spirit—was more important than material and financial comfort.

The world is full of pleasant, relatively content, and comfortable people who lack substantive meaning in their lives. As a result, they often possess no measurable depth. Without depth, they fail to maximize the growth of their gratitude, empathy, and adaptability muscles.

Because being comfortable is overrated, many drunk with the numbness of stable contentment never become incentivized to risk their efforts in pursuit of meaningful, professional, artistic, spiritual, or relational depth. Because they are bound and beholden to the gods of safety and stability, urgency doesn't break through for anything. Drive catches no traction.

Meaning deprivation can often produce a heavy deficit of wisdom acquisition, enlightenment experiences, and reward appropriation. Being too comfortable can cause one to forfeit the satisfaction gained from inner life struggle. It can cause one to miss out on the deep relational fulfillment gained by joining others in justifiable risks.

Clinging to comfort was never something that was attractive to inventor and entrepreneur Elon Musk. Elon always believed that to actualize one's capacity to develop technology and to invent was to literally create magic in the world. From his early days of promoting electronic payments with PayPal, to his endeavors with electric cars through Tesla, straight through to his relentless pursuit to create planetary redundancy with SpaceX, Elon has always chosen to *"eat glass and stare into the abyss of death"* instead of slowing down and embracing the comforts available to one who has already wildly succeeded.

Elon not only fully understands **Failure Rule #2: *Nothing Is Safe*;** he deliberately chases the most unsafe paths to maximize the meaning of his unique, history-shaping *calling journey*. And failure is no stranger to Elon, even in his reinvention pursuits. When he set out to build his first rocket, he failed three times before finally succeeding on his fourth launch—just when he was poised to run out of funding.

True success doesn't rest. It keeps moving forward, expecting new failures to emerge as defeatable obstacles. True success keeps moving, embracing discomfort and danger as it evolves.

In my own *calling journey* of creative, entrepreneurial authenticity, I've embraced discomfort many times to chase meaning. Maxing out my credit cards to create my first record label as an unemployed father leading a single income household. Abandoning my home in Ohio to chase an insecure promise of prosperity in the northeast. Assuming high risk by partnering in an online lending business and purchasing a fitness center—when I could've settled for the comfortable path of a mediocre job with mediocre pay. I've known what it's like to stare into the proverbial abyss of death many times and taste the crunch of eating glass with each difficult decision.

With a storied legacy replete with white prostitutes, fighting social Darwinism, defying cultural racism, and punching through his calling, legendary boxer Jack Johnson knew what it was like to live a life of embracing discomfort in an unsafe world. No matter what the obstacle, Jack Johnson never flinched. He never fell back on the deceptive comforts that may have come along with bowing to the societal expectations of the time. Instead, he moved *"like a jellyfish"* because *"rhythm don't mean nothing."* In this, he went with the flow and never stopped.

I've always been attracted to boxing. This is strange, given I know very little about the sport and rarely watch any matches start to finish. It is less the actual mechanics of what happens in the ring that I gravitate toward and more the stories that are so often wrapped around the fighters themselves that intrigues me. Their stories of struggle. Of determination. Of grit, guts, and glory. Whether it's a Rocky flick or the story of Micky Ward or Muhammad Ali, it's always the indomitable spirit exuded that I am drawn to.

In a larger sense, I've always felt that the imagery of boxing was a fitting metaphor for so much of life itself. Life often necessitates a harnessed fighting spirit to get through the difficulties and tumult that so often encumber it. This is why I have a set of boxing gloves tattooed on the topside of my left forearm with a banner that reads *"Never Give In"*—to perpetually remind me to harness my fighting spirit as I walk through life.

Jack Johnson's entire life was emblematic of the *"Never Give In"* spirit. He became the first Black heavyweight champion of the early twentieth century by embracing discomfort and confronting the obstacles of an unsafe world. Jack had many obstacles to overcome. As a Black man living in the early twentieth century, he was inherently branded as an outcast of society simply because of the color of his skin. As a boxer, he aligned his reputation with a sport that, at the time, was under heavy scrutiny by society. Boxing was viewed as nothing but a lowly sport of barbarism. Jack Johnson, by association, was viewed as nothing but a lowly barbarian.

Jack was also a visceral violator of the sexual mores of the time. No, he wasn't gay—he just loved to have sex with white women. White people hated him for this. Black people hated him for this. But Jack never let the criticism stop him. He knew reputational comfort was overrated. He ignored the noise and kept punching in the ring. He kept his pedal to the metal in his beloved fast cars. And he kept his arm around white women.

It's been recorded that from the time Jack was young, he was a restless kid. It is said that he had always bubbled with ambition. That he was known to speak with great confidence—as if he was destined for great things. These great things all represented ambitions distinctly outside the expected reach of his inherited confines—a distinct culture of Black laborers.

It was this tough Black labor culture that conditioned Jack to be a fighter—in the ring and in life. Bred in the discomfort of pervasive racism, Jack was conditioned from early on to eschew judgment, eschew barriers, and punch his way through life. This spirit caused him to follow the dictates of his *internal spirit voice* and live out his *calling journey* with unsafe authenticity.

Jack came up as a fighter during a time in which the nation was entrenched with the rhetoric of social Darwinism. The zeitgeist of the time had Jack viewed as inferior. Social Darwinism had its grip on the culture, and many oriented their worldview around the idea that the white race was superior and dominant. Jack took this discomforting context and converted it into fuel. He defied the dogma of social Darwinism and displayed his bravado loudly as he mocked his detractors for being inferior to his athletic prowess.

Jack's entire universe was unsafe. As he navigated the seedy underground world of boxing culture, temptation and deception was all around. Rampant corruption. Hustlers. Prostitutes. Drugs. Pimps. Crime.

Most boxers lost ground in this environment. Many drowned in these seductive trappings. But Jack didn't allow any of this contextual negativity trap him or slow him down—except for, maybe, prostitutes. Well, only one white prostitute in particular. The one he married: Lucille Cameron.

It was this move that sent him into exile. Jack was sentenced to jail for violating the Mann Act, which forbade the interstate transport of any girl for the *"purpose of prostitution or debauchery, or for any other immoral purpose."* The underlying crime of that time was that he was specifically traveling with a white woman. Effectively rendered an outlaw, Jack then fled the country with his white wife and went to Europe. Now overseas, Jack still kept it moving, never stopping to be comfortable. He kept hustling, fighting, and moving forward.

Jack Johnson lived a remarkable life of charging headfirst into discomfort within the unsafe worlds of boxing, of cultural racism, and of exilic danger. Jack rounded out his adventurous life with a stint as a musician, memorializing his fighting career by storytelling in dime museums and playing small roles in films. Jack ultimately exited this world with the same velocity and intensity in which he lived—by dying in a high-speed car accident.

Jack Johnson punched his way through his unsafe life—never stopping to seek a comfortable life. His legacy went on to inform and inspire the career of Muhammed Ali. In 2018, under influence by Sylvester Stallone and other advocates of Johnson's legacy, President Trump finally did what both Bush and Obama failed to do—he posthumously pardoned Jack ninety-seven years later.

If your decision-making process is too heavily governed by the dictator of stability, the realization of your calling will be more than difficult. Toxic stability will stunt your achievement of maximum purpose. The fictional character of Gus Lobel knew this and chose meaning over the dangled carrot of a comfortable retirement.

Big thinking, vibrant dreaming, and bold living do not bow to the gods of stability and easy comfort. Look no further than the ongoing testament of Elon Musk's boldly prolific entrepreneurial output.

An undue regard for security and safety does not produce loud, authentic living. Jack Johnson's legacy proves this. Whether fighting in the ring, defying the cultural racism that enshrouded him, or fleeing in exile to Europe to maintain his interracial marriage, Jack Johnson lived loudly and authentically.

As you wrestle with direction while unwinding your *calling journey*, remember that an undue regard for comfort is the hobgoblin of small living. Remember Gus Lobel, Elon Musk, and Jack Johnson.

Remember that nothing is safe.

Remember that being comfortable is overrated.

CHOOSE THE HARD WAY

"Self-raised, self-made
Nothing was ever handed to me
I tasted pain, the gutter hugged me
Till I stood up and embraced the flames
Always pushing, always searching
Always crossing the line
Try to hold me back
I swing the hammer of inner strength
Always the hard way"

—SCOTT VOGEL, FRONT MAN FOR THE AMERICAN HARDCORE PUNK BAND TERROR, FROM THE SONG "ALWAYS THE HARD WAY"

> **LESSON:** Choose the hard right way over the easy wrong way even if suffering and hardship follow.

Those who swing the hammer of inner strength and who always choose the hard way do so because the easy way is rarely the right way. And it takes inner strength to choose the hard right over the easy wrong. Because **Failure Rule #2: *Nothing Is Safe*** stands, choosing the hard way because it's right isn't safe either. Choosing the hard way can often produce deliberate suffering. Sometimes it may mean you are maligned, targeted, and demonized. Those who choose the hard way do it despite all of this. They do it because they understand what the metal band Hatebreed sings: *"I'd rather suffer for the truth/Than prosper from a lie."* So they take the arrows, scrutiny, and blowback that comes against them—and they keep moving forward. They move forward because they typically carry a *Portfolio of Pursuits* mindset. With this mindset, any consequence of failure that occurs from embracing the hard way collapses into a pre-positioned waterfall of plans backed by a long thought-out idea stack.

One day, while working as a partner in the online lending firm, I just left. Resigned. In an instant, I withdrew from the partnership and forfeited that portion of my income by self-selecting out of my employment arrangement as chief operating officer (COO). With that long-developing decision, I chose the hard way and temporarily crucified the perception of my stability.

I loved the online lending business. I was constantly looking for ways to optimize, future-enable, and grow the business. I didn't know I was going to resign that day. I had wrestled violently with the decision points that fed into the culminating decision for months. That day, I fell flat on the mat and quit the wrestling.

Tumult had ruled the day within the four-year young startup. In its short life, it had already experienced changes of control, investor turnover, and tightening regulatory headwinds. One day, we received a cease-and-desist order from the attorney general of a state in which the majority of our loans were made. Our concentration risk issues had come to roost before we could properly diversify. This shattered the stability of the business. On that same day, a competitor falsely accused us of stealing sensitive customer information stemming from an employee who had worked previously with the competitor. Along with receiving a legal complaint from the competitor, this also led to a costly, grueling federal criminal investigation (that was ultimately dropped). Other issues were hovering. Misjudgments were made in our transition to automation that cut deep to the bottom line. Archaic operational processes, modernized too late, collided with the eager strangulation of increasing regulation (*Operation Chokepoint*).

The company had lost, and was losing, a lot of money.

It was within this vortex of unflinching bearish negativity that my position as partner and COO was placed firmly in the target scope of my majority shareholding partner. I volunteered and had implemented a 30 percent reduction in pay, but it wasn't enough. The hard truth was that the business could no longer afford to pay me, and I could not afford to work for any less and still support my family.

Because the business was circling the drain, the payroll line item with my name on it had to be struck if there was ever to be a chance for it to survive. My partner knew this. He had a lot of money invested in the firm. Instead of confronting the issue honestly with me to seek a creative approach to the problem, he instead chose to methodically build an erroneous case against me. The purpose was to avoid having to let me go as COO and instead simply push to significantly reduce my role and compensation while somehow retaining the full benefit of my efforts. The campaign included ridiculous charges of incompetence, allegations of lack of devotion, absurd accusations of malfeasance, and a host of other carefully crafted but poorly argued false aspersions. He chose to manufacture lies because he couldn't have an honest dialogue about the realities facing the company. It would've been too painful, too complicated, and too emotional.

When this became evident, I had a choice to make: security or integrity. Ease would have had me clinging to what little security was still there while accepting a total stripping of my dignity. And in the end, the path of ease would have revealed no material security anyhow.

I didn't choose the path of ease. I chose the hard way. I chose integrity. And all hell broke loose. Because the easy way is rarely the right way. And it is better to suffer for the truth than prosper for a lie.

John Joseph McGowan, who you know well by now through this book's foreword and previous mentions, has known hard times all too well and also knows how to choose the hard way and suffer for the truth. As singer for the legendary hardcore punk band the Cro-Mags, John has anthemized the hard times ethos worldwide for over thirty years. In the song titled *"Hard Times"* he sings:

*"Hard times coming your way
You're gonna have to rise above them someday
Organize your life and figure it out
Or you'll go under without a doubt"*

This song has become a perennial anthem of my life.

Along with being a consummate conqueror of hard times, John Joseph is also a relentless seeker of the truth. I was fifteen when I first heard the Cro-Mags. The raw, dirty, rumbling hardcore terror that they put forth rocked me to the depths of my soul. Never before had I felt the distilled core of human frailty. Never before had I been sucked into the deep reservoir of pain from which humanity groans for the truth. This was all manifested saliently in thunderous music as John Joseph growled and shouted into the microphone. I was a teenager doing what teenagers often do—questioning everything. I was searching. Seeking. Looking for something real. Trying to figure out how inner life was going to match external life. I stumbled upon the Cro-Mags at the right time.

I have a tattoo on my right elbow of a bomb with a banner that reads *Age of Quarrel*—the title of the Cro-Mags first album. It was released in 1986. That record still moves me as ferociously today as it did when I first heard it. *Age of Quarrel* brims with a distinct, boiling angst and agony that could only emanate from the seeker's heart of John Joseph.

As John has recounted the story behind how Cro-Mags began, he recalls a conversation he had with H.R., the front man for the Rastafarian hardcore band Bad Brains. He describes the conversation as a deep, spiritual interchange that he'll never forget. It was this conversation that ultimately led John to adopt the Hare Krishna faith. From that conversion, Cro-Mags lyrics became riddled with spiritual themes and descriptions of John's restless search for the truth. It is a search guided by the urging of his *internal spirit voice* and his unwavering attentiveness to it.

As a young, hardcore punk kid, these songs stirred me deeply. And like the conversation in which John was moved spiritually by the words of a Rastafarian to find his own faith, I was moved, in part, by the gnarled words sung by a Hare Krishna devotee to seek my own faith-path, which I ultimately discovered in contemplative Christianity—the notion that the emphasis on internal attentiveness to our soul's intuitive response to God's dimension within us guides the ongoing transformations of our spiritual path.

Years later, I interviewed him for a music magazine. We talked for an hour and a half about how his spirituality helped him overcome hard times. I'll never forget the conversation. Above all else, John continually emphasized the need for one to *"roll with the punches in the material world."* Sometime after that phone conversation, I finally met John in person at a show at The Trocadero in Philly. We had a good chat. I was wearing an A-shirt, also called a wifebeater. After looking at my arms, he nicknamed me "Diesel."

John, also known as JJ or Bloodclot, was conditioned by hard times from an early age. Abusive foster homes. Crack cocaine addiction. Homelessness. Incarceration. Drug dealing. And a variety of other assorted wanderings into confusion, depravity, crime, and difficulty.

He dug deep and excavated all of his pain, his past sins, and his journey to spiritual redemption and revealed it to the world in his book *The Evolution of A Cro Magnon*. The late Adam "MCA" Yauch of the Beastie Boys described JJ's book this way back in 2007:

> As I read the first few chapters, tears welled up in my eyes. A lot of people talk about coming from the streets, when Bloodclot says it, shit is real. I have tremendous respect for John, all that he's endured, and who he's become, and I would recommend this book to anyone in a heartbeat. So if you want to remember what New York City was like in the '70s and '80s, if you are interested in selling fake acid at Madison Square Garden, or dressing up like Santa Claus in a wheelchair to hustle money for the Hare Krishnas, or for that matter, if you are just interested in some of the best of the eight billion stories that New York City has to offer, put a read on this.

Through it all, John Joseph remains the quintessential hard times' hero—fully conditioned by difficulty, yet fully in tune with his *internal spirit voice*. John has always chosen the hard way. He has always chosen to suffer for the truth rather than prosper from lies.

John now competes regularly in Iron Man competitions. He is obsessively devoted to his health (see his book *Meat Is For Pussies* on his plant-based diet philosophy). He travels across the country speaking in gang-affiliated high schools, prisons, and lockups around the principles of a positive mental attitude that has helped him overcome hard times (see his book *The PMA Effect*). In his late fifties at the time of this writing, he also still rocks out all around the world fronting his current band, Bloodclot.

John Joseph has lived his life choosing the hard way in accordance with the dictates of his own conscience. As a triathlete, he's embraced veganism in sharp contrast to a hyper-masculine sports culture that often views veganism as inferior to meat-based protein consumption. As a Hare Krishna devotee, John's response to the rampant corruption he found in the organized structure of that religion was to distance himself from the external group and to instead practice and retain his faith individually. As a survivor of child abuse and drug addiction, he's chosen to document his pain and vulnerabilities through cathartic writing that can bless others rather than bottling it up inside.

Buddha said that three things cannot be long hidden: the sun, the moon, and the truth. If you are living a lie in your current occupational manifestation, find a way to transition into one that aligns with your *calling journey*. If you are in a dead or toxic relationship and you fear leaving because of a degradation in lifestyle or an uprooting of your stability, choose the hard right way and get out even if suffering travels with you. You can only cover up and hide the lie of such incongruence for so long. At some point, the truth will overcome your situation. When it does, choose the hard way and align yourself with the truth even if it is accompanied by suffering.

It is always better to suffer for the truth than to prosper externally from joining yourself with a lie.

Some people seem to inherently understand this wisdom. From the time he was a child, Winston Churchill seemed to live and thrive within the knowledge of **Failure Rule #2: *Nothing Is Safe*.** When he was a young boy, his mother found his erratic, rambunctious energy difficult to manage. She found it especially difficult that he gravitated toward situations with a distinct element of danger.

It was Churchill's propensity to work and live comfortably within the reality of an unsafe world that helped him develop the spine to call out and confront Nazism. He did this in the face of a culture that was prone to believing Hitler's lies of promised peace. Churchill contrarily saw the world with a profound sense of realism and clarity. Churchill's personality had long been shaped to suffer for the truth rather than go along with a lie in the name of elusive, false prosperity. He swung the hammer of inner strength and deliberately chose the hard way.

But Churchill also knew failure just as well as he knew victory. He is famously quoted as saying, *"Success is the ability to go from one failure to another with no loss of enthusiasm."* While I have no doubt that embracing enduring enthusiasm was his normal, consistent response to failure, he wasn't always able to harness that enthusiasm.

When Churchill lost the election after the war in 1945 to the Labour Party, he was not able to harness immediate enthusiasm to transition to his next formal pursuit. Plagued by what his neurologist diagnosed as cyclothymia, a mild version of bipolar disorder, Churchill suffered from mood swings and depression. He called it the Black Dog. And when he lost reelection, the Black Dog got the best of him for a while. He retreated to the south of France and indulged in the restorative creative hobbies of painting and bricklaying, which had always proved to be uniquely therapeutic for him.

But Churchill's depression-tinged interlude into exilic hobbying in the south of France was not for naught. He used that time to reframe his ambitions as the official leader of the opposition. While he didn't particularly enjoy this role, he still embraced it. Churchill had a deep idea stack to leverage as he reinvented himself. Like most who choose the hard way, failure eventually stimulates a reinvention plucked from a well-cultivated *Portfolio of Pursuits* mindset. It took him a little over a year, but he finally overcame the Black Dog, strengthened his give-a-damn muscle, and immersed himself back into politics. This re-immersion was catalyzed by him accepting Truman's invitation to give the "Iron Curtain Speech" at Westminster College in 1946.

Instead of resigning from the online lending company, I could've absorbed all the lies and all of the diminishment that would've come with staying. I could've cowered and accepted the crumbs I was being offered. The path of ease would've had me cling to as much stability as possible. It really would've been easier on many levels. I would have avoided so much discord in my family. I might have reduced the amount of tension in my first marriage. But settling and staying for less would've been a fraudulent and weak move.

Sometimes you have to accept, even encourage, temporary collapse in order to fall into the beauty of the next unfolding step in the mysterious tumult of your unique *calling journey.* **Because the easy way is rarely the right way.**

Trading authenticity for nominal financial and material stability never works in the end. Knowing it meant immediate uncertainty and necessary chaos, I made the decision to walk away. Because it is better to suffer for the truth than prosper for a lie.

If you're facing a decision in which you can clearly delineate between a hard right choice and an easy wrong choice, don't let security and stability bully you into the easy wrong choice. Don't permit the promise of mediocre comfort to steer your decision. It's an illusion. Because nothing is safe anyway.

Instead, let the retention of your integrity and authenticity drive your decision as much as is pragmatically possible. Even if it's not recognized or visible to anyone else.

When you do this, you need to always have an idea stack ready to deploy. When good faith intentions are not reciprocal. When push comes to shove. When you realize you are at the end of the day, a line item in the payroll budget.

You need to have a disaster recovery and continuity plan ready to activate.

When I resigned, I had a waterfall of plans waiting in the ready. A well-positioned idea stack. I implemented them in parallel, with haste, in the coming weeks after walking away. There were multiple threads that all bore discernible fruit in various timelines. You never know when disaster may strike, or you may need to willingly open your door to it. So make plans.

As you navigate into your *calling journey* knowing that **Failure Rule #2: Nothing Is Safe** is true, swing the hammer of inner strength. Like me when I walked away from a character assassination campaign and a meager offer of stability. Choose the right hard way instead of succumbing to the temptations of comfort and nominal security reflected in the easy wrong way. Like John Joseph has done in music, writing, athletics, and religion. Embrace just suffering for the truth instead of false prosperity in the name of lies. Like Churchill embraced as he confronted Nazism among the backdrop of Chamberlain's cowardly appeasement.

LEVERAGE CHAOS AS AN IDEA ENGINE

"One of the key qualities a leader must possess is the ability to detach from the chaos, mayhem, and emotions in a situation and make good, clear decisions based on what is actually happening."

—JOCKO WILLINK, RETIRED NAVY SEAL, PODCASTER, AND AUTHOR OF *EXTREME OWNERSHIP*

LESSON: When chaos surrounds or befalls you, leverage it as a springboard for forward-enabling ideation.

Folk legend Bob Dylan sang about how chaos was a friend of his. Ancient Chinese military strategist Sun Tzu observed that, "In the midst of chaos, there is always opportunity." Similarly, because we know that a crisis is usually accompanied by chaos, Democrat mayor of Chicago, Rahm Emanuel, explained amid the 2008 global financial crisis that, "You never want a serious crisis to go to waste. I mean, it's an opportunity to do things that you think you could not do before."

In a world in which **Failure Rule #2: *Nothing Is Safe*** stands true, you can expect to encounter chaos as you struggle to unite with your *calling journey*. When you collide with chaos, you need to make sure you are prepared to leverage it as an idea engine. Prepare to use, harness, and mold the energy of your chaos into a shape that newly resembles a deeper push into the inertia of your *calling journey*. Don't resent the chaos. Don't unnecessarily fight against it. Use it, appropriate it, and orchestrate it into new habitable order that catalyzes ideas into action that otherwise sat immobilized.

The wise of us rightly set out to orient our lives to avoid crises and the chaos that failure-driven crises often produce. No one sensible seeks to induce chaos into their lives for amusement and thrill. But this doesn't mean that when chaos inevitably descends upon you after some failure of analysis, some failure of contingency thought, or some failure of execution, that it cannot be embraced with thrill, discovery, and a sense of open possibility. It doesn't mean that it cannot be duly purposed to ignite previously infertile ideas into sudden fruitful blossoming.

In order to embrace uninvited chaos with a deliberate sense of thrill, discovery, and open possibility, you need to detach from the cyclone of emotions that activates in chaos. This is the key to owning your chaos before it owns and swallows you. This is key if you are to leverage chaos as an idea engine.

As the ex-commander of the Navy SEAL Team 3 Unit Bruiser amid the chaos of the Iraq war, Jocko Willink knows the importance of emotional control amid chaos. As the *New York Times* bestselling author of books such as *Extreme Leadership* and *Discipline Equals Freedom*, Jocko coaches, writes, and speaks a lot about emotional control amid chaos. To be a leader—of either a team or simply your own life—you need to learn how to pre-decide to detach from your emotions when chaos falls upon you. This premeditative approach will help you act on that decision more readily when chaos blindsides you. Because it will.

In this chapter's anchor quote above, Jocko stresses the importance of detaching from one's emotions and the surrounding chaos itself in order to gain a clear objective line of sight on a chaotic situation. It is only then, with emotion in check, that a leader or an individual can make a sound decision in a time of chaos. And it is only then, with emotion subdued, that one can see the potential and reshaping possibility of opportunity that exists in chaos. This is how chaos becomes an idea engine—birthing new realities and direction for those who learn to affect chaos before it affects them.

Chaos, opposition, and division all bring opportunity along with their challenges. Amid the chaos and uncertainty of the 2020 election, in an interview on Fox News, Jocko noted how emotional control was the key for Americans in the aftermath of the election. In this post-election chaos, Jocko suggested a new opportunity existed for us all to freshly find a way to listen to each other and discover common ground with those who think differently than us about the election, politics, or the world at large.

Pointing to the exasperated state of the country, Jocko explained:

> With exhaustion comes heightened emotional states. We have to watch out for getting emotional and letting emotions drive our decisions. We don't make good decisions when we're emotional.

He went on to explain how sometimes chaos is a positive hallmark of living in a free country. If we weren't free to have diverse opinions, we would be trapped in the imposition of autocratic order and uniform thought. With freedom, we must learn to embrace the challenge to treat each other with respect and kindness amid the messy chaos that comes with open diversity of thought. The opportunity in this chaos, Jocko explained, was to learn how to listen intently to those who think differently and then to find common ground and build on it.

As an entrepreneur, when your revenue is down by 20 percent and your expenses have increased by just as much, step back and think about what opportunities lie in your chaos. As a creative, when you get stuck halfway through a project and its current evolving iteration no longer resembles your original vision, think about how that chaos can be used to birth new, better ideas for a different vision endpoint. As an authentic, when others ostracize you for being eccentric and original, shape that emotional chaos into ideas that even more sharply bolster your uniqueness in the world.

Make productive chaos a feature of your life, not a bug.

I resigned from the online lending firm on June 13, 2013. Father's Day was June 16. My ex-wife agreed that we would all go down to the Jersey shore for Father's Day and spend it on the beach. She even drove, which was very nice of her, and I appreciated it very much. I sat shotgun, reading. Thinking. Praying. Planning. Knowing myself better with each new thought.

She kindly allowed me that reflection time, and she graciously attended to the kids. She was not happy that I made the decision to resign and walk away. And she didn't really understand my logic, but she acted as if she trusted me and knew that I trusted God.

Still, she very much would've preferred that I be normal. She would've preferred that I just had a job that was stable, predictable, and wasn't too taxing. My happiness, my applying the full width of my talents and gifts, my seeking maximum indelible impact through my efforts, my being conscious of the pulling of my mysterious *calling journey*—these considerations really didn't matter to her.

Security mattered. Predictability mattered. She did not understand the truth of **Failure Rule #2:** *Nothing Is Safe.* She wanted nothing but safety, real or not. Meaningful or not.

And I understand that. Truly, she is like most people. I am the strange one. Safety has its place, but it does not rule me. It is not my highest value.

So I had about a three- or four-hour period of time that day on the beach in which I did nothing but reflect and pray. Contemplating how I would leverage the chaos of my new circumstances as an idea engine to reshape my future closer to my *calling journey* destiny. I swam like a beast. I took long walks up and down the beach. I smoked a cigar. I nipped on some bourbon.

She was hoping that the fruit of my reflection would be some magical job I would pull out of the sky. Or two jobs. Or a list of ideas about possible jobs from which I would eagerly join the W-2 world exclusively and abandon all other pursuits. Essentially, I imagine, she thought I'd finally just focus wholly on getting a normal job and being normal for the sake of normality's false facade of security.

Identifying a strategic, logical W-2 job was definitely a part of the fruit basket of ideas rendered from my beach reflection interlude. But it was only one, largely utilitarian and pragmatic piece of the vision. In hindsight, I am amazed how the primary idea for a W-2 job hatched that day bore long-term fruit and grew into a wonderful, meaningful piece of my *calling journey* tapestry over time.

On that day, as my swimming body crashed into the waves, and the chaos of my tenuous life hovered over my consciousness, I leveraged that energy to hatch a variety of ideas to start new businesses and to repurpose and accelerate existing ones. Other immediate ideas also bubbled up into actionable clarity along with the W-2 job pursuit and new business ideas. I resolved to cut personal expenses. I strategized how to reconfigure unique temporary income sources. I engaged in measured borrowing for investment purposes. I took bold next steps in my pursuit of completing and releasing my first spy novel.

From the entire lot of these ideas, three very tangible ones were captured in three documents I produced in the month following the Father's Day beach reflections on my chaos. Looking back, all of these ideas—born from the idea engine of my chaos—generated measurable results.

The first document was an updated resume that reflected my net new experience gains in financial services. The resume touched on new COO experience, knowledge acquisition in the fintech space, non-bank lending experience, management competencies, vendor management abilities, and many other skills.

Within six months, this document (and all it represented and reflected) led to my corporate banking career in the payments space. Several conversations with a key business acquaintance from the cigar lounge that I faithfully frequented led to interviews in which I was able to animate the contents of the document. This animation and competency demonstration opened up the opportunity.

The second document was a promotional one sheet detailing consulting services I was offering in the online lending space. Leveraging a steadfast friendship with a previous business partner, I was connected within weeks to another online lending firm that had need of my unique insights and consulting services.

Within two months, I had produced more income from this consulting engagement than I would've settled for if I had remained with the partnership in the online lending firm. Quickly, this relationship lurched soundly into the adjacent possible. The consulting engagement evolved into a proper business partnership in a leads-generation company. My income from that company almost reached parity with my W-2 income in corporate banking, before ultimately dissipating due to unnavigable regulatory headwinds.

The third document was a sales one sheet for my first spy novel, *BLAZE: Operation Persian Trinity*. I had worked on this book for five years. It was finally ready for release at the time my core income had disappeared and my marriage was marred with irreversible chaos. This vortex of instability only drove me to lean in more to this thread of my *Portfolio of Pursuits*. This chaos ignited my idea engine and I leveraged it into actionable efforts to realize the next steps of my *calling journey*.

I met with publishers, attended writing conferences with famous authors, and cobbled together my self-publishing plan. This resulted in negligible sales but led to an opportunity to become a columnist for a niche news and commentary website. That then evolved into an eventual publishing deal to reissue the book. One fallen domino later, I managed to land a co-authorship deal with an established *New York*

Times bestselling author to write *CALIPH: Ottoman Rising*, my second novel. He had developed a consistent sales history and cultivated a strong following with a niche loyal audience. This made for a great partnership opportunity.

To prepare to rise out of chaos and reestablish sustainable order in your life, you need to structure, stage, and mobilize multiple latent pursuits with different paces, priorities, and probabilities of success. Start now to diversify your pursuits, interests, and ambitions, and you will be best positioned to maximize future income and fulfillment redundancy. This is how you leverage chaos as an idea engine in a world in which nothing is safe.

Amid the tumult, these three pursuit paths—the commercial banking career, the online lead-generation company, and the novelist career—all bubbled up to the top. They had each developed at different inflection points to craft a new future for me that has become wildly colorful, lucrative, fulfilling, and diverse. This was a future I never would have imagined on that day when my stomach revolted with intestinal volcanic anxiety—that day when I walked away from the security of my partnership position in the online lending company. This unimagined future came to being because I leveraged chaos as an idea engine and mobilized a multipronged disaster recovery plan for my life.

There was one more idea that rose to my mind on that Father's Day beach reflection besides the three I just outlined. This fourth idea was the most overarching of them all and carried the longest tail. It was the idea to write this book.

The preliminary ideas that came to me that day on the beach served to convict me with an utter compulsion to begin working on this manuscript. The pains and resurrections I had experienced, the complexities of my journey, and the depths of emotion that encompassed all of my failure stories boiled inside me like scorching hot lava. Crisis, failure, and the anvil of change was forming something new in me. I felt the pressure deep within, like birth pangs that evidenced something was growing inside that imminently needed to be nurtured to its release. The failure stories, and the precepts of *Failure's Rules*, needed to be excavated and put on paper for others to pick at. So for the past seven years, amid many other projects and life changes, I have followed through with that relentless commitment.

Not everyone sees chaos as an opportunity to creatively generate new ideas and push them into actionable reinvention. Some people succumb to the chaos rather than using it as a springboard to a newly imagined reality. Irish malcontent and unemployed house painter Michael Fagan lived a life plagued with chaos and failure in the summer of 1982. While living in an Irish enclave of North London, Michael found himself spiraling into a series of cascading failures. He lost his job, his wife, his confidence, and then his privileges to see his children. These cascading failures ushered in swift doses of high chaos into his life.

But Michael did not handle his failure stack or the chaos it wrought well. He didn't know how to step back, see the energy of the chaos around him, and find a way to harness it into new ideas that could facilitate reinvention. Because doing that is hard. And you need to be pre-oriented to react with such intentionality when failure's chaos strikes.

Instead, Michael peered outward to the macro political climate of Britain at the time. He cast his gaze of blame on the Royal Family. And the Prime Minister. Michael was convinced that Maggie Thatcher had poisoned Britain and that her policies had caused or exacerbated the high unemployment rate that was at the very root of his suffering. And for this, Michael wanted answers from the Queen. And he set out to get those answers by breaking into Buckingham Palace, plopping himself in her bedroom, and asking her face to face. After a bet with some lads at the pub, a taxi to the palace, a climb up a twenty-foot wall, and a pull up a drainpipe straight to a balcony, Michael achieved this objective. He hoisted himself smack dab in the middle of the Queen's bedroom. He then asked her for a kiss and a cigarette. And some answers on his political grievances.

And fair enough to a degree. We all have the right to act on our convictions to try to enact political change where we see fit. I'm not sure Michael's strategy was sound, but his intent otherwise was understandable.

However, when it comes to trying to absorb and optimize your failure experiences, pointing to macro political impetuses simply is not helpful. To leverage failure's chaos as an idea engine that helps you push into your *calling journey*, you need to utterly detach from political thought altogether and view your circumstances through a politically agnostic lens. You need to narrow your focus specifically to how you will decide to react, engage with, and attempt to shape the circumstances you find yourself in. Immediate engagement in macro political causes will not help you quickly or with any high degree of probability.

Michael didn't help his unemployment by seeking political answers from the Queen. He didn't get any closer to seeing his children or regaining his confidence by dropping himself into the Queen's bedroom—except for maybe his confidence in his ability to successfully trespass and break into the palace. Michael would've been better served by compartmentalizing his political grievances and curiosities, putting them aside for another day, and simply focusing on generating ideas to appropriate his life's chaos and reshape it into closer alignment with his larger *calling journey*. Who knows what transformative, actionable ideas he may have come up with if he'd utilized his creativity toward personal reinvention instead of devising a methodology to break into the palace? Who knows how he might have *Third-Doored* his way into a viable adjacent possible had his focus been different?

When failure thrusts chaos into your life, don't distract yourself from leveraging that chaos as an idea engine by pointing to external or distant macro sources as the cause of or solution to your chaos. Even when it's true, it's not immediately useful. What's useful is taking inventory of your latent ideas, dreams, and reinvention instincts and applying them to the fresh new circumstances that you find yourself in now that the ground has shifted. Now that chaos has challenged you. Now that failure has provoked you. And now that your *calling journey's* next step is hidden somewhere in plain sight.

When my financial planning practice was declining due to the 2008 financial crisis, my political feelings on that reality didn't immediately matter. They weren't going to help me find the best way to recalibrate and fold back into my *calling journey's* inertia. In 2013, when the Department of Justice's (DOJ's) *Operation Chokepoint* lived up to its name and began choking out small to midsize players in the online lending space, my political opinions on the legitimacy of the regulatory initiative weren't going to help my online lending business figure out how to pivot. In 2014, when *Operation Chokepoint's* impact followed me into corporate banking and my team struggled to adapt to a consent-order environment, my political thoughts on the operation didn't matter. Pointing to any external event, force, or policy as an escape mechanism from facing reality was not useful in any of these circumstances. What was useful was determining how the chaos of imposed disruption would inform behavior that would find a way to survive, mold, and grow. And how I could effectuate shape-shifting into viable adjacent possibles.

Sometimes it's the chaos of confusing stagnancy that ignites our idea engine. Sometimes our chaos is merely the threatening, paralytic stillness of not knowing what direction we need to begin moving into. Author and speaker Alex Banayan was suffering with directional chaos as he sat staring at the ceiling in his college dorm room. The son of Jewish Persian immigrants who fled Iran as refugees, Alex's parents had high and very specific hopes for him. He jokes that he pretty much came out of the womb with MD stamped on his behind. But the tracked normality of the college curriculum and the subsequent life it promised just didn't grip Alex. In fact, it pushed him away. It pushed him into viable adjacent possibles.

Alex found himself deeply curious how those with unorthodox career paths found their hook into success. There was no college course that taught students how to think differently and forge their own career path in unorthodox ways. The ways that have led so many to greatness and uniqueness.

Alex thought of Bill Gates. *How does a college dropout find success as an entrepreneur and then become, for a time, the richest person in the world?*

He thought of Lady Gaga. *How did she land her first record deal at nineteen years old, while waiting tables in New York City?*

And Steven Spielberg. *How did someone who was rejected from film school become the youngest major studio director in Hollywood history?*

Alex became obsessed with this curiosity. And in his obsession with those who created unorthodox career paths with no formal blueprint to guide them, Alex did the same. He decided *he* was going to be the one to study such individuals and present their lessons and mindset to the world. This was Alex's unorthodox path. This was what he calls the *Third Door*.

As referenced earlier in the Definition of Terms, the *Third Door* is the door that someone can bust through when the front door is too crowded and the back door is open only to those with special, privileged access. As Alex describes it, it is *"the entrance where you have to jump out of line, run down the alley, bang on the door a hundred times, crack open the window, sneak through the kitchen—there's always a way."*

Alex went on to employ the *Third Door* approach to find his own unique path. First, he used a *Third Door* approach to get himself on *The Price Is Right* game show with Drew Carey. Then he used the *Third Door* to win on the show. The winnings then fueled his project. He went on to *Third Door* his way into interviewing Bill Gates, Larry King, Steve Wozniak, Tim Ferriss, Larry King, Pitbull, Lady Gaga, and more. Never fulfilling his parents' dream of becoming a doctor, Alex took the *Third Door* by writing the book on it and building a career around educating others how to find, and break through, their own *Third Doors*.

Alex leveraged the directional despondency he felt in his college dorm room by igniting his idea engine. He turned the chaos of his confusion into a crystallized idea that joined him succinctly into his own unique *calling journey*. The world is full of doctors. There is only one guy who teaches the *Third Door* concept.

When failure's chaos befalls you, detach from the triggers of heightened emotion and find a way to view the opportunities in your chaos. Like Jocko Willink would urge you to do. When chaos strikes, make sure you've cultivated a healthy idea stack to leverage and activate that will help you reshape your direction *because* of your chaos, not just *in spite* of it. Like I did when I walked away from my partnership in the online lending firm. When chaos, fear, and poverty plague you, don't first point your finger at macro political or external sources, like Michael Fagan did. This will not immediately help you use the inertia of your chaos to reshape your way into your *calling journey's* mystery. Instead, be more like Alex Banayan and ignite the creative curiosity inside until it becomes an actionable pursuit defined by its unorthodox uniqueness.

Channel Bob Dylan and let chaos be your friend. Remember Sun Tzu, and find the opportunity in your chaos. Knowing **Failure Rule #2: Nothing Is Safe** is real, you need to prepare to leverage chaos as an idea engine to more succinctly wrap yourself into your tumultuous *calling journey*.

WHEN UNLOVED, SING YOUR OWN LOVE SONGS

"This day, I vow to myself to love myself, to treat myself as someone I love truly and deeply—in my thoughts, my actions, the choices I make, the experiences I have, each moment I am conscious, I make the decision I LOVE MYSELF."

—KAMAL RAVIKANT, AUTHOR OF *LOVE YOURSELF LIKE YOUR LIFE DEPENDS ON IT*

> **LESSON:** When you feel unloved, change your internal monologue to one that reinforces the uniqueness of your created Being; do this until that mode of self-talk becomes your new reality.

After the Father's Day beach reflection time, I told my ex-wife what had come to me.

"Is that it? That's what you've come up with?" she said with a look of disappointment, annoyance, and confusion.

The answer, of course, was, *"Yeah, what did you expect?"*

Fourteen years of marriage, and she still expected something different. She wanted to hear something that would comfort her and let her know that everything was going to be okay. That things would get easier. Safe. Dependable. Predictable. That I'd somehow become Joe-Suburbia. You know, buy some khakis, cover up my tattoos, and obediently spend my Saturdays mulching.

She certainly didn't want me to explain to her the reality of **Failure Rule #2:** *Nothing Is Safe*.

She didn't want new ideas to repurpose existing businesses, another book project, another new startup business or a plan to begin consulting work. She didn't want any of that stuff. She wanted to know what job I was going to get, how I was going to get it, and when I would start. And she wanted me to say I would be okay with whatever it was for good because it would be stable and safe and would have a "future."

The very last thing she wanted me to say was that I was committed and inspired—above all else—to write a book on the value of failure.

Before Chris Gardner became a successful stockbroker, he was broke and on his way to homelessness. But his idea engine was revved up. He knew how to leverage chaos. But his wife wasn't interested in his ideas anymore. She no longer believed in his ability to reinvent himself.

Neither did Bob Carr's wife. The original founder of Heartland Payment Systems, and now also Beyond Payments, didn't always know success. Before he met success, he was first wedded to failures. His early ventures ended up falling apart. Bills went unpaid. Credit cards were canceled. And eventually his wife didn't care about his ideas. Her faith in his resilience was empty.

Both Gardner and Carr knew what it was like to face spousal disillusionment in the midst of failure. They both knew what it was like to look into their partner's eyes and know that their ideas were no longer valued. They both knew that they would have to sing their own love songs, orchestrate their reinvention, and press on alone.

At least for a while.

* * *

Fast forward just two days after Father's Day to the evening of June 18, 2013.

The ambulance came to our house.

It had been humid as hell that evening. I had been lying in bed trying to read. It was a Brad Thor novel. I love the way that dude writes. I had worked out that day and did a heavy chest workout. My breathing became heavy and, with the weight of my circumstances, my mind equally so. The more I was conscious of the humidity (despite having the A/C on), the more I became conscious of my troubled breathing. And the more the heaviness of my chaotic life dug into my thoughts. My chest began twitching and tightening. Muscle spasms and shit.

My mind and heart, already burdened with the uncertainty and complexity of the directional issues I was contending with, followed suit and swirled into their own spasms. All conditions were compounded.

Then I couldn't breathe at all. And my mind went berserk with envisioned scenarios of heart attacks, panic attacks, death, dying, and all imaginable horrors.

I went to my wife and asked her to call the ambulance. I was panicked. Freaked out of my mind. Her eyes rolled. She dismissed everything I said. She refused to call the ambulance. She treated me with complete and utter indifference. Then she accused me of being dramatic and exaggerative.

Maybe so, but my disposition still created a real condition. It turned out that the issue was muscular inflammation in my chest, but my reaction to its effect on my breathing was a minor panic attack—a real condition.

She had responded with demonstrative coldness. She eventually called 911 after I pleaded and screamed for her to please help me. Of course, this all served to exacerbate my condition.

As I was being lifted into the ambulance, she was at the edge of the truck telling me I should get out. She said that she should drive me instead because the ambulance was too expensive.

There was no love in her eyes. There was no compassion or empathy in her words. I thought I was going to have a heart attack simply by peering into her loveless eyes.

It was at that moment—lying in the ambulance and wondering if that night would be my last—that I vowed to always and totally love myself and to run from anyone whose influence served to dismantle that love. I vowed, that night forward, to always sing my own love songs to myself no matter what.

If your path as an entrepreneur, a creative, or an authentic leaves you unloved, you need to pen love songs to yourself. Sing them loud. proud, and often. Make them anthems that sustain you and empower you. They will become an echo of your *internal spirit voice.*

* * *

Fast forward once again to August 2020. I was now remarried. Once again, I had done a heavy chest workout that day. But I had also had a big meal and quite a bit of bourbon, which I reckoned may have been an issue. I woke up in the middle of the night, struggling to breathe. I tried mental exercises to calm my body and breathing. I did this for about an hour. No relief. I still couldn't breathe well. I didn't want to wake my wife up and bother her. Why did I hesitate to go to her? Was it PTSD from the last time I was in this situation? Who knows? Maybe.

Finally, I woke her up and told her what was going on. She didn't roll her eyes. She didn't tell me I was exaggerating. She treated me with love. We got in her car, and she drove me to the emergency room. Because of COVID-19 hospital protocols, she couldn't go in with me. She said she would wait in the car. Knowing it would be hours at a minimum before I would be released, I told her to just go home. I told her that I'd take an Uber. I didn't want to ruin her sleep by asking her to wait for me. She refused and told me she would wait in the car. In love and loyalty, she waited in the car for three hours for me. I was released sometime around three in the morning. It was the same issue I had seven years prior when I was with my ex-wife. Muscular inflammation in the chest. But this time, it wasn't compounded by a minor panic attack. Because this time, I wasn't unloved.

Just because you're unloved now doesn't mean you will always be. Sing your own love songs to yourself but be open to finding those who will join you in those songs.

Silicon Valley entrepreneur and author, Kamal Ravikant knows what it's like to wallow in the misery of an unloved mindset. Kamal had failed as a CEO and found himself broke and living off his credit cards. His depression became so deep that it affected him physically. He could barely get out of bed. He ignored outreach from friends. He was slipping into the abyss.

Along this downward spiral, however, Kamal found a way to turn it all around. At a certain inflection point, he made a deliberate decision that he was going to learn how to love himself—because he believed his life depended on it. In order to learn to love himself, he reckoned he needed to change his pattern of thoughts. He needed to disrupt the story loops about himself that kept running through the tracks of his mind. Kamal recalls what he had discovered this way:

> This I know: the mind, left to itself, repeats the same stories, the same loops. Mostly ones that don't serve us. So, what's practical, what's transformative, is to consciously choose a thought. Then practice it again and again. With emotion, with feeling, with acceptance. Lay down the synaptic pathways until the mind starts playing it automatically. Do this with enough intensity over time and the mind will have no choice. That's how it operates. Where do you think your original loops came from?

Kamal continued, no matter how difficult in his state of depression, to deliberately choose his thoughts. He chose thoughts and attendant self-stories that reminded him of who he was before and in spite of all of his failures. He heard his *internal spirit voice* break through failure's tumult. He affirmed, amplified, and echoed this voice consciously. *Daily*. Until it disabled the suicidal tendencies that had been attacking him.

Along this transformation, Kamal did something else. He used the energy of his failure to shape him closer to his *calling journey*. Like many creatives, he leveraged failure's chaos by turning it into meaningful and impactful art that could bless others. He documented his transformation from being stuck in an unloved mentality to embracing positive self-love. He did this in his book *Love Yourself Like Your Life Depends On It*. Still broke, with no income and living off of his credit cards, Kamal self-published the book. It was only eight thousand words. He sold it for $2.99. But he went on to sell half a million copies. The early sales from the book allowed him to very quickly stop living off of credit cards and even live generously and comfortably. Kamal has since fully wrapped himself into his *calling journey* by becoming an entrepreneur again, by writing more books, and by speaking to audiences on how to overcome suicidal thoughts through the practice of loving yourself.

You cannot actualize the promptings of your *internal spirit voice* if you don't love yourself. It is a hard prerequisite. You cannot give the world what you were created to give it if you are stuck accepting an unloved mentality.

You must, like Kamal did, feel the weight of your self-doubt, let it go, and then consciously create new self-story loops in your mind that reinforce your unique value. We are fearfully and wonderfully made. Know this and move forward in the world accordingly with boldness.

Reject the temptation to accept an unloved mentality when those around you genuinely do not love you. As I did when lying in an ambulance waiting to be carried onto a stretcher, my ex-wife's coldness crystallized in front of me through her loveless eyes. In such moments, join the chorus of those who sing love songs for the unloved—and then sing them to yourself eternally, if necessary.

Because **Failure Rule #2:** *Nothing Is Safe* is true. Including your closest relationships.

KNOW YOUR OPERATING SYSTEM AND OWN IT

"I think self-awareness is probably the most important thing toward being a champion."

—BILLIE JEAN KING, FORMER WORLD NUMBER-ONE TENNIS PLAYER AND GENDER EQUALITY ACTIVIST

> **LESSON:** Define the internal operating system that regulates you; rely on it when failure strikes.

Investor and author Tim Ferriss points to the ancient wisdom of stoicism as his operating system. Stoicism, to Tim, is what informs how he reacts—or deliberately doesn't react—to the unfolding events of his *calling journey*. Punk rocker, Hare Krishna devotee, and triathlete John Joseph has an operating system that includes a strict commitment to veganism. This stands true even as he trains rigorously for Iron Man competitions. Personal finance guru Dave Ramsey's operating system is Christianity. This operating system compelled him to continue to tithe 10 percent of his income even as he marched toward, into, and out of Chapter 7 bankruptcy. Tim, John, and Dave all know their operating systems. And they all take full ownership of them.

My ex-wife and I separated in October of 2013, a few months following my minor panic attack. The divorce path had been set, and there was no turning back. Regardless of the complex culpabilities that both of us carried, key components of our operating systems simply grew to be irreconcilably incompatible.

I understood **Failure Rule #2: *Nothing Is Safe*.** Therefore, I subordinated safety well below my faith, which is the overarching core code of my operating system. Within this operating system, I follow the mysterious promptings of my *internal spirit voice*, which I recognize as *The Spirit*. This voice calls me to take accelerated risks of faith in pursuing my *calling journey*. Listening to this voice helps me eliminate the possibility of future regrets. Because what burns deep inside, I must pursue. I cannot suppress this core attribute of my operating system. I know it intimately and I own it explicitly.

My ex-wife's operating system could not integrate into my system, after years of being exposed to its code. Unfortunately, there was no proverbial engineer who could build a philosophical API (application program interface) to successfully connect her to call into my system. I understood her operating system and accepted it. She valued safety, comfort, and stability above all else. Specifically, material comfort and financial stability. I tried to provide this sufficiently, even as these values remained appropriately subordinated within the programming of my operating system. But ultimately the gaps were unacceptable to her.

Several months after the separation, because I vowed to always sing love songs to myself no matter what, I memorialized the separation by getting a "Love Songs for the Unloved" tattoo on my calf. This is the title of one of my favorite albums about heartbreak and recovery by the seminal New York hardcore punk band Sheer Terror. I once released a DVD/CD of their reunion show at CBGB's in New York City on my label Thorp Records. The tattoo is the album's cover art. The title track had become an anthem that buoyed my strength daily in this period. The tattoo symbolizes the perennial, God-empowered undergirding of self-love that carried me through that hard time. And many other hard times since.

The truth is that long before that day on the beach when I still provided her with the wrong answer or the night of my muscle-spasm-induced panic attack—in which her lovelessness was on full display—her ship had sailed. She had already given up on me, on us, and any thread that was still hanging on was weak. Almost a year prior she had already confessed that she did not love me and wanted a divorce.

The split was painful, and I didn't want it, but she had made up her mind. We both contributed to the schism between us. But the impenetrable truth was that I was never going to have the right positions. I would never have the right answer. It's not within me. Because I had developed a vastly different operating system than she had.

America's former world number-one pro tennis player Billie Jean King knows her operating system and has owned it.

Now I confess, the first time that I heard Billie Jean King's name, it wasn't at all in relation to her legacy as a tennis star. No, it was by watching the film *Fletch Lives* in which *LA Times* reporter Irwin Fletcher, played by actor Chevy Chase, uses her name as an alias while impersonating an exterminator, wearing a G. Gordon Liddy disguise, and rambling on about how insects multiply by masturbation.

Since that first impression, I have now learned exactly who Billie Jean King is. She is an extraordinary woman whose operating system has always been unique. But her system never integrated well with the tennis establishment. Billie Jean experienced the discomfort of placism from the onset of her tennis career. One of the earliest signs of her system being disparate from the tennis establishment was when she was in her youth. She was forbidden from being in a group photo among her tennis peers because she was wearing tennis shorts sewn by her mom instead of the nice tennis dress that was deemed a requisite. This clash with the sport's establishment, and expected etiquette, was the beginning of what would be a consistent thread of her life. One that she embraced and owned.

Billie Jean had, as a key attribute of her operating system, an aggressive playing style on the court. This created friction with the tennis establishment's expectations for women players. But Billie Jean didn't throttle back her style. Because she knew her operating system and owned it.

Billie Jean was not content with the way tennis was viewed in America. She compared the respect the sport of tennis received in Europe versus its status in America and was indignant. She spoke out about how tennis was ignored in America. She put it this way:

> In America, tennis players are not people. If you are in tennis, you are a cross between a panhandler and a visiting in-law. You're not respected, you're tolerated…you work all your life to win Wimbledon and Forest Hills and all the people say is, "That's nice. Now what are you going to do with your life?" They don't ask Mickey Mantle that. Stop twelve people on the street and ask them who Roy Emerson is and they're stuck for an answer, but they know the third-string right guard for the Rams. I'd like to see tennis get out of its "sissy" image and see some guy yell, "Hit it, ya bum," and see it be a game you don't have to have a lorgnette or a sash across your tuxedo to get in to watch.

Billie Jean's operating system rejected the elitism ingrained in the culture of American tennis. She boldly advocated for the democratization of the sport in ways that would appeal to the working and middle classes of America.

Simply being a woman—a part of her operating system informed by her very biology—also caused friction for a time with Billie Jean's *calling journey* as a tennis pro. Billie Jean was a staunch advocate for gender equality. She owned this piece of her operating system publicly. This led her to competing in the *"Battle of the Sexes"* match, when she was twenty-nine years old, against Bobby Riggs, who was fifty-five at the time. The match attracted a massive amount of publicity. It was considered a critical event that could increase recognition and respect for women's tennis. Fulfilling that end, Billie Jean won. But instead of gloating that she'd beat a fifty-five-year-old guy, she instead expressed that she was just happy to have exposed more people to the sport.

As Billie Jean King explains in the anchor quote above, you need to have strong self-awareness to become a champion.

As an entrepreneur stepping out in an unknown path, you need to first take a sober look at your operating system and define its attributes. Then know how those attributes fit uniquely relative to your pursuits. As a creative, you need to learn to own the strange code of your unique operating system. Then leverage that strange code to put unmistakable art into the world. And as an authentic, you need to learn to thrive when your operating system clashes with the establishment of every space you enter. This means that you smile and bugger on when your Being clashes with the world around you.

Be self-aware, and know your operating system. Then own it, even when friction is strong, like Billie Jean King did.

Because **Failure Rule #2:** *Nothing Is Safe* is true—whether you prepare for failure or not—you need to have a strong operating system. When failure strikes or friction heats up, it's imperative that you know and fully own your unique operating system. Like I did when I moved forward with strength after the failure of my divorce. Or like Billie Jean King did when she pressed forward against the tennis establishment and fulfilled the glory of her *calling journey* as the world's number-one tennis pro.

Think of Tim Ferriss, John Joseph, and Dave Ramsey. Like them, know and own your operating system. Then use that knowledge to discover the unraveling narrative of your mysterious *calling journey*.

MAKE REINVENTION YOUR UTMOST SKILL

"This is life. Things get taken away. You will learn to start over many times—or you will be useless."

—FROM THE BOOK *THE MAGIC STRINGS OF FRANKIE PRESTO* BY MITCH ALBOM

> **LESSON:** Because circumstances are subject to fluidity and volatility, you must cultivate strong reinvention skills.

Since **Failure Rule #2:** *Nothing Is Safe* is true, you must make reinvention your utmost skill.

Industries, jobs, and sectors that appear safe—and may even be safe from a safetyphile perspective—often are at risk of becoming factories of increasing mediocrity, bastions of stale thinking, and targets of blindsiding disruption. When these symptoms bubble up, or you see them on the horizon, you need to draw plans for confronting or escaping them.

The quote above is right. Things get taken away. You have to learn to reinvent. You have to learn to shed the debris and start over. You need to be prepared to do this over and over. If you don't, you will be useless. Buddha urged that all conditioned things are impermanent and that when one sees this with wisdom, one can then turn away from suffering.

Christians and Jews know well the expression found in the book of Job advising that the Lord giveth and the Lord taketh away.

If any of this is true, it means that reinvention must be your utmost skill. If life is conditioned in impermanence and things can be taken away, you need to prepare to adapt.

The transformational change from a physical to digital delivery system in the music industry forced me to reinvent. iTunes didn't exist when I created my first record label. There was no dominance of Spotify and Apple Music in the year 2000. Now music delivery has changed. When was the last time you purchased a compact disc?

The rapid transition from physical delivery to digital delivery almost destroyed my business. This profound industry transition was a quintessential example of the beauty, devastation, and inevitability of creative destruction. It forced me to step back and comprehensively reassess my model in light of the changes. I was compelled to stretch myself, diversify my skills and interests, and reshape the purpose and vision for my record labels.

As a financial planner, I thought I would be able to build a safe business. But I was living in northwest Ohio in the auto belt. This was the lifeblood of my client base. And that industry began rapidly contracting. Then the financial crash of 2008 came before I could get any real traction in building my practice. My reinvention muscle flexed easier this time. I had done it before. I instinctively knew how to break down my assumptions, reconfigure my strategy, act swiftly on immediate adjustments, and push hard into new pathways of change and promise.

Later, I found myself in the online lending business. The business was notorious for its high margins. I easily saw a future that was endless and bright. But deep within I also knew that I had to make sure my reinvention muscle never atrophied. I had learned that nothing was safe. Three years into it, nasty regulatory headwinds blew the industry's way and demolished most small to midsize players. I got out and nestled into the supply side of the business through the lead-generation space. This reinvention move bridged the gap to subsequent next moves.

My reinvention muscle had become limber, responsive, and agile.

I had also diversified into the fitness business while I was running the online lending business, consulting in the music industry, running the record labels, and writing my first novel. My partner and I bought a functioning fitness center with roughly nine hundred members. But we failed to identify that the gym was built on an outdated model when we purchased it.

Quickly, with the help of consultants, we constructed a plan to retool the model and transform the company—from the receivables model to the service offerings, to the facilities strategy. We had access to the necessary capital and began implementing the plan. It was working. Progress was measurable. But it was slow, and the source of capital abruptly became no longer viable.

So we shut it down.

Reinvention came to the rescue. Detachment from sunk costs enabled decisive action and we exited. Collateral damage and consequence followed, but the pace and effectiveness of diversified reinvention was stronger than the strength of consequence.

Sometimes reinvention doesn't necessitate taking decisive action but instead requires merely loosening oneself to adapt to fluid circumstances. In these times, perspective on priorities and values is important.

During one season in my life, I had to step back, minimize the role of my ego, and allow fluid circumstances to play out and reveal my best next steps. I was dealing with multiple challenges simultaneously that forced me to slipstream into the fluidity of the times. Only then could I smoothly steer into a reinvented life.

I was mired in legal disputes with my ex-wife that carried challenging financial implications. I was mired in an unpredictable, drawn-out legal battle with an artist on my record label. It was a battle that, at one inflection point, had the potential to threaten the entire business and the twenty-year legacy it had established. At the same time, I was mired in a crisis at my day job that required hyper-focus on a chaotic situation, keeping me at the office with hands-on TCB, sometimes until 3:00 a.m. And at the same time, my wife and I were living uncomfortably with 90 percent of our belongings in boxes due to a planned move that fell through unexpectedly.

During this time, I set aside deliberate time to take long walks at state parks. I used this time to decompress, reflect, and plan the reinvented ways forward. Music helped. And I might have carried a flask with me too.

In that particular season, and as a result of those long walks, several events entered my awareness that helped level-set my perspective.

A colleague at work had recently gone through a tragic loss of a granddaughter. Her granddaughter was less than a year old and was murdered at a daycare facility—suffocated intentionally by a daycare employee. It was all captured on video. Nothing I was dealing with mattered at all as I juxtaposed my challenges against the dark corridor of pain she was navigating through. And she returned to work several weeks later—diligently resuming her role with grace, composure, and a smile. This was a lesson.

I had also been struck by an account I heard of a Yazidi woman. After living through the murderous atrocities ISIS had committed on her community, this woman had found peace in jettisoning any attachment to the tragic history of her community. She spoke about letting it all go, moving on, and harnessing small daily goodnesses more than being weighed down by massive historic losses. Somehow this story gave me strength and perspective.

My reinvention during this time materialized by disconnecting myself from ego in my negotiation approaches to the legal battles with my ex-wife and the disgruntled artist on my record label. I chose to make decisions that lubricated my future path instead of stubbornly trying to preserve the past status quo paradigms. My future path emerged soon after. It included a new home, which on multiple fronts provided a richer life for my wife and me. The path also brought me into close proximity to my son. It allowed conditions to enable me to focus on and finish the first draft of my second novel. By holding my challenges with a lighter grip, I found myself more calmly solving each one as I focused on the new priorities of my emerging reinvented life.

Reinvention takes many forms. Many people think about the so-called sin businesses—alcohol, gambling, tobacco, porn, strip clubs—as being depression-proof. Maybe so, but they're not all quarantine-proof. During the 2020 COVID-19 shutdowns, strip clubs across America found themselves shutting their doors, and their dancers found themselves putting their thongs back in their lingerie drawers.

The Lucky Devil lounge in Portland, Oregon, was one exception to the full-blown impact of the COVID-19 shutdown-induced economic depression. They found an adjacent possible to lurch into that helped mitigate the full economic effect of the shutdown. They decided to bastardize the Uber Eats moniker and create Boober Eats—a stripper delivery service bringing pub food and boobs to your door for a fee. The dancers donned face masks, carried sanitizing wipes, and traveled with bodyguards. Their incomes were still badly damaged, but the owner's creative pivot helped mitigate total disaster for many of the women—many of whom were single moms who relied on their dancing tips to support themselves and their children.

Learn how to advance when things are falling apart, when chaos emerges, and when you feel like you're under attack.

Keep moving and make reinvention your utmost skill.

Because nothing is safe.

ALWAYS BE BUILDING SOMETHING (ELSE) FOR YOURSELF

"Learning to view yourself as being in business rather than merely an employee brings enormous benefits in its wake. You gain a tremendous sense of security. Also, you're no longer subject to the capricious whims of your employer."

—RABBI DANIEL LAPIN, AUTHOR, PUBLIC SPEAKER, AND PODCASTER

> **LESSON:** Understand that it is not your employer's job to take care of you; that is your job. Therefore, you must soberly build contingency pursuits on the side in an attempt to create financial and fulfillment redundancy.

A good friend of mine worked with relentless zeal for a company for twenty years. He is a consummate, perennial professional and a disciplined workhorse. His credentials are impeccable and his reputation unmarred. He showed up earlier than anyone else and stayed later each day for his entire tenure. His loyalty and commitment were extraordinary. He contributed above and beyond because it wasn't about the biweekly check for him. He viewed the company as a permanent work home and his approach reflected that.

The problem was that he was wrong.

The company did not reciprocate. They didn't view him as a permanent resident employee. They were good to him while he was there. They benefited from the value of his work. But at the end of the day, he was a line item. Ownership and management structures changed. The line item with his name on it found itself under the microscope and changes were made. He was laid off. He thought he was safe. He was wrong.

Failure Rule #2: *Nothing Is Safe* reared its sobering head.

His trust in the job-for-life dream was shattered. The myth was busted. And the company continued to reap many of the residual benefits of his talent, labor, and intelligence long after his departure. Long after the company had any obligation to reward him for it.

This is not wrong. It's how employeeism works.

A company has to pay you less than the value of your contribution or they will not be profitable. With this being understood, you must not lock yourself into siloed employeeism by funneling all your energy into only building something for someone else.

My friend did this. He didn't mind his own business. He only minded the company's business. There was no cultivation of anything outside of his day job that would benefit him long term. There was no ancillary pursuit that had a chance to potentially set him free or build reasonable redundancy to guard against the realities of an unsafe world.

He job-hopped for a while. He experienced a few more layoffs and false starts. He endured salaries at half his old rate. He was fortunate in the end, and finally found a role with a salary commensurate to his legacy job.

But not everyone is that fortunate. Because nothing is safe.

Don't only build something for someone else and neglect to simultaneously build something for yourself.

If your industry is trending and feels safe, think of it as unsafe. If your company is flourishing, think of it as unsafe.

When you view everything as unsafe, you will push yourself to be better than you are.

If you love your job, think of ideas to generate income outside of your job anyway. Even if you're convinced you'll never want to leave and you'll love it forever.

And while you're doing that, go interview several times per year. Test your viability in the market. Practice selling yourself to new gatekeepers. Keep your sights ever focused on the width of potential new horizons.

This mindset will cause you to become better at your job. You'll learn and grow tremendously from engaging in other endeavors and periodically exploring what else might be within your reach. You will learn to naturally see opportunities to cross-pollinate your skills, and you will constantly challenge your perception of what possibilities are all around you.

Develop a *Portfolio of Pursuits Mindset* around your work life. Honorably isolate your time. View your W-2 job as just one of the pursuits that spiders out of the business entity of *you*.

Heed the words of Rabbi Daniel Lapin and view yourself as being in business rather than merely being an employee. You are in the business of *you*. Know this and orient your decisions accordingly.

And no matter how diverse your pursuits spread—knowing the constancy of **Failure Rule #2: *Nothing Is Safe***—make sure you are *always* building something, or *many* things, *somewhere* for yourself.

THE PORTFOLIO OF PURSUITS MINDSET

BE AN OCTOPUS

"It's better to be an octopus than a fish. If an octopus loses a tentacle to a predator, the octopus will survive with seven tentacles left to itself."

—GENE SIMMONS, ICONIC SINGER FOR KISS, ENTREPRENEUR, AND AUTHOR OF *ME, INC.*

> **LESSON:** Diversify your pursuits, not just your savings and investments; this way, you increase the probability of both your financial and fulfillment continuity.

Over the years, as I became increasingly aware that nothing was safe, I intentionally began to develop what I call a *Portfolio of Pursuits Mindset*.

In the apartment I kept before I got remarried, I had a whiteboard wall where all my notes and ideas found themselves. I would chunk out each active, developing, and aspirational vertical that was relevant in my *Portfolio of Pursuits* and write it on the whiteboard wall. This became a constant reminder of my commitment to building a diversified, iterative set of pursuits. Each one a tentacle.

Rock god Gene Simmons is an octopus. He has built an astounding *Portfolio of Pursuits* with many tentacles. Okay, maybe he's a super octopus. His tentacles definitely count more than eight—music, restaurant chains, comic books, business books, an insurance venture, professional sports team, record label, reality shows, and licensed merchandise. That's at least nine, and I'm doubtless missing many more.

Gene Simmons didn't become this way in a vacuum. His mentality was shaped from his earliest days by living in the unsafe rubble left by his father's parental failure—his dad left when he was seven. Gene responded to the failure conditions his father left him in by accepting **Failure Rule #2:** *Nothing Is Safe*. He then built the strengths of his life around that premise.

Gene's Hungarian parents both survived World War II and escaped to Israel only six months after its historic rebirth. His mom had been imprisoned in the Nazi death camps at age fourteen and witnessed both her mother and grandmother walk into the gas chambers together. Gene's mom survived the concentration camps and shortly thereafter met Gene's father. Hard times shaped Gene's parents—through the grueling horror of evil ethnic genocide.

The marriage did not last long. When Gene's father walked away, he left them to contend with poverty all by themselves in the newly formed Israeli nation. In his book Me, Inc., Gene describes his father's failure flee this way:

> Once the rug had been pulled out from under us, it was up to my mother—and then, eventually, up to me—to make a living.

They lived in a one-bedroom apartment riddled with bullet holes—collateral damage from Arab-Israeli conflicts. They had no bathroom—just an outhouse that was nothing but a hole in the ground. They had no toilet paper—they used rags that they washed and reused. No toothbrushes or toothpaste. No shower or bathtub. No car. No telephone.

Nothing was easy. Nothing was safe. And Gene believed it was up to him to build a different life for himself and his mother.

Gene and his mother found their way to America when he was eight and a half years old. His uncle had bought them plane tickets. Once in America, Gene's early entrepreneurial roots really began to sprout. He joined the Junior Achievement at age twelve and learned the core principles of business and capitalism that no public school would ever teach him. He learned about cost of goods, profit motive, taxes, stock, budgeting, and corporate org chart creation. And the criticality of mastering language skills for communication, persuasion, and relationship building.

It was from this foundation—being paternalized at an early age and being immersed in the principles of capitalism—that Gene became the business giant and super octopus he is today. But Gene didn't have a straight path at this. Like anyone else attempting difficult things, Gene confronted failure. He opines on the topic this way:

> Don't feel bad when you fail. You're no different than the most powerful, the most intelligent, and the most entrepreneurial among us.

> When you buy a car, it comes with five wheels. The spare isn't there for **if** you get a flat tire—it is there for **when** you get a flat tire. Because you will get one…But as long as you've got a spare tire in the trunk, you can keep going.

If you're just breaking out as an entrepreneur, make sure you design your plan with a spare tire. Or two. Or eight. Build a plan that encompasses a *Portfolio of Pursuits* from the outset. Diversify your passions, interests, efforts, risks, and goals so that the evolving composite survives and satisfies regardless of how it adjusts over time.

If you're setting sail on the rough seas of life as a creative, you must have a *Portfolio of Pursuits* that includes strong noncreative pursuits. Back up and load balance your creative ambitions with supportive pragmatic and clinical skills and assets. Success as a creative is one of the most difficult paths to succeed on. And it is worth doing—because its intangible rewards are predictable amid the unpredictability of its tangible rewards. So design your path safely with practical back-up support. Build belts and suspenders that can allow you to sustain your creative pursuits when the runway to tangible rewards is long, winding, and unpredictable.

To live consistently as an authentic, you must also build in layers of pursuits that sustain you. Being an authentic intrinsically carries with it a higher risk of rejection than the way of soft conformity. Some power brokers will not like your style and will not hire you. Some people will not appreciate your eccentricities and will choose not to work with you. Some colleagues will feel threatened by your authentic approach and may set out to sabotage you. So learn to build redundancy in your plans and talent stack. And be sure to build on—with deliberate intent—the key relationships you hold that are dynamic, strong, and have sustainable chemistry.

Fish die easily. So build a *Portfolio of Pursuits,* become an octopus, and die hard.

To manage my *Portfolio of Pursuits*, I would update the status and next steps of each pursuit periodically as things developed—all prominently on my whiteboard wall. Part of the composite included entre-employee goals within a W-2 role. These goals have been crucial to strengthening the bond position that is the maintenance of a W-2 career.

Within my W-2 career, I am also conscious of maintaining a sort of sub-*Portfolio of Pursuits Mindset*. While under a confining regulatory consent order, the firm I work for needed to find new and creative ways to create revenue and leapfrog into a future-enabling business model.

So within my sphere of influence and controllable work output, I strove to help realize this goal. In conjunction with my boss, I had helped reignite an innovation idea I germinated years prior. The idea had initially died on the vine with the departure of a former executive. This initiative would create new revenue from dormant corporate assets that had been overlooked and unutilized for years. It was one of many initiatives that I was eager to work on and contribute to in order to help widen the firm's overall *Portfolio of Pursuits*, as well as those attributed to my department.

Because Failure Rule #2: *Nothing Is Safe* is true, sitting still is death. You must stretch yourself to find and display your unique value. If your primary assigned value diminishes, let your new imprints out survive them and guide your forward path. The adjacent possible is everywhere. Even inside your corporate job.

The whiteboard wall in my old place also outlined a long-term passive income pursuit. Further, it showcased active, developing, and aspirational pursuits in e-commerce, IP rights, lead generation, publishing/media and other spaces. All pursuits carried different paces, priorities, partners, purposes, and probabilities of success. This is how you emerge in the world as an octopus.

You must plan and develop each tentacle, knowing that they all carry different risks and purposes. Expect many tentacles to be cut off. Never stop thinking about new tentacles to pivot to as replacements for those that will inevitably be severed.

This is how you begin to view yourself as an actual living, breathing, business entity that hosts various lines of business. This is how you establish, as Gene Simmons has termed it, *Me, Inc.*

Like any portfolio, you need to monitor and evaluate each tentacle on an ongoing basis as you rebalance with changing times. Income redundancy and fulfillment diversity is the goal. If one income stream changes adversely for any reason, you shift toward others, adjust, and accelerate. If the meaning output from one tentacle gets low, you rely on a tentacle with higher meaning output to satiate you.

Because **Failure Rule #2:** *Nothing Is Safe* cannot be fully gamed, nothing will ever grant you an assurance of bulletproof safety in perpetuity.

Neither will the *Portfolio of Pursuits Mindset*. Because nothing is safe. But it is a great strategy for building up resilience toward unexpected change and a sound recipe for wealth creation and fulfillment abundance across time.

Don't sleep with the fishes. Instead, grow a *Portfolio of Pursuits Mindset* and become an octopus.

HOW CAN YOU GIVE THE WORLD WHAT FEW OTHERS CAN?

"I have a personal philosophy in life: If somebody else can do something that I'm doing, they should do it. And what I want to do is find things that would represent a unique contribution to the world—the contribution that only I, and my portfolio of talents, can make happen. Those are my priorities in life."

—NEIL DEGRASSE TYSON, ASTROPHYSICIST, PLANETARY SCIENTIST, AND AUTHOR

> **LESSON:** Learn to identify the unique chemistry of your individual talent composite; then, use that composite to create outputs of blessing that no one else can create in the way that you can.

In order to complete your strategy to fortify yourself in a world in which *Nothing Is Safe* and **Failure Rule #2** does not relent, you need to know exactly what you are uniquely made of.

We are all individuals. We are all crafted, molded, and formed mysteriously in our mother's wombs. We are all born with our own mix of genetics, dispositions of temperament, environmental conditions, and unique physicalities. So, too, were the accomplished astrophysicist Neil deGrasse Tyson, and Elgin James, the former leader of a violent street gang.

Disparate as these two subjects would appear, they have something profound in common. They have both learned how to take their exclusive composites of human manifestation in the world and mobilize them into unmistakably unique contributions. They both have given the world what few others can. And what no other can in the specific ways that they have.

This is what you need to focus on as you explore the contours of your *calling journey* path.

Neil deGrasse Tyson felt the tug toward an extraordinarily clear and unique calling as early as the age of nine. This happened after he visited the sky theatre of the Hayden Planetarium. Tyson recalls that visit and the power it had on him this way:

> So strong was that imprint [of the night sky] that I'm certain that I had no choice in the matter, that in fact, the universe called me.

The *Divinity of Purpose* got its grip on him in that moment. Tyson was giving lectures on astronomy by the age of fifteen. At age seventeen, he applied to Cornell University with an application that was overflowing with his passion. That application ended up in the hands of famed astronomer Carl Sagan, who, in turn, sent Tyson a personal letter. Sagan later invited Tyson to spend a day with him in Ithaca. Tyson now points to that day, remembering that it was the day he learned from Carl what type of person he wanted to become.

Tyson channeled his passion for astrophysics into developing a portfolio of talents that allowed him to make contributions to the world that few others could. He went on to author many books. He served on President Bush's 2004 "Moon, Mars and Beyond" commission to help implement the US space exploration policy. He became director of the Hayden Planetarium—the very source inspiration that catalyzed his wonderful *calling journey*. He narrated the documentary *400 Years of the Telescope* on PBS. Then he hosted the show *Nova ScienceNow* on PBS. He was a regular guest on The History Channel's *The Universe*. Tyson then partnered with comedian Lynne Koplitz, and later comedians Chuck Nice and Leighann Lord, to launch the podcast *StarTalk*. To round out the application of his unique portfolio of talents, he co-developed the video game *Space Odyssey*.

Don't shy away from identifying and developing your unique talents because you're afraid to feel the familiar sting of failure. Because **Failure Rule #2:** *Nothing Is Safe* is true, it is best to obey Benjamin Franklin and *"hide not your talents. They for use were made. What's a sundial in the shade?"* In this, find the most distinctly unique application of your portfolio of talents, channel Neil deGrasse Tyson, and chase that as a priority.

> **REFLECTION: TAKE INVENTORY OF YOUR UNIQUE TALENT COMPOSITE**
>
> If you've never really taken inventory of your talents through this lens (of unique impact) before, don't worry. This is a normal place to be. It takes deliberate analysis to do this. And many of us are time-poor, overextended, and just trying to hang on. If this is you, take a step out of that paradigm for a minute and try to reflect on the following questions:
>
> - In your current work life output, to what degree are you utilizing your most effective and unique skillsets to maximize positive impact, blessing, and contribution to the world?
> - Think of the work you do or the role you fulfill. How many people can do what you do with very little difference in how they do it and little difference in the type of impact they have? If you're not able to answer this with "very few people," then you might not be doing what aligns with your *calling journey*.
> - Think about what the world might need that only you can give it in the way that only you are able to offer it. Whatever that looks like. Are you working to find a way to give that to the world? If not, how can you?
> - If you know what you could give to the world that no one else can, are you developing your strategy to deliver it to the world? If not, why? Are you bowing to the false gods of security and stability instead of creating habits of audacity? What intentionality must you apply to your life to begin building this strategy?

> - Are you rigorously pursuing creative detours that might grant you a platform to maximize use of and impact with your most uniquely valuable and effective skills? If not, what can you do to map these paths out and get started on the first affordable step in pursuing them?
>
> **No one can answer these questions for you. But you need to ask them of yourself.**
>
> If, after meditating on these questions, your unvarnished, intellectually honest conclusion is that you are right where you ought to be—no matter the job or whether you have a boss, are a boss, or are exclusively your own boss—then you need to home in and accelerate that dynamic. This means that you're joined with your *calling journey* already. This means you merely need to home in, step on the gas, sharpen your focus, and give the world what few others can in the way that you can.
>
> If the answer is not clear, if your honest assessment of these questions reveals a distance from a definable *calling journey*, then you need to step back, struggle to hear your *internal spirit voice*, and do the hard introspective work of mapping out a path to collide into your *calling journey*.

Elgin James once played guitar in a hardcore punk band with retired Navy SEAL Jocko Willink. In a former life, Elgin was the founder of the street gang FSU (Friends Stand United). Then he did the hard internal work of identifying his unique talent stack. Because he did this hard work, he was able to break away from a stale life of crime and violence. He was able to pivot and reinvent himself so he could pursue a fresh life that would enable him to give the world what few others could.

Elgin James had angst and conflict brewing inside him from the earliest of ages. Bouncing from orphanages to foster homes for a time as a child, Elgin eventually landed himself in a farm home owned by civil rights activists. Elgin, who is mixed race, internalized and reacted strongly to many conditions of his upbringing. His curiosity with civil rights began there. After mirroring his adopted parents' affinity for the pacifist beliefs of Martin Luther King, Elgin eventually pivoted to studying the revolutionary messages of Malcolm X and Stokely Carmichael. Elgin deliberately contrasted the lifestyle of his adopted parents in other ways. After watching animals get slaughtered on their family farm, Elgin took shelter in the vegetarian lifestyle. After witnessing his adopted parents abuse drugs and alcohol, Elgin took on the cloak of militant, straight-edge philosophies, a subculture of punk rock.

Elgin's decision to craft a unique set of beliefs that contrasted his upbringing led directly to him becoming the default founder of a violent street gang. FSU, which was equally known to mean *Fuck Shit Up* along with *Friends Stand United*, had in its unofficial mission statement to target drug dealers, drug users, and white power skinheads for violence. Throughout punk shows across the US, FSU became a feared presence that initiated violence wherever they went—often indiscriminately, despite their stated goals. They had chapters in Philadelphia, upstate New York, and many other cities extending out from the founding city of Boston. FSU's notoriety went on to be documented in *Rolling Stone* magazine and an episode of the TV show *Gangland* on the History Channel.

FSU ended up causing Elgin to be punished both for his sins and by them. In 2009, he was arrested on extortion charges involving an incident with a member of the punk band Mest. In 2011, he was sentenced to a little over a year in prison. At sentencing, Elgin said, *"The last few months have been a juxtaposition of the best and worst of my life. Today I faced my day of reckoning...I have accepted responsibility for my past."*

The juxtaposition Elgin referenced was profound. For years leading up to his sentencing, Elgin had done the hard soul searching necessary to rebuild a failed life and align with his unique *calling journey*. Elgin had publicly distanced himself from FSU and violence. He and his girlfriend jettisoned the northeast and moved to Los Angeles so Elgin could pursue the core of his *calling journey*: screenwriting. In the ashes of a stained reputation attached to gang life, Elgin heard the *internal spirit voice* calling him to screenwriting. It was on the day of his sentencing that the contrast of his old life and new life was the most evident. Because it was on his day of sentencing that Elgin was also hired to write a screenplay for Brian Grazer and Universal Pictures. His new life was also on contrasting display at sentencing through the support of his new Hollywood mentors. Among many other letters written to the judge, actors Ed Harris and Robert Redford penned messages of support for Elgin, noting the transformation that had taken place in his life. Redford, who Elgin specifically cites as being instrumental in helping him turn from violence, wrote the following about him:

> I believe that Elgin has the potential to make a difference. He has an important message for people of all ages on the possibility of change (and) the power of nonviolence.

Elgin endured his earned prison time and continued to dig deep on honing his unique screenwriting skills. He went on to give the world what few others could. He went on to bring to life projects, such as the film *Lowriders* and the TV Series *Mayans M.C.*, the highly anticipated spinoff to FX's hit show *Sons of Anarchy*.

Do not delay in seeking to hear your *internal spirit voice*. You will need to hear this voice clearly if you're to take an accurate inventory of your unique portfolio of talents.

You will need to fully understand your unique portfolio of talents if you're to find a way to give a unique contribution to the world, as Neil deGrasse Tyson did. If you're not sure what your unique portfolio of talents is, maybe start by reflecting on the questions posed above in this chapter.

If you've wandered off into moral failures in life that have left you far behind the path of your *calling journey*, remember Elgin James.

No matter how misaligned you've found yourself, your *internal spirit voice* still yearns to be heard and followed. Nothing is safe, including your reputation. But by listening to your *internal spirit voice*, doing the hard work of reinvention, and building a plan to give the world what few others can, you can throw away the stale reputation sketch of the past and ink an entirely new one that aligns with your *calling journey* future.

Indeed, you possess the power to sketch a fresh reputation that enables you to give the world what few others can.

BE THE INERTIA

MAKE YOUR ENVIRONMENT A PRODUCT OF YOU

"I don't want to be a product of my environment. I want my environment to be a product of me."
—JACK NICHOLSON AS IRISH AMERICAN GANGSTER FRANK COSTELLO IN THE DEPARTED (BASED ON THE LIFE OF GANGSTER WHITEY BULGER)

LESSON: Find ways to reasonably extend your imprint on your circumstances or they will unreasonably force their imprint on you.

Your work environment bends to the reality of **Failure Rule #2: Nothing Is Safe** just as much as any other environment. But that doesn't mean you can't also work to make it bend more toward you.

Don't allow yourself to slip into the numbing contentment of being a product of your work environment. Instead, appropriate your environment into your Being and return yourself into that environment to shape it more toward your way of Being.

Channel your inner Irish gangster and strive to make your work environment a product of you.

Afford yourself serious time to reflect on every nuance, interaction, and contextual observation in your work environment, your work life, and within your career decision-making matrix. See the whole chessboard.

Take inventory of how you act, react, and feel throughout your workday.

Pay the most attention to the words you say. And the words you hear. Be sure to listen intently, with as much emotional intelligence as you can muster, to the words others speak. Listen more than you speak, as much as your role will allow.

Guard your external and internal attitudes toward your tasks, your trajectory, and your ever-flexing work vision. Unpack these attitudes and apply reason and analysis to them, lest they run amok and own you in unhealthy ways.

Mind your thoughts around the time clock, the structures you are bound to work within, and the choices you make about how you are going to feel. Wherever you sit within an org chart or within the ecosystem of your chosen space as a self-employed person, you need to stagger your day in such a way that leaves margins of time for you to catch your mental breath. This will allow you to calibrate your emotions and put forth your Being with precise intent instead of allowing your Being to manifest as it feels.

If you find yourself being led too much by the inertia around you, then you need to change the way you walk into and through your work each day.

You need to preset your attitude each day so that you become the prime mover that catalyzes the inertia of your work environment.

If you're an employee, take on new initiatives that you can uniquely deliver on outside of your prescribed role. Maybe this means you build a sound case for an innovative initiative and galvanize the appropriate executive support to get the initiative approved for resources. Or maybe making your work environment more a product of you is as simple as arranging your workspace to minimize intrusions and distractions so you can own the physical space that informs how you feel throughout the day and ultimately informs the quality of your work product.

If you're an entrepreneur, maybe you need to brainstorm a new manifestation or offshoot of your brand and begin planning a way to prove out the concept. Or maybe you need to rethink how you represent your company, its image, and its message in your marketing to extend your imprint with more precision. Maybe you need to find more efficient ways to delegate and outsource pieces of your operations to allow you to spend more time on shaping your business for wider impact.

If you're a creative, consider finding a new format to bring your art to the world and pursue it with earnest. Art is in its essence a message. Maybe you need to diversify the mediums by which you deliver your message to widen your footprint and make the environment of your market more receptive to your vision. Walt Disney was drowning in financial failure with his initial motion picture releases. It wasn't until he diversified the delivery of a piece of his message, by productizing Mickey Mouse's image on a watch, that he tapped into the financial success that would help underwrite his next projects for years to come.

If you're an authentic, maybe making your environment more a product of you means that you need to lean in more and find a way to telegraph your authentic way of Being to the world that might be inspirational to others. This could take the form of using more personalized language in a corporate environment that has grown stale with buzzword speak. Maybe it means that you finally take the first step to creating and sharing content online that reflects the uniqueness of your authentic Being's interests and perspectives.

If you're an employee, an *entrepreneur*, or a *creative* and you have a fixed workspace, you will optimize your reach as an *authentic* if you decorate your workspace with art, images, or slogans that reflect your ethos. **What you look at while you're working is important.** Ex-mixed martial arts (MMA) fighter, entrepreneur, host of History Channel's *Hunting Hitler*, and current US Army soldier Tim Kennedy has a Venn diagram posted in his office that states in its center what he believes is his core purpose for living. That purpose, for Tim, is to preserve and protect human life and to expand freedom. He filters all of his decisions through that purpose test. If an action he's contemplating doesn't tie back to that purpose, he doesn't do it. If it does, he moves forward. Having this posted in his office causes him to constantly be reminded to think of new ways to act on his purpose to make the world at large more a product of his mission. What is your mission? How can you decorate your workspace to keep you focused on expanding it?

To make your environment a product of you, you need to be constantly bending out of your lane and claiming new territory unto your environment. This will increase your run-ins with failure but also maximize your impact in the world. Because **Failure Rule #2: *Nothing Is Safe*** is unavoidable, making your environment a product of you—one that bears as much of your imprint as possible—is also not safe. But it is worth pursuing both for your own fulfillment and for multiplying the ways in which you can bless others.

In a podcast interview with Heather Parady on her *Unconventional* podcast, author and motivational speaker Joshua Coburn urged listeners to make their environment a product of themselves this way:

> If you don't belong, make others belong to you.

Now Joshua is obviously not talking about literally *forcing* others to belong to you. He is talking about showing up in the world in such an authentic way that you cannot be bent into your environment, but rather that your environment bends toward you. And the more you project strength and confidence in your Being, the more your environment will attract itself to your way of Being. This naturally results in others bending their behavior in accordance with yours.

Joshua Coburn grew up in a small Midwest town in Iowa. At a young age, he was attracted to tattoos and piercings. Joshua's modified appearance made him an utter freak during the mid-nineties in his small Iowa town. He was told constantly that he was disgusting, ugly, and should never have children. He went to his grandmother's home on holidays and found that every one of his cousins had their picture framed somewhere in the house. But there were no pictures of him. Society's rejection of Joshua was just as strong and evident within his own family.

Joshua was kicked out of his mother's house at age twelve and forced to live with his broke recovering-alcoholic father. He had no anchoring platform of encouragement to launch him into adulthood. Failure, depression, anxiety, and even suicide were all that he could foresee at the time.

Joshua continued through much of his early life with a posture bent toward accepting himself as a failure. At one inflection point, Joshua woke up to get himself breakfast and realized he didn't have any milk for his cereal. This discovery brought Joshua to tears. Not because he loved milk so much that he couldn't bear to not have it but because the weight of the cumulative rejection that society had hoisted upon him day in and day out—merely for the fact that he manifested his authentic being through his appearance—had fully now fallen upon him. Joshua felt this weight unbearably upon him as he thought of going to the grocery store to buy milk. He couldn't imagine going to the store one more time to endure yet another barrage of stares, insults, and judgments for being tattooed and pierced.

With the aggregate weight of society's rejection bearing down on him, Joshua sat down to write his suicide note. Ninety minutes ticked on by and the note was not yet written. His *internal spirit voice* was screaming with resistance.

Joshua heard that *internal spirit voice* reminding him of all the things he wanted to do in life. Travel. Write books. Speak. And inspire others to find strength in their authenticity. Yet in that moment, Joshua had no strength in his own authenticity.

But then, he asked himself a pivotal, life-saving question:

> If I can take responsibility for ending my life, why the fuck can't I take responsibility for living my life?

In that game-changing moment, Joshua decided to turn away from victimism. He decided to detach from the optics of failure. With a clear vision of his *calling journey* in his mind's eye, he turned away from suicide and committed to taking responsibility for his life.

From that moment on, Joshua lived his life in such a way to make others belong to him because he inherently knew that he didn't belong to, or fit in with society. I imagine Joshua could have related well many times to the lyrics from the song "I Was Wrong" by the punk band Social Distortion:

"I got society's blood running down my face
Somebody help me get outta this place."

While society's blood metaphorically ran down Joshua's face, he did ultimately help himself find a way out of that suicidal place. He still encountered times of depression, anxiety, and failures, but he has still found a way to fulfill his *calling journey* ever since. In this, he's learned to make his environment a product of himself.

He has written several books including *Through the Eyes of an Abstract Mind* and *Shit That Needs Said So You Can Kick All The Ass*. He has become an entrepreneur by founding Dissident Cigars. Through his company *Manners and Motivations*, Joshua speaks at schools and businesses on the topic of authenticity. His message focuses on ways to create cultures of kindness, inclusion, and success based on human connection.

Within reason and with the right intent, it is better to make your work environment a product of you than to allow yourself to become a product of an environment in unnecessary flux. Get control and project your best reach.

This is hard, I know. On a good day, I may do this adequately for half of the day. Some days, or even weeks, when I do this better and with more consistency, I can't help but deeply feel and notice the contrast. Engaging in your workday with a calm, deliberate, and philosophically guided intentionality will completely change who you are and the satisfaction you derive.

Reject the failure messages that tell you to only stay in your lane. Or worse, to sit still within your lane and willingly get run over by the traffic of a judgmental society.

Instead, confront this unsafe world and work to shape it more to belong to you. Think of Joshua Coburn as you do this and take responsibility for living and shaping your life as an authentic. Reject a victim mentality, hear your *internal spirit voice* and embrace the danger of your *calling journey*.

Whatever your role, be the inertia.

Wherever you are in your *calling journey* discovery, craft an environment that can be more recognized as a product of you.

ABOVE ALL ELSE, FIND A WAY TO GIVE A DAMN

"Suffering is people not caring about your work. Pain is you not caring about work."

—DRAGOS BRATASANU, AWARD-WINNING SCIENTIST AND RESEARCHER, FILMMAKER, AND AUTHOR OF *PURSUIT OF DREAMS*

> **LESSON:** Find a way to manifest enthusiasm in your work, even if it's painfully manufactured.

Intentionally generating enthusiasm for your work will help you find strength in your unsafe work environment that is ever subject to **Failure Rule #2**.

Whether you're an entrepreneur or an employee, you need to find a way to give a damn about your work. For the entrepreneur, this is pretty much instinctive and implied. If you are an employee, this may not be so easy.

When someone close to me made the difficult decision to leave a job that was filled with meaning, this person was left with a deep void to fill. The job they left increased their competency daily. It provided a mission-based work environment rich with significant relationships. But the leadership was wildly deficient. Observable bias existed. And there was no transparent structure to follow for anyone to achieve career growth and development. So this person left.

The new firm my friend joined didn't have these leadership issues, but it was also not clear if it would ever deliver on the fulfillment attributes of the previous role. My friend felt mission-hungry and disconnected from a team decentralized by remote work. My friend excelled quickly, developed relationships fairly easily, and earned validation for contributing value within months. But there was still a deep emptiness hovering heavy beneath the surface. *Will I ever feel connected to this firm? This industry? This team? This audience? This content?* my friend wondered.

Indulging in nostalgic feelings around previous endeavors is dangerous but natural. Especially on the front end of a new pursuit. Letting go of the verified positive elements of the familiar recent past to embrace the unverified quality of a slowly unraveling fluid future is difficult.

I was stuck in this long tunnel when I exited the online lending space as a partner in the firm. As I entered the payments space to begin my banking career, the lure of nostalgic thinking weighed me down amid the emptiness of the new unknown.

I lived in this space for the first two years. Maybe three. The new role felt flat, safe, dry, and unstimulating. I felt conflicted constantly. I *wanted* to care. I *wanted* to give a damn. I *wanted* to dive in with passion and enthusiasm. But there was nothing taking root to consistently align me the way I desired. All the external accoutrements of a great job were present: generous salary, nice office conditions, easy commute, friendly culture, great health benefits. Plus, paid time off—something I had literally never had in my entire adult life. And I had an amazing boss who had evolved into becoming one of the best mentors I would ever have.

Yet in those early years, I still missed the chaos. I longed to recapture the visionary mindset. I craved the impulses of aggressive creativity. I longed for the daily adrenalizing. I hungered to achieve the autonomy to constantly chase a new adjacent possible. I missed working in a perpetual **VUCA** environment—which in this context is typified by the:

- *Volatility* of a dynamically evolving opportunity environment.
- *Uncertainty* of perpetual unexpected challenges.
- *Complexity* of consistent multi-input decision-making.
- *Ambiguity* that allows for the freedom to apply subjective judgment to determine the paths forward.

All of these elements existed in my previous pursuit stacks.

This dangerous nostalgia hung on me like rusty barnacles on a sunken ship. I knew I had to find a way to shed them.

Early on, sometime within my first year working for the bank, I was sitting in the corporate break room eating my lunch. I was feeling incomprehensibly disconnected and lonely. I was living in the pain that Dragos Bratasanu references in this chapter's anchor quote. I was feeling the deep pain of not knowing how to care about my work.

As I simmered in this pain, I ate my chicken and broccoli and tried to distract myself with reading. I was reading *Lone Survivor* by Marcus Luttrell in my iBooks app on my phone. In the section I was reading, Marcus was describing his experience during Hell Week at the beginning of his pursuit to become a Navy SEAL. He was feeling demoralized. He was in pain physically and mentally. He wanted to quit.

There was a captain named Joe Maguire from Brooklyn who challenged Marcus in his dwindling thoughts of resignation. Captain Maguire tried to help steer Marcus away from the unnecessary failure of premature resignation. He told him to not give in to the powerful pressures of the moment. He reminded Marcus that whenever he was hurting bad, he ought to just hang in there. *Finish the day*, he would urge him. He advised Marcus to wait out his feelings. He told him to see how he felt the next day, and if he was still feeling bad, he should still think long and hard before deciding to quit.

The captain also reminded him to take it one day at a time—the oldest advice in the book. Further, he told him to take it one *evolution* at a time—because you can't judge the totality of a pursuit over a small corridor of experience. Accurate judgment of the totality of a pursuit requires stepping back from your experiences and objectively reflecting on them after a long passage of time.

But it was the closing thoughts that Marcus recalled Captain Maguire sharing with him that both caused Marcus to hang in during Hell Week and strengthened me to keep going in my new banking career. The captain admonished Marcus:

> Don't let your thoughts run away with you, don't start planning to bail out because you're worried about the future and how much you can take. Don't look ahead to the pain. Just get through the day, and there's a wonderful career ahead of you.

Marcus Luttrell took Captain Maguire's advice to heart. He did not bail. He decided not to look ahead to the pain. Instead, he took that day's pain for just that day. He did this day in and day out as he forged a valorous career as a US Navy SEAL. He went on to receive the Navy Cross and Purple Heart for his heroic actions against the Taliban amid Operation Red Wings. All of Marcus's fellow warrior friends died in that operation. Marcus went through hell to stand as the lone survivor of the mission. And in 2013, the film *Lone Survivor* was released, with Mark Wahlberg playing Marcus, to give the world a cinematic view into Marcus's heroism.

I had no evidence on that day in the break room that there would be a wonderful career ahead of me. That evidence didn't even begin to start accumulating with substance for a good three years. Yet somehow that line—*just get through the day and there's a wonderful career ahead of you*—lodged itself inside my soul for the entirety of those three years. While I had no evidence that things would change, I could hear my *internal spirit voice* reassuring me with certainty that it would. Reassuring me that I wouldn't be trapped in a box of corporate mediocrity and dull safety if I stuck in there. My interpretation of my *internal spirit voice* could've been wrong. But I trusted my interpretative instincts, invoked my faith, and held on—eventually being validated for my decision.

Every time I felt like I needed to aggressively begin looking elsewhere or reorient my prioritized commitments, that line would bubble up inside my head. I knew to recognize this voice as my *internal spirit voice*. I chose to listen to it, and I kept badging into the office day in and day out—with an open mind and an eager work ethic—hoping to discover the conditions of meaning I was seeking.

It was a faith play. I *believed* there was a purpose for my being there, but I didn't know. Because **Failure Rule #2: *Nothing Is Safe*** is ever applicable, my calculated bet on my future was not safe either. I could have been wrong. There may have never been a basket of meaning conditions greeting me along the way just because I hung in there. But in this case, there was. The *Divinity of Purpose* finally showed its face.

Somewhere within my fourth or fifth year at the bank, *everything* began to change. The compounding effect of my acquired knowledge and skills began to show exponentially.

I was starting to get regular exposure to and with colleagues who were officer level. Intellectual stimulation somehow became the order of every day. New work relationships formed that held a higher degree of quality in the substance of collaborations. I began to meet more colleagues who I began to learn from and admire. The bank assumed new executive leadership that installed a deliberate philosophical culture of excellence that was inspiring. I was challenged with wider, more consequential initiatives to lead and assist on. I started to develop a passion for future-enabling tech and the promise of a banking world that would be ubiquitous with immediate, digitized domestic and cross-border payment activity.

Additionally, my boss continued to grow and shine in his role. He increasingly became an inspiring mentor to work with and follow. I became an officer and was promoted several times. I came to thoroughly enjoy the challenge of cultivating a team of direct reports who could digest the downstreaming of strategic enterprise vision-casting.

My meaning bucket had miraculously filled up. I embraced an exciting enterprise vision and was given opportunity to develop the adjacent possible with new payment product initiatives, and every day was now an exciting cauldron of challenging VUCA. I no longer had to struggle to give a damn.

Don't give up when you're fresh into a new pursuit or endeavor unless you are absolutely certain that your *internal spirit voice* is urging you to do so. Only you can judge your interpretative accuracy on this, like I did when I walked away from my job at the wholesale mutual funds shop in my early twenties before I even finished training. Absent of clear signaling from your *internal spirit voice,* you need to allow yourself time to internalize the full gamut of your feelings, your observations, and your evolving analysis of your role over a long experience period before judging your purpose in the new pursuit.

Your pursuit may never give you the meaningful conditions you need. But it may. If it doesn't, you will know when that hope needs be abandoned. Just allow enough time to pass before reaching that decision.

In the interim, find a way to give a damn. Take one day's pain at a time. And be open to the idea that you may end up with a wonderful career in the very space or place that you feel so lost in.

As you work to find a way to give a damn each day, do not silo yourself only to the role and tasks for which you've been assigned. Position your skill acquisition strategy in such a manner that you are the one looked upon to dive headfirst into a crisis, to tackle unique projects, to solve complex problems, and to lead on stand-alone opportunities. Be the one called upon to plug and play wherever you are needed. This is one way to be failure repellent and it may be the key to cultivating your conditions of meaning.

Do your job to the best of your ability and with enthusiasm, if possible. If you need to manufacture that enthusiasm, learn how. If not, be the person known for constantly performing with dispassionate excellence. Doing this deliberately and with discipline may paradoxically create the passion within you that you need to meet your conditions of meaning.

As a matter of habit, train yourself to be ever-conscious of the entire flow and dynamic of your team, your department, and the enterprise at large. Broaden your impression and information intake. Look for ways to leave marks of value outside of your job description as much as possible. *Third Door* your way into new opportunities if you have to. This could be an unsolicited insight you offer, an outside-the-box idea you promote, or simply an act of informally assuming a leadership role when none was ever assigned to you.

Cultivate a high-octane contribution mentality, and then forget that you are even working for someone else entirely. Own your ambition, and act on logical initiative every day. Treat your role as if you gave it to yourself. Within realistic boundaries, act as if it is yours to grow, shape, and develop. Appropriate it like it was your own business.

Because who you show up as, what mark you leave, and what benefits you garner within your work environment—whether you own it or not—are your own business. Mind them.

It *is* painful to not care about your work. But don't give up easily or quickly on the hope that your work might someday provide the meaningful conditions you need to align with the *Divinity of Purpose*.

Whatever your pursuit, whatever form you file your taxes on, and whatever your current feelings around your work may be—above all else—you need to find a way to *give a damn*.

One painful, unsafe day at a time.

You never know—like Marcus Luttrell or me, you may have a wonderful career ahead of you.

A SOUL ON FIRE IS A SOUL ALIVE

"The only people for me are the mad ones, the ones who are mad to live, mad to talk, mad to be saved, desirous of everything at the same time, the ones who never yawn or say a commonplace thing, but burn, burn, burn, like fabulous yellow roman candles exploding like spiders across the stars and in the middle you see the blue centerlight pop and everybody goes 'Awww!'"

—JACK KEROUAC, AMERICAN CATHOLIC AUTHOR, ICONOCLAST, AND BEAT POET

> **LESSON:** Learn to mind many fires inside. Cultivate these fires so they burn maximally.

Burn, burn, burn, like fabulous yellow roman candles exploding across the stars. Live your life hot. As you collapse into your *calling journey's* flames, burn with every next achievable step. May each of your actions breathe fresh oxygen into your glorious fire. May your fire embolden you with energy, desire, joy, and life-affirming fear. Always be on fire. Because a soul on fire is a soul alive.

Burn with passion and spread out your fire into new and dangerous territories because by now you know well that **Failure Rule #2** is true: *Nothing Is Safe*. So don't let others dampen, contain, or temper your flame. Defy such efforts and deliberately write your own story with unbridled tenacity instead.

Whatever your story is, write it with fire. It could be the story of building the business of *you* within the framework of being an entre-employee inside a company. It could be the strategy that enables you to build a *Portfolio of Pursuits* in which your W-2 job is one tentacle of the octopus of you. It could be seeing that creative project through to the end without having any social proof validating its viability commercially. It could be holding fast to your distinction as an authentic in an environment that carries an unspoken frown upon such a way of Being. Whatever the story line, you will find more satisfaction, more depth, and more unexpected opportunity and adventure by writing it with fire.

Write it with color, audacity, and imagination. Draw outside the lines when your hand guides you to. Write with heat. Avoid yawning and saying commonplace things in your story. If it's lukewarm, life will spit it out, and it will likely never resemble your *calling journey*.

The more you live your story this way, the more alive you will feel and the more empowered you will become. You will generate ideas often and organically. You will have a pregnant stack of ideas on standby should they need to be birthed in your next chapter.

Build a *Portfolio of Pursuits* as you write your story with burning passion. This will help you limit the number of people in your life who have the power to make a decision about you, on any given day, that can radically affect your future and fate.

This is important.

Move toward getting that number down to zero. Then your future and fate will rest more and more in your hands and not on a limited number of people for whom your best interest is not their incentivized priority.

To do this, you have to build up your idea inventory and then leverage those ideas to create and maintain multiple streams of income, no matter the difficulty. The average multimillionaire has between seven and fourteen streams of income. To become an octopus like them and build a *Portfolio of Pursuits* that provides a redundant defense against an unsafe world, you need to have fire in you every day.

As I continue to join myself with my *calling journey* path and develop my *Portfolio of Pursuits*, I struggle to do this. But somehow, I find a way each day to build that fire. Even on days when creating that spark is agonizing and forced. You need to manufacture the fire if you have to. Light as many matches as you can find. Get up early. Or stay up late. Spark a new idea to chase in the wake of every failure. Do whatever you have to do to keep oxygen flowing toward the flames of your *Thing Two* dream (see **Failure Rule #4**).

Be one of the mad ones and make sure your soul burns, burns, burns.

Because a soul on fire is a soul alive.

American Catholic author Jack Kerouac was an authentic who lived his life hot. Kerouac burned with the flames of a well-heard *internal spirit voice*. Eight days into his life in the Navy, Kerouac found himself on the sick list. The structures of Navy life were not a fit for a creative like Kerouac. He simply could not find himself able to conform to the group discipline rigors of the military. He was honorably discharged after being diagnosed with dementia praecox—a dated term for an iteration of what we now know to be schizophrenia. While that was the diagnosis, the truth is Kerouac just didn't belong there. He burned for a hotter life. The medical examiner quoted him as saying, "I just can't stand it here. I like to be by myself."

After Kerouac was discharged, he continued to listen to his internal spirit voice and press on as a writer and an adventurer. He joined the collective of writers associated with the Beat generation. Yet in his true authentic form, Kerouac never felt aligned with the term and would reject it saying, "I'm not a Beatnik. I'm a Catholic."

Kerouac's raw authentic approach to life punctuated everything he did. In his book *On the Road*, in which Kerouac details "a story about two

Catholic buddies roaming the country in search of God," he lays down a narrative that uncovers the pulsating underground culture of 1950s America, replete with jazz, sex, illicit drugs, and open-road exploration. Kerouac often evoked controversy for his dichotomous expressions. Juxtaposing the contrast between Catholicism and promiscuous underground sex and drug culture was one of them. But Kerouac also divided critics with his political expressions. The right scorned him for his associations with drug use and sexual liberation. The left held him in contempt for being outspoken against communism. This duality was most typified by his cheering on anti-communist Joseph McCarthy on television while smoking pot.

Whatever iteration you examine of Kerouac's extraordinary life, it's clear that he lived his life authentically hot. From his stubborn attachment to an unorthodox life to his refusal to conform to rigid labels of association, Jack Kerouac was a soul on fire. He was a soul truly alive.

It is often within the incubation stage of an idea or a pursuit that the fire burns hottest. It is also in this stage that the fear of failure, the instincts of self-doubt, and the white noise of negative external voices can easily put your fire out. It is in this stage, at the onset of conception and imagination, that you need to protect your fire the most.

I knew this to be true decades ago when I stood holding down the production line at the steel plant and the fire emerged around the idea of competing in bodybuilding, I instantly protected the idea. I told no one until the pursuit was already in motion. Before I told anyone about it, I had already hired the trainer, put my diet in flight, and committed to the date of competition. It was already real when others found out. It was no longer a baby idea with a delicate flame susceptible to reflexive, countering input. It was by then a well-nourished roaring fire.

As the vision for starting my first record label came to me, I guarded that fire with caution. I eschewed the impulses of self-doubt. I more feared failing to launch than failing to succeed. I cultivated the idea's fire fully conscious that a future regret of having never started was my highest fear.

Late at night, after the kids were asleep, I would fire up the laptop and my imagination to sketch out the character descriptions and plotlines of my first spy novel. I did this in secret, telling hardly anyone for some time. Once I sufficiently built the fire for sustainability, I slowly revealed what I was working on to others as I began to more formally chart the pursuit.

As your fire first emerges and your incubation stage begins, remember that creation is its own reward. Remember that you are the primary shepherd of your idea. Solicit strategic input and enlist partnered help when appropriate but guard the fire that rose with your idea. You are the keeper of those flames.

Neil Gaiman, author of *Make Good Art* and creator of *Coraline*, knows the rewards that are enjoyed by cultivating the flames that birth creation. Gaiman has explained that he's never been involved with a project that was done just for money that was ever worth it. He describes such projects as bitter experiences. Because Gaiman is a soul on fire, he only comes alive when he's engaged in a project that he's inherently drawn to help push into the world. He describes such engagements this way:

> The things I did because I was excited, and wanted to see them exist in reality, have never let me down, and I never regretted the time I spent on them.

Burn, burn, burn like fabulous roman candles exploding across the stars. Capture and protect the fires that burn within and protect them from the elements that would snuff out those fires. Be the keeper of your flames so that they burn away the possibility of future regret. Because creation is its own reward, nourishing your fires into launched realities will make you feel alive.

As you leverage the fire of your excitement to enable your ideas to exist in reality, remember well **Failure Rule #2:** *Nothing Is Safe*. Because this is true, you need to mind many fires. While each fire becomes its own reward at the point of creation, not all will last long enough to keep you warm forever. So build a *Portfolio of Pursuits* and mind many fires. Let each fire contribute to the blazing path of your *calling journey*. Let each fire inhabit you and drive you.

Because a soul on fire is a soul alive.

DON'T TETHER YOURSELF TO NOTIONS OF PERMANENCE

"Practice experiencing everything in a state of non-expectancy and nonattachment. The beauty of living will suddenly become clear."

—STEVE LEASOCK, AUTHOR OF *SIMPLICITY OF LIFE: WHY DOES BEING HUMAN COMPLICATE EVERYTHING?*

> **LESSON:** Learn to detach yourself from that which may be lost, destroyed, or taken away; instead, attach yourself to the beauty of living in all circumstances.

Don't tether yourself to notions of permanence. Because **Failure Rule #2** is real—*Nothing Is Safe*. Nothing is permanent. And guess what?

This is good news!

If you want it to be. You choose.

If you take Steve Leasock's advice, you will see the clear beauty in life even when things are taken away from you. Even when your failures cause loss, heartache, and grief. If you choose to embrace your unsafe life without the entanglements of permanence, you will learn to find joy in all circumstances. This does not mean that you do not mourn. It does not mean that you don't acknowledge disappointment or temporary regret. It *does* mean that you choose, through decisive nonattachment, to focus on joy in spite of circumstance. And then you choose to move on and leave behind the remnants of old attachments with peace.

Buddhism teaches nonattachment through the renunciation of the world's lusts, cravings, and desires. This view can help put temporary attachments in perspective. In the biblical book of Philippians, the apostle Paul expresses a nonattachment approach to life by declaring, "*I have learned the secret of being content in any and every situation, whether well fed or hungry, whether living in plenty or want.*"

Whatever underlying philosophy empowers you, know that you have the agency to choose how you view your circumstances. You can view every loss and color every change with fear, dread, anxiety, regret, and terror, *or* you can anticipate every mutation of circumstance with excitement and wonder.

Cultivate a backlog of ideas to draw from when circumstances mutate among change and loss. Develop this backlog until each idea is ready to be tested. Test each idea at the right time. With the right circumstances. And the right mix of enthusiasm and tactical strategy.

I've been blessed with lots of loss in my life. Material things. Relationships. Money. And more.

That's right, I used the word *blessed*.

Every loss has taught me how to be more adaptable. Taught me how to grow my idea muscles. Stretched me in ways that would not have occurred in static financial times. Or in stable relationship circumstances.

As previously mentioned, over the course of my adult life, I've lost businesses, a home, lots of money, friends, a marriage, my credit, jobs, clients, and customers, and I was estranged from my son for a period of time.

Every ebb of life teaches me the value of detaching my identity from anything except my God-given unique blend of ever-evolving, experience-formed, idea-based skillsets and personality.

I've learned that dissatisfaction, discomfort, and a repulsion from the undesirable circumstances of failure's exhaust, when coupled with pain and loss, can light the brightest flame of ambition.

Swimming in this space (of repulsion from failure's exhaust) can refine your focus in such a way as to resurrect long latent desires, seemingly impractical dreams, and well-developed ideas into actionable realities.

In these valleys I've created things that otherwise would not exist.

Stephanie Land, author of *Maid* and inspiration for the Netflix TV series adaptation of the same title, also created things that otherwise would not exist without the valleys of her life. Stephanie leveraged her dissatisfaction with poverty by mobilizing her idea to document the pain of her experiences. She refused to tether herself to her impoverished circumstances. She refused to view her poverty through a lens of permanence. She rejected the placism that she encountered all around her.

Stephanie cleaned houses as a struggling single mother and often found herself crying in her clients' bathtubs. At the grocery store, while using her electronic benefits transfer (EBT) card, she could feel the burning stares of judgment from those who believed that any use of government assistance automatically translated to a lazy person unwilling to work.

Repulsed by the struggles of poverty that she found herself contending with, Stephanie chose to uncover meaning in the chaos of her circumstances. She chose to instill order into the labyrinth of her emotional haze by distilling the lessons she was learning onto paper.

Because Stephanie chose to see her discomfort through an artistic and opportunistic lens, she not only memorialized and elevated the value of her life experiences in her book *Maid*, but she also became blessed with the byproducts of success—her book attracted an agent and ultimately achieved commercial traction, paradoxically lifting her out of the very poverty she acutely shines a light on in her book.

Traversing through spaces of pain into the resurrection of bootstrapped prosperity will increase your inner satisfaction. It will raise your quality of life to new hilltops. Removing yourself from any attachment to expectations of permanence will strengthen your position in the world. It will fortify the stability of your soul. It will ground your approach to relationships. And it will help you learn how to shed losses and keep moving forward without unnecessary weight.

High school basketball coach Ray Drecker, the main character in the HBO TV series, *Hung*, moves through the serial tragedies and failures of his life with a sense of effortless nonattachment. Ray is a divorced dad who is trying to maintain his role in supporting his twin children along with his ex-wife, who is remarried. The downward spiral of Ray's luck is kicked off when his house—that he let the insurance lapse on—burns down. His immediate response? With a smile, he jettisons his emotional attachment to the physical home, puts his economic concerns on pause, and encourages his kids to help him build a tent out back to sleep in. Ray assures the kids with words to the effect of, *"It'll be great... we'll camp and make breakfast!"*

While none of us ever wishes to be in a position in which we choose to moonlight as a prostitute (as Ray ended up doing) to get our financial boat floating again, there is still an attitudinal lesson in Ray's bouncy reaction to loss. When loss and misfortune fall upon you, think of ways you can detach, proverbially build a tent, go camping, and look forward to making breakfast.

Hold tight to your desire to see the beauty of living in all circumstances. Because **Failure Rule #2: *Nothing Is Safe*** sometimes acts as a thief, hold loose all the temporal attachments in your life that can be lost, destroyed, or taken away. Learn the secret of being content in any and all circumstances. Learn to manifest a worldly nimbleness. Like both Stephanie Land and Ray Drecker did, don't tether yourself to notions of permanence.

GET USED TO UNSAFE SPACES

"You build on failure. You use it as a steppingstone. Close the door on the past. You don't try to forget the mistakes, but you don't dwell on it. You don't let it have any of your energy, or any of your time, or any of your space."
—JOHNNY CASH, SONGWRITER AND OUTLAW COUNTRY LEGEND

> **LESSON:** When you abide by the promptings of your *internal spirit voice*, expect to travel into messy, unsafe spaces.

Sometimes your *internal spirit voice* will beckon the essence of **Failure Rule #2: Nothing Is Safe** to usher itself into your path—for your *calling journey's* sake.

When your *internal spirit voice* is consistently heralding a path for you that defies the advice of those you love, it can cause deep conflict within you. This conflict, if poorly understood, can cause you to make decisions that invite unnecessary chaos and failure into your life. Incongruence of the soul can do that to a person. When your life's trajectory is pulling you away from the will of your *internal spirit voice*, detaching from that trajectory to deliberately align with your *calling journey* can be messy.

When I quit student teaching—abandoning the aimed result of four years of college study—to follow the prompting of my *internal spirit voice* into the mystery of my *calling journey*, things got messy. When I abruptly quit my job at an investment firm in my early twenties to pursue helping at-risk kids, things got messy. When I maxed out my credit cards to start my first record label while I was unemployed, things got messy. When I walked away from my partnership and position in the online lending firm and invited necessary temporary chaos into my life, things got messy. In each one of these instances, I embraced the mess. When you're truly hearing and acting in accordance with your *internal spirit voice*, you'll need to get used to stepping out into messy, unsafe spaces.

As I sit typing this, I am drinking a hot, bold cup of black Death Wish brand coffee. It is my preferred cup of joe while writing because it's so damn strong. As I sip the rich black elixir, I can't help but reflect on the probability that in the eyes of many, the unsafe life that outlaw country legend Johnny Cash lived must have made him look like he had a death wish. Johnny is famous for stepping out into messy, unsafe spaces.

Early on in his first marriage to Vivian Liberto, Johnny's *internal spirit voice* was in conflict with the inertia of his life. He was working as a traveling salesman. He was settling into the expected structure of normal family life and nine-to-five compliance. The illusion of the safe life was pulling him away from the urgings of his *internal spirit voice*.

But Johnny Cash was a man whose soul was on fire. He was a soul alive. His *internal spirit voice* was pushing him to detach from the lure of the supposed safe life and instead pursue the making of immortal music. When Johnny rejected an offer to work a stable job for his father-in-law's company, he was obeying the directives of his *internal spirit voice*. This was a pivotal decision. It represented Johnny fully embracing his *calling journey*—a life of music. And from that point on, Johnny's story unraveled as if he had a death wish. He recognized that **Failure Rule #2: *Nothing Is Safe*** was clear, and he chose the highest pursuits worthy of his life instead of meager offers of safety.

As Johnny began to follow his *internal spirit voice* and embrace an unsafe life, his internal conflicts increased. As touring became his life, his wife remained back at home raising four kids. This disconnect was not sustainable. His marriage crumbled. Simultaneously, his ability to internalize the implications of fame was immature. This immaturity made him susceptible to substance abuse. Johnny fast became an alcoholic and an amphetamine junkie. He lived like he had a death wish.

But Johnny's marital and addiction failures weren't the end of his story. It turns out that deep down, Johnny's will to live was stronger than his death wish impulses. As Johnny's second marriage to June Carter evolved, Johnny got clean with her help. As he kicked his addictions, he also got religion. As he got religion, he was able to manifest deeper meaning and impact through his life and music.

After tumbling through danger and tragedy during Act 1 of his *calling journey,* Johnny rose to perform in Act 2 with grace, wisdom, and inspiration. He continued to represent the broken, downtrodden, and forgotten by wearing black to remind us of *"the ones who are held back."* He befriended evangelist Billy Graham and began expressing his faith journey explicitly in his music. He did this in an unvarnished way that integrated the totality of his imperfection with the totality of the mercy of God.

Johnny's music would not carry the weight, meaning, and eternal impact that it does today if his life wasn't wrought with tragedy, addiction, and failure. From the ashes of Johnny's failures, beauty and strength ultimately emerged.

As you contemplate how to best resist the inertia of a faux safe life, be mindful that following your *internal spirit voice* may cause confusion, internal conflict, and pain before it leads you to maximized meaning and fulfillment.

If you're an entrepreneur, you should expect things to go wrong and prepare to embrace complex and consequential problems before you enjoy the fruits of creating something out of nothing. If you're a creative, you should know that digging deep into the recesses of your soul to produce unmistakable art can sometimes stir difficult emotions that would otherwise lie buried. As an authentic, you should prepare to square your shoulders as you ignore expectations of conformity and animate your true Being.

As you struggle to hear and properly interpret the messaging of your *internal spirit voice,* know that if you choose to follow it, you will need to get used to unsafe spaces. Following your *internal spirit voice* will often require you to *deliberately* enter unsafe spaces. Like when Johnny Cash rejected his father-in-law's job offer and crashed into his tumultuous musical *calling journey.* As you navigate these unsafe spaces, know that you must learn to use your failures as steppingstones and learn to close the door properly on the past. Don't give your failures your energy, as Johnny advises in this chapter's anchor quote.

Most importantly, know that if you choose to follow your *internal spirit voice's* direction, you will also be deliberately entering into spaces of highest meaning. Like Johnny Cash proved as his music went on to bless the souls of over ninety million listeners and counting.

GET BUSY LIVING

"If you're not busy living, you're dying."

—VINCE FLYNN, LATE, GREAT THRILLER
AUTHOR OF *AMERICAN ASSASSIN*

> **LESSON:** Time is not your friend, so get busy living to the fullest—and remember that you must die.

Get busy living or know that you're dying.

The ultimate manifestation of the truth of **Failure Rule #2: Nothing Is Safe** is your death. And it will visit you at its mysterious convenience, not your thoughtful appointment. So seize abundant living as much as possible before it shows up.

Yesterday I woke up with debilitating pain in my lower back. It is in a spot that I injured doing heavy squats at the gym weeks ago. Until I awoke yesterday, I thought it was firmly on the mend. Yesterday also happened to be the day I had a scheduled colonoscopy. So I woke up with back pain that rendered me immobile on the same day I had to go have a doc insert a tiny camera up my anus. All kinds of fun.

As I sit typing—loaded up on muscle relaxers and painkillers—I can't help but be conscious of the fragility of life, the mortality of humankind, and the need to seize each moment. At the time of this writing, I am approaching my forty-seventh birthday. As I think about the years I have left, my *internal spirit voice* is loudly urging me to get busy living and fulfill the visible next steps of my *calling journey* with haste.

In 2013 geopolitical thriller author Vince Flynn died after years of battling prostate cancer. He was only forty-seven. While his family and his readers would've wished he had more years in his life, Vince certainly packed a lot of life into his forty-seven years on this planet.

Vince's origin story reveals a man who understood that time was not his friend. He was busy living right up until his untimely death.

Armed with a degree in economics, Vince left college and found himself immersed in macaroni and cheese—he became a marketing strategist for Kraft General Foods. But mac and cheese wasn't really something that was going to fulfill Vince's meaning bucket for the long term. In accordance with his *internal spirit voice*, Vince left Kraft in 1990 to accept an aviation candidate slot with the US Marine Corps. Vince had always been attracted to a life in the military. But as it turned out, Vince's interlude into military life was just a detour that routed him instead to his ultimate *calling journey* fulfillment. His military ambition failed when he was medically disqualified as a result of several concussions and seizures that he had suffered as a kid.

Vince didn't let the failure of being disqualified derail him from digging deep and pursuing his *calling journey*. He understood **Failure Rule #2: *Nothing Is Safe***. His military dream was not safe. But his failure mutated into an adjacent dream. That dream was to become a full-time fiction writer of geopolitical spy thrillers. It was adjacent because the story that was bubbling up in his mind's eye involved an ex-Marine-turned-CIA agent (Mitch Rapp). Vince wasn't going to become a Marine, but he was going to perpetuate that spirit in the hearts of his readers.

Vince's writing dream was an unusual and unexpected one. It did not seem suitable because he had struggled his whole life with reading and writing because of his dyslexia. But while Vince felt as if he was *born to lose* with dyslexia, he still chose to *live to win* and overcome his condition's limitations.

Still licking his wounds after his disqualification from the Marines, Vince took on the burden of the ordinary nine-to-five grind. He began working for a commercial real estate company in his hometown of Minneapolis. Vince used the day job for some stability as he leveraged his spare time to shape his ideas for his first novel.

Vince held down the nine-to-five job for two years until fully embracing the dangerous promptings of his *internal spirit voice*. Vince quit his job, moved to Colorado, and worked full time on the novel we now know as *Term Limits*.

This period was not an easy and open success path for Vince. There were no early indications that his *Thing Two* dream (see **Failure Rule #4**) of writing full time was going to work out. But creation is its own reward first. The external rewards creation produces often come much later, if they come at all.

For Vince, it took five years of writing all day and bartending all night before the fruit of his writing labor materialized. After more than sixty rejection letters, Vince bypassed the literary gatekeepers, chose himself, and self-published his first novel, *Term Limits*. The book shot to number one in his hometown, Minneapolis. Within just a week, Vince landed a new agent and a two-book deal with Pocket Books, a Simon & Schuster imprint.

From the time that Vince inked his deal with Pocket Books up until his untimely death, he was busy living and writing. He released fourteen bestselling novels around the Mitch Rapp story. His book *American Assassin* was adapted to a film starring Michael Keaton and Dylan O'Brien. And he consulted on the story lines for the TV show *24*, featuring Kiefer Sutherland.

Vince's story was one that inspired me to vigorously pursue writing spy novels. His perseverance through failures spoke to me. He overcame being disqualified from the Marines, outwilled the limitations of his dyslexia and ignored the negativity of publisher rejections. Disqualified, dyslexic, and rejected, Vince leveraged his failures into success and proved that after it sucks, *Failure Rules!*

> **REFLECTION: MAXIMIZE THE LIFE IN YOUR YEARS**
>
> **How might Vince's story inspire you right now to engage with whatever version of failure you are contending with? Consider the following questions:**
>
> - What are the failures you are confronting right now? Are you allowing these failures to have too much power over your unfolding story?
> - How can you leverage your current failures, like Vince did, to swerve more succinctly into the organic current of your *calling journey*? How can you get your power back from your failures?
> - Knowing time is not your friend, how can you get busy living and ensure you have the highest amount of life in your years? How can you own your time with authentic fullness and use it in alignment with your *calling journey*?
> - Are you living each day with the message of memento mori—*remember that you must die*—driving each decision you make so that you maximize your time as you live in the flesh?

Decide right now to orient your priorities so that one day when someone asks about you, "Whatever happened to her?" the answer will instead explain *what happened to the world because of her*. Don't let things just happen *to you*. Be intentional in your *calling journey* alignment quest. Make things happen *to the world*.

As I approach my forty-seventh birthday at the time of this writing and reflect on Vince's death at the same age, these are the questions I ask myself. Think of Vince and ask yourself the same questions. The nature of your answers may be as important as the difference between an obituary that highlights selling macaroni and cheese versus one that champions a career as a bestselling author.

THE COSTS OF ALIGNING WITH YOUR CALLING JOURNEY ARE WORTH IT

"We all learn lessons in life. Some stick; some don't. I have always learned more from rejection and failure than from acceptance and success."

—HENRY ROLLINS, SINGER, AUTHOR, AND ACTOR

> **LESSON:** Even though a departure from the safe path may come with high costs, if bearing those costs helps join you with your authentic *calling journey*, it is worth it.

The reality of **Failure Rule #2: *Nothing Is Safe*** often kicks into high gear when you actually begin acting in accordance with the promptings of your *internal spirit voice*. It's almost as if disobeying your *internal spirit voice* keeps a strong portion of **Failure Rule #2**'s challenges at bay. And aligning with your *calling journey* through following your *internal spirit voice* instantly activates the unsafe truth bomb of **Failure Rule #2**. It becomes the cost of your authentic journey. Because obeying the directives of your *internal spirit voice* will usually come with a cost. Because boldly embracing the meaning of your *calling journey*'s next steps often requires a new and distinct adoption of responsibility. And it's usually in that newly formed responsibility that your cost is found.

If you move from a meaningless high-paying job to a meaningful job with an average salary, your cost is the reduced salary. If you migrate from being an employee to being a self-employed entrepreneur, your cost is the full burden of isolated autonomy. If you are a creative sharing your work for the first time, the cost for your courage may be fielding waves of rejection—of the very art that reflects the deepest parts of your soul. When you're an authentic who shows up in the world precisely as who you are, you may carry the costs of nonconformity in the deepest of ways.

As I have continued to embrace growth in my banking career, the costs have been the burden of simultaneity, chaos, and juggling multiple high-stakes responsibilities. High rewards come with the cost of a responsibility stack that stretches upstream in consequence, horizontally in footprint, and downstream in management accountability. This cost dynamic means that I contend with the intensity of a VUCA work environment and all the stress that it carries. Personally, I embrace this cost and find thrill and pleasure in the grip of a VUCA work environment. It is a just and acceptable cost for the high rewards I receive.

One of the practices that helps me dive into the VUCA environment each day is the consumption of strong black coffee coupled with listening to fast, driving music. Motivational speaker Tony Robbins's morning routine may include doing a hot-sauna-to-cold-water-plunge, but mine includes strong black coffee and strong punk rock. This is what prepares me for the everyday VUCA of my job.

I recently got a tattoo of a coffee pot with the symbol for the seminal punk band Black Flag within the design showing as negative space. The four bars Black Flag symbol has been known to represent never backing down, the opposite of the surrender meaning of a white flag. My tattoo is a nod to the song "Black Coffee" by Black Flag. The song describes a maddening jealousy and heartbreak experience that is exacerbated by high consumption of black coffee. However, for me, I simply like the song's intensity and the way it exalts the strength of my favorite morning elixir.

Henry Rollins is the most well-known singer for Black Flag. It is his voice barking passionately on the song "Black Coffee." But long before Henry was touring the world screaming on stage as the front man for Black Flag, he was paying bills by scooping ice cream as the assistant manager at a Haagen-Dazs store in Georgetown.

At this time, Henry had his own band, SOA (State of Alert), but had become a huge fan of Black Flag. He went to see Black Flag play at an impromptu show at a New York bar when then-singer Dez Cadena asked Henry to take the mic on stage to sing the song "Clocked In." This was apropos since Henry had to drive back to DC to work the next day. Someone needed to scoop the ice cream.

Henry had impressed the band with his stage demeanor and vocal style. He had inadvertently *Third Doored* his way onto Black Flag's talent radar. Dez wanted to switch from vocals to guitar, so the band needed a singer. Henry performed at an informal audition the next day and then was formally asked to join the band. He accepted.

Knowing that this represented a pivotal moment in his *calling journey*, Henry embraced the risk of punk rock poverty. He quit his job at Haagen-Dazs, sold his car, and moved to LA. He was all in.

But as I stressed earlier, obeying your *internal spirit voice* usually carries a cost. There were no more petty staychecks from the ice cream shop for Henry. No more certainty in his transportation or lodging. He would be married to the road, hunting day in and day out for sustenance and shelter in concrete jungles spread across the country.

Black Flag were road warriors who toured their faces off to survive. Unlike today, touring in a punk rock band in the eighties was brutal. Things often didn't line up or go as planned. No cell phones, GPS devices, e-mail, Square payment apps, or high guarantees.

Henry has famously told the story of how they had to resort to eating dog food on tour when there was no money for food. This was part of the cost for Henry embracing the thrilling tumult of his *calling journey*. Henry recalls those tumultuous times with his bandmates this way:

> We were broke and at each other's throats, but every song we wrote was first-rate.

REFLECTION: EMBRACE THE COSTS OF JOINING WITH YOUR CALLING JOURNEY

Do you want to extract something actionable from Henry's story? Then here are some questions you need to think about:

- What is that thing in your life that you aspire to that is akin to writing first-rates songs (your *Thing Two* dream—see **Failure Rule #4**)? Have you begun to chase it?
- What is the proverbial dog food you need to eat as part of embracing the thrill of your *calling journey*? If this is your highest cost, are you willing to pay it?
- What is the full cost of chasing your *Thing Two* dream (see **Failure Rule #4**) in earnest? What is the full cost of *not* chasing your *Thing Two* dream? Which one of these costs is most worth bearing?
- What is the ice cream job in your life that you cling to so tightly that you're effectively deaf to the sound of your *internal spirit voice*? How can you plan to *break free* from this stranglehold of safety and *break into* your unsafe *calling journey*?

Henry bore the cost of joining his *calling journey* because he believed **Failure Rule #2: Nothing Is Safe** was obvious. He followed his *internal spirit voice*, jettisoned any illusions of security, and he got in the van to tour with Black Flag.

Over thirty years later, Henry's *calling journey* has unfolded to prove well worth the hard costs of poverty and pain that the early years required. With a resume that boasts countless albums with Black Flag and his own act, Rollins Band, a Grammy for his audio reading of his book *Get In The Van*, a TV talk show, and acting gigs in movies such as *The Chase*,

Johnny Mnemonic, and *Heat,* I doubt he has regrets about leaving the ice cream store.

Henry is a soul on fire. He is a soul alive. He followed the directives of his *internal spirit voice* to chase his *calling journey* as a creative in music, writing, and acting.

If you're hesitant to embrace your *calling journey's* next step because the cost is clear and scary, take a step back and evaluate what truly carries meaning for you. Reflect on Failure Rule #2's reality. Know that *Nothing Is Safe* and that the costs are worth bearing if they allow you to crash into the authenticity of your unique *calling journey.*

And then remember Henry and know that dog food rules and ice cream is overrated.

DON'T OUTSOURCE YOUR STORY

"Can we continue to argue that our lives are an unfolding novel written from afar...are we not writing the script interactively throughout this novel, page by page by page?"

—JAMES HOLLIS, PSYCHOANALYST AND AUTHOR
OF *LIVING AN EXAMINED LIFE*

> **LESSON:** Live your life in such a way that you know exactly what your book would look like—one you want those left behind to read.

Knowing that **Failure Rule #2: *Nothing Is Safe*** is a nonnegotiable reality, you don't need to seek safety in the innocuous micro-narratives that others write for you, about you.

No, write your own story—*no matter fucking what*—or others will write it for you, *at your expense*, for the benefit of their feelings, their interests, and their entombed vision of who they need you to be.

You need to own each emphasis, each hero arc, and every suspenseful cliffhanger to each chapter of your story regardless of the optics of failure, pain, and debris that might muddle the prose within.

Never, ever let anyone else's reflexive judgments and perceptions taint the agency you have over your story.

When my financial planning practice was dying, nothing in my life was safe. Every unforeseen delay in a sales cycle or abrupt account closure threatened my personal economy and my family's stability.

I chose to harness the terror and pressure into grit toward multiple pursuits with varying timelines.

Confucius waxed poetic about the value of planning for different target harvests. He advised that if your plan is for one year, you should plant rice. If your plan is for ten years, you ought to plant trees. And he calculated that if you're looking for a real long game of one hundred years, then you should educate children.

First, the rice. The degradation of my financial planning practice prompted me to jettison the Midwest and its rustbelt ways and move back to the Northeast. We moved with nothing secured on the other end. Three kids, as young as three. No anchor or promise of replacement income waiting to greet me—only the belief that the economic soil of opportunity in the northeast would be more fertile. Months after relocating, my belief was validated as I entered the online lending space and that wild journey commenced. Within the year, the planted rice was ready for harvest. I repressed fear. I embraced nonattachment to material things and left my home of seven years. And I left the safe nook of an established community to write a new chapter of my story for the benefit of myself and my young family.

Then, the trees. As my financial planning practice was declining, I used the cracks in my schedule to retool the models for my inactive record labels. Capital was secured. Plans were refined. We signed five new bands to each label and planned a robust release schedule to stimulate growth and near-term revenue. Not all of these trees grew strong, but over the next ten years, about half did. This wouldn't have happened if I had let immediate concerns of safety concern me. If I had been preoccupied with the temporary negative optics of my unfolding story, there would have been no enthusiasm for such an initiative.

Then, the education. The legacy seeds. Not rice, not trees. No, this was my long-tail pursuit. A piece of content to be available immortally. In this empty space of flux and uncertainty, when everything was collapsing within the machinations of my primary income source, I collapsed into my dreams and imagination. As I detailed earlier, late at night, when the children were sleeping and the house was still and hauntingly quiet, I wrote. Seven years later those writings became my first published spy novel, *BLAZE: Operation Persian Trinity*.

I decided I wasn't going to wait until retirement to act on my dream of writing books. I started in the midst of absolute personal chaos instead.

I was going to scribe the contours of my life. My circumstances weren't going to write the rest of the story. We all have the choice to decide how forcefully we are going to interact and impose our will into the unfolding narrative of our lives.

You get to make that choice.

Like James Hollis proposes in this chapter's anchor quote, we all get to write our life's novel interactively page by page.

Don't outsource your story to others.

Don't outsource your story to the whims of your circumstances.

Comedian and actor Kevin Hart addressed this in his own way on the *Joe Rogan Experience* podcast. *"What's your book look like?"* he rhetorically asked. It sounded like a simple question for Rogan's audience. Simple, sure. But it's a powerful question.

Live your life so that it would translate into a book you would want those you leave behind—and love the most—to read.

If your life does not feel like an unfolding novel that you intentionally interact with and shape—in partnership with some notion of a higher power or movement of Providence—then you need to take back your story and own it.

And if cascading failure surrounds you, find the soil in the sidewalk cracks of your life, and find a way to plant rice, trees, and the long-term education seeds that bear your legacy.

Because *Nothing Is Safe* anyway.

And because **Failure Rule #2** is a good thing.

ALWAYS REMEMBER FAILURE RULE #2

NOTHING IS SAFE

The world is constantly reminding us that it is unsafe. Just read the news on any given day. We are always being reminded of **Failure Rule #2**. Nothing is static. Nothing is truly stable. Everything is subject to some sort of risk or failure. Because you now fully know how true this is, it behooves you to decisively find your meaning, fulfillment, survival, and prosperity as an *entrepreneur, creative, or authentic* in holding tightly your internal attachments and only loosely gripping those external things that can be lost, destroyed, or taken away.

Since **Failure Rule #2:** *Nothing Is Safe* imposes fragility on our choices, you must choose pursuits worthy of your life. As author and podcaster Srinivas Rao did when he discarded external societal expectations and abandoned his habit of corporate job hopping. He instead infused the spirituality and freedom he found in surfing into his own brand of creative ideation through his writing and podcasting. Similarly, because **Failure Rule #2:** *Nothing Is Safe* teaches us life's unchanging fragility, you must not let false feelings of fear derail you from enjoying the ride you were created to take. This means that you must channel the spirit of Motorhead's Lemmy Kilmister and deliberately attack life with an *intent to win* even when you feel as if you were utterly *born to lose*.

Don't inappropriately glorify safety in your life. Because **Failure Rule #2:** *Nothing Is Safe* applies also to structures of power, you shouldn't unwisely outsource your safety either. Remember the words of the crab boat captain that Mike Rowe recalled: *"If you want to be safe, that's on you."* Also, make sure to remember that because nothing is safe, you ought to base your decisions more on making an impact with pursuits worthy of your life. Never forget the lesson of the fictional character Gus Lobel (Clint Eastwood) in the film *Trouble with the Curve*—*being comfortable is overrated*.

Choosing the easy way may sometimes feel like the safe route, but it's not because nothing is safe. Instead, be sure to choose the hard right way instead of the easy wrong way in times of consequential decisioning. Do this even if it causes you to welcome suffering into your life for upholding the truth. Like Winston Churchill did when he confronted Nazism at a time when others were happy to appease the Nazis instead. Sometimes when you choose the hard right way, the consequence of your decision is that chaos emerges around you. When this happens, you need to detach from the cyclone of emotions that naturally bubble up in times of chaos. As you detach, you need to find a way to see the creative, reshaping opportunities that lie within circumstances of chaos, just as retired Navy SEAL Jocko Willink advised.

Because **Failure Rule #2: *Nothing Is Safe*** is omni-operative, your access to being loved is also unsafe. When this access is severed and you find yourself unloved, you must choose to vigorously love yourself. As investor and author Kamal Ravikant did, you must flip the script on your internal monologue and reinforce the unique value of your created Being until those truths anchor deeply into your new self-talk reality. Doing this will also help you to define the operating system that regulates your decisions along with your view of self. It is this defined operating system that you must engage with when failures strike so you can make your failures rule in accordance with your operating system. You get to design this operating system just as Billie Jean King, Tim Ferriss, John Joseph, and Dave Ramsey have. It will be your operating system that will guide your steps toward reinvention when failure strikes. It is because circumstances are subject to fluidity and volatility that you must make reinvention your utmost skill. A skill I have employed many times in the music business, in banking, finance, in the fitness space, and in writing. Your reinvention skills are necessary if you are to view yourself as a business entity with multiple lines of business under your management—a *Portfolio of Pursuits mentality*. Since nothing is safe and failure in some form is inevitable, you need to learn to cultivate this and be an octopus, like rocker Gene Simmons has.

To help minimize the failures of mediocrity, work to identify the unique chemistry of your individual talent composite. Follow Neil deGrasse Tyson's philosophy, and find the mix of talents and competencies you possess that aggregate into a distinct offering to the world. If you do this, you will be better prepared to make your world and work environment a product of you, like motivational speaker Joshua Coburn has learned to do. Finding a way to do so will help you to extract more meaning out of your work. It is one step that will help you maintain a will to give a damn about what you do, which, as you learned from retired Navy SEAL Marcus Luttrell, is necessary for short-term endurance and long-term success.

When you accept and realize that **Failure Rule #2: *Nothing Is Safe*** can enable freedom, then you will be empowered to live as a soul on fire. Because a soul on fire is a soul alive. Remember how American Catholic iconoclast Jack Kerouac knew and lived this.

As you navigate the unsafe world that reflects **Failure Rule #2**, know that there is high value in traversing through spaces of pain with a deliberate sense of nonattachment. Approaching pain and failure spaces with a nonattachment mindset will help you bootstrap yourself into new positions in the world as you shed losses and turn your pain into art. Like author Stephanie Land did as she converted the pain of poverty into inspirational words. Use your failures as steppingstones and build on them as you travel through unsafe spaces, like country legend Johnny Cash did.

Failure Rule #2: *Nothing Is Safe* reminds us also that we must die, and time is not our friend. With this, you must get busy living life to the fullest, like the late thriller writer Vince Flynn did before cancer took him at age forty-seven. And like punk rock icon Henry Rollins chose to do when he quit his job scooping ice cream to embrace the adventure of punk rock poverty by living in a van to tour with Black Flag.

As you digest the truth of **Failure Rule #2: *Nothing Is Safe,*** don't seek false safety in the unsolicited narratives others write for you or about you without your consent. Write your own story instead—*no matter fucking what*—so that others do not write it for you. Because if you let them write it, *it will be at your expense,* for the benefit of their feelings, their interests, and their entombed vision of who they need you to be. Find courage in this unsafe world. Know **Failure Rule #2** well and choose pursuits worthy of your life. Choose to live your life in such a way that you know exactly what your book would look like: one you want those you love and leave behind to read.

FAILURE RULE #3
MONEY IS SPIRITUAL

"You've got to be able to understand how money is created—that money is spiritual. It is essentially the result of doing things for other people...and there is no limited pie in the sense that the only way for me to get a dollar is to take it from you. That is absurd."

—RABBI DANIEL LAPIN, AUTHOR OF *THOU SHALL PROSPER*

> **PRINCIPLE:** Money is an elusive, versatile tool loaded with spiritual power. If misunderstood, it can fuel envy and greed and ultimately the failure of self-inflicted emptiness, but if viewed and used properly, it can be a multiplier of blessings and an enabling thank-you note that can help lift valued recipients up and out of their failure valleys.

REJECT BOTH ENVY AND GREED

"Envy and greed starve on a steady diet of thanksgiving."
—REV. BILLY GRAHAM, EVANGELIST, PRESIDENTIAL SPIRITUAL ADVISOR, AND FRIEND OF MARTIN LUTHER KING JR. AND JOHNNY CASH

> **LESSON:** Focus on that which is eternal by embracing gratitude and rejecting envy and greed.

If you fail to apply the inherent power of **Failure Rule #3: *Money Is Spiritual*** to your financial perspective, you risk being entrapped by the alluring emptiness of envy and greed.

Many people, often non-entrepreneurs, seem to think that being an entrepreneur is entirely about chasing money. They think it's about greed. That it's about an insatiable desire for more that never ends.

But this is not true. Greed rarely pays off. It usually has a steep cliff in front of it. In fact, greed often leads directly to failure, and not the good kind. Because real greed—the real disingenuous pursuit of money only for the sake of it—almost always goes off the rails. It almost always fails to deliver the value needed to maintain true success. And it almost always leaves an unsatisfied mind.

There's a space of consciousness and perspective that lies soundly and rationally somewhere between the disdain and willful disregard for money and the unbridled worship of money. It is in this space that currency can be seen for what it is, what it was meant to be, and how it ought to always be. It is in this space that gratitude and thanksgiving live. It is in this space that both envy and greed are rejected.

Like many things in life, it's not the item that signifies good or evil but the disposition of the end user, the intentions of their heart, and the actions that emanate from their use of free will. A knife can be used to kill or spread butter. Fire can be used to cook food or burn down an entire neighborhood. You get the point.

This is a simple and intuitive truth to grasp. Yet with money, it seems so many people never find that balance. Instead, many sit more to the edges of envy or greed instead of in the rational bucket seat of controlled respect. It's in those dangerous edges of envy and greed that failure waits to strike. Envy and greed are both poisonous spirits that often cause failures of many varieties over time—spiritual bankruptcy, discontentment, fractured relationships, lifestyle dysfunction, and sometimes tangible economic (and potentially even physical) harm to oneself and to others.

In the film *Wall Street*, released in 1987, Michael Douglas famously plays the nefarious, crooked stockbroker Gordon Gekko. Douglas's role as Gekko has become the quintessential pop culture symbol for greed and financial corruption. In the film, Gekko explains his deep affinity for greed this way:

> Greed, for lack of a better word, is good. Greed is right. Greed works. Greed clarifies, cuts through, and captures the essence of the evolutionary spirit. Greed in all of its forms—greed for life, for money, for love, for knowledge—has marked the upward surge of mankind.

It doesn't take a lengthy analysis of Gekko's statement to discern that he has casually conflated the concept of healthy desire with unhealthy greed. The former being a positive driver of the evolution of developed society and collective cooperation. The latter being a selfish attribute that corrupts desire and goodness, overrides justice and charity, and prioritizes personal gain over competitive fairness.

Yet those who drift into the realm of greedy behavior often don't fully wear their new stripes immediately. The drift is innocuous. The drift typically occurs one small, compromised decision after another; then, after a while, people find themselves operating primarily on selfish principles.

You need to avoid this. You need to preemptively erect guardrails around your decision-making to prevent this drift. Else, you will ultimately find yourself bereft of true meaning in your work and life. Else, you slowly corrode your closest relationships over time. Else, you conclude your path with a conflicted heart and a stained conscience. All the gains in the world won't purchase the reversal of such consequences.

But it's not just greed that you need to watch out for as an entrepreneur seeking to make your imprint in the world. Envy is equally as powerful, destructive, and seductive. Envy is greed's malevolent twin sibling.

The Greek philosopher Democritus observed that *"an envious man pains himself as though he were an enemy."* Those who latch onto envy develop a poisonous disdain for those who have more, but the only real poison dispensed is the portions that the envious themselves swallow and suffer from. Envy is a poison that kills only the one who carries it. This is true for all kinds of envy. Envy of money, lifestyle, status, privilege, position, love, and even community.

In the aforementioned film bearing the name *Envy*, starring Jack Black as Nick Vanderpark and Ben Stiller as Tim Dingman, Stiller as Tim is suffering with the self-administered poison of deep envy. After Tim's neighbor and best friend, Nick, strikes it rich by inventing a spray can that makes dog shit disappear, Tim is stuck grinding away as a working stiff at the sandpaper factory. But he is forced to witness the newfound opulence of his best friend and neighbor—high resolution in his face. During a performance review conversation with his boss, Tim explodes. All of his bubbling envy is released. His boss asks him if there is any reason that his focus has been off kilter. Tim confesses:

No. No reason. No. I mean, nothing I can think of. I mean—you know, other than every day, I get into my little shit-box car and there he is—with the wind in his hair—on his great big shiny horse. And I drive off to do what? To make sandpaper. To make paper with sand on it. I'd love to see you try to turn your weasley little mouth into a fake smile, day after day after day while you have to wave toodly-fucking-do to your best friend who's rearing up on a big white horse like he's the Lone Ranger. Then I'd like to take a peek at your performance chart, you beady-eyed little shrimp-boat bastard. Is that a reason? I mean, is that a reason? Shit doesn't just disappear.

Dingman may be right that shit doesn't just disappear. But he's wrong to allow his roaring envy to overcome him. Yet there is no denying that life is difficult. There is no denying that much of the work that people do, not just making sandpaper, is grueling. And there is no denying that it can be difficult to not point at those who appear to have it better and to not become covetous. It is difficult to see those with more and instead study them, try to learn from them, and see if there is merit to becoming inspired by them.

Comedian and podcaster Adam Corolla touched on the modern acceptance of envy on his podcast. Corolla lamented the envy our culture has widely embraced and admonished those who buy into it. He harkened back to his childhood when instead of envy, people responded with respect toward, and being inspired by, those who may have earned more. His rant aired as follows:

> You took guys who built something, and you said, "there's a guy who accomplished something." You didn't say, "that guy didn't pay his fair share." That guy paid millions of dollars last year, and you paid shit and you're pissed at him? It's this envy and shame, and there's gonna be a lot more of it...It used to be back in the day, a father was walking his son and they'd see a guy go by in his Rolls Royce and you said, "There goes Mr. Jenkins. Look up to him." What do we do now? Oooh, look at him. Does he need that car? Why does he need to drive that car? Let's throw a rock at it.

Most accomplished people who have been blessed with more do not operate in the mold of Gordon Gekko. Most are not driven by, rewarded for, or sustained by greed. So do not view those with more through this lens. Even in the instances in which it may be true, viewing them this way will not help you. Envy doesn't build anything good within you. Envy only promotes excuses, vitriol, and discontentment.

In the country song "Grass is Always Greener" by Jake Owen with Kid Rock, the singer's point of view focuses on an observational comparison of his life with his neighbors. Along the lines of Theodore Roosevelt's assertion that *"comparison is the thief of joy,"* the song begins with:

"Neighbor got a brand-new Cadillac
Still got my old Ford truck (But it runs)
Got a sweet saltwater pool in the ground
We got a three-footer sittin' above (Splish splash)
Got a new John Deere, just ridin' around
With a cold beer in his hand (Hell yeah)
While I'm still pull, start, push
Hell, but it gets the job done, amen."

You need to remember that your self-worth is not tied to your net worth. Whether you're the one with the Cadillac or the Ford, you need to take the highest pleasure in the true blessings of your life. Identify those things that transcend the material. Those things that are eternal. The quiet contentment of your inner spirit. The trusted relationships you have cultivated. The gift of every bite of food taken. Focus on these things and give thanks.

Remember, as Billy Graham reminds above, both envy and greed starve on a steady diet of thanksgiving. Take Jake Owen and Kid Rock's advice when they sing:

"If you're mad at the man or you're mad at the hand
You were dealt, well then, you're missing the point
Grass is always greener in somebody else's joint."

Reject both envy and greed. Wherever you are in the trajectory of your career, your *calling journey*, and your net worth status, you must always find your balance in the midspace of contented thanksgiving.

Remember that money is only as good as the good it facilitates.

Because **Failure Rule #3**: *Money Is Spiritual* abides.

MONEY IS A THANK-YOU NOTE

"No transaction happens unless it is voluntary. It only happens if both of you think you win."

—JOHN STOSSEL, CONSUMER TV PERSONALITY,
LIBERTARIAN PUNDIT, AND AUTHOR

> **LESSON:** Honor the transactions you engage in; strive to fully earn each payment you receive in honor of the inherent thank-you note it represents.

There's one principle that I've learned to internalize that seems to keep me grounded regardless of where I may be on the continuum of trying to wed money with meaning. This, again, is the understanding that the exchange of currency is nothing but a thank-you note.

If you do not value the thank-you notes you receive, you will fail to maximize the meaning of your business, employment, or daily transactions. This failure will diminish the fulfillment of your life. Because life is inextricably connected to work, business, commerce, and the continual engagement in transactions. When this inextricable connection is stripped of proper reverence, dissatisfaction and the distortions of envy and greed take hold. Because **Failure Rule #3:** *Money Is Spiritual* cannot be ignored without consequence.

No one forced your employer to hire you or you to accept the job. No one put a gun to your customer's head forcing them to commission your service or purchase your product. Transactions are not compulsory.

Transactions are mutual and voluntary. Transactions are a good faith bet between buyer and seller that the exchange will be good for both sides. Completed transactions, by structural design, are evidence of a bilateral win-win calculation. Even when one party is wrong in their win-win calculation, they enter the transaction believing that they're right. Transactions only happen, as John Stossel suggests above, if *"both of you think you win."* Unlike non-transactional business interactions (credentialing, credit attribution, etc.), transactions tangibly strengthen relationships. Author Nassim Nicholas Taleb explains it this way in his book *Antifragile: Things That Gain From Disorder*:

> My experience is that money and transactions purify relations; ideas and abstract matters like "recognition" and "credit" warp them, creating an atmosphere of perpetual rivalry.

To work and live with integrity you need to ensure your work product reflects the value you receive in the thank-you note of your salary. Or as an entrepreneur, the thank-you note of your revenue. This will purify your business relations because transactions are sacraments.

This requires choosing to manufacture enthusiasm if it's not naturally bubbling up. It means that you need to do your best at what you do even on days when you are not interested in it. Doing this will honor the entire transaction of your employment or the efficacy of your entrepreneurial output. It will strengthen you in ways you may never have thought possible in a role, field, or set of circumstances you are struggling to align with.

It means casting aside your own feelings and focusing instead on earning the merits of each thank-you note received in each payroll or receivable deposit. This is extremely difficult if you have not found a way to maximize efforts to marry meaning with your money. If you find yourself in this space, choose to embrace dispassionate excellence. Deliberately showing up with dispassionate excellence can often birth portions of the meaning you need to carry through to the larger, more uniquely aligned meaning you ultimately desire.

Intentionally approach your work with a service mentality that honors the risk taken by your employer on you. Or as an entrepreneur, the risks your clients, partners, and customers have taken on you. While doing this on your own time, diligently mind your own, or other, businesses on the side. Harvest shadow careers, and find small ways each day to move the needle on developing meaning in and monetization of your calling-driven passions.

If the way you're currently earning or making your money doesn't carry with it sufficient meaning, you need to chase something that has a higher chance to deliver the sustainable meaning you ultimately need. This may be in a distant dream pursuit—or what you will learn, as you keep reading, to call your *Thing Two* Dream (See Failure Rule #4: *Build Your Thing One and Thing Two Dependency*). If your *calling journey* has you strategically wading through a means of earning money that carries low meaning, just make sure you understand its enabling purpose: to sustain and empower you while you make gains toward a higher meaning pursuit in alignment with the whisperings of your *internal spirit voice.*

And if you're still traversing through a low- or no-meaning occupational manifestation, you must still find value and satisfaction in validating each thank-you note you receive. If you don't, the failure of dissatisfaction and emptiness will enshroud you.

Because Failure Rule #3: *Money Is Spiritual* ultimately makes the world go 'round, give each transaction an earnest attempt at delivering value that allows the other side to win as much as you do.

TRANSACTIONS ARE SACRAMENTS

"We make a living by what we get, but we make a life by what we give."
—WINSTON CHURCHILL, NAZI DEFEATER, PAINTER,
WRITER, POLITICIAN, AND CIGAR LOVER

> **LESSON:** Viewed properly, transactions are sacraments—earthly expressions of the spiritual connectivity that exists in exchanges of measured thankfulness.

Money is Spiritual.

And transactions are sacraments.

At least when viewed correctly.

Because when **Failure Rule** #3 is operative, it makes the world go 'round better.

If money is not viewed through this lens, it is a weakened tool that will cause a failure of motivation. No matter how hard you work for it and how much you make, if you do not view money—and the transactions you apply it to—through the lens of it being a meaningful tool for the exchange of service and value for expressed gratitude, your expectations around money will most likely fail you. Because an isolated love of money is an empty fuel source.

However, if you rightfully choose to utilize money as a tool to enhance fair exchanges of service and value for gratitude in all of your affairs, your relationship with money will be fulfilling and sustainable. It will bless you and most of those with whom you transact. And it can be a mechanism for helping you, or those you deal with, overpower circumstances of failure with a sense of pride and meaning.

Our life is sustained by what we get, but it is made by what we give.

The transactional exchange of money bears the qualities of a sacrament—an earthly mechanism for spiritual connectivity. The exchange of money, or any other exchange of value, represents a recipient's expression of thankfulness for a product or service. The agreed price in the exchange is the very essence of the recipient's placed level of thankfulness—what we simply call value—for the product, service, or measure of usefulness received.

Placed value is measured thankfulness. And we go about our days placing our measured thankfulness one purchase at a time.

The exchange of money is a transactional event that attaches value to the utility of someone else's efforts, time, or applied skillsets. The exchange of money, when used in charitable giving, is the consecration of love, compassion, and specified giving from one to another. In his book *Thou Shall Prosper*, author Rabbi Daniel Lapin explains this principle as follows:

> Not only is money not bad, but it often can be a result of self-improvement. You receive money in proportion to how helpful you can make yourself to other people.

Examine the quantifiable impact of those who operate at the top of ethical hierarchies of competency, and you will discover that they often exhibit a work approach that maximizes help for their colleagues, direct reports, shareholders, partners, and customers. Contrary to popular perception, most do not climb success ladders and receive high financial reward without proportionately delivering help and utility to others. Those who climb the ladder by shortcutting such contributions rarely stay there long.

I love getting a good, full-service car wash. I'll pay top dollar for the most complete express service that details the inside of the car—deep dash cleaning, vacuum and shampoo, windows, door jambs, etc. Where I take my car, White Glove Car Wash, this service is called *The Elite*. It costs about twenty-five bucks and takes about thirty minutes.

One day I was feeling especially grateful. I left work a little bit early to get to the car wash before it closed so I could get my favorite service. It was payday, and my thank-you notes were more abundant than before as a tax cut took effect that pay period.

The man who detailed my car was called Prince. Fondness for the origin of the naming inspiration and the associated sonic work of *Purple Rain* aside, I instantly liked the guy. He enthusiastically cared for my vehicle. It was February, and it was freezing. Five o'clock struck; the quitting bell rang. Every other car wash employee left, but Prince kept at it. He wasn't done with my vehicle. He wanted to make sure it was cleaned to his satisfaction and my pleasure.

As I watched him, I remembered the days, over twenty years prior, in which I worked at a White Glove Car Wash during winter after dropping out of college for a semester. I rode my bike there each morning, at nineteen years old, with my lunch swinging in a brown paper bag from my handlebars. I didn't have a driver's license or a car yet. Most days were so busy I didn't even get to eat my lunch. By noon, my hands were often frozen to near numbness. I would warm them next to a heater, hovering my hands around it with my fingerless gloves on—the fingerless aspect being a necessary feature to collect the cash I received from paying customers. Yet every day, I smiled with gratitude as I struggled to offer the best service to each customer. Even then, I knew earning money was spiritual. And you received it in proportion to your ability to help and serve other people.

As I watched Prince work on my car, my gratitude for his service escalated. I told him I needed to run to the ATM to get his tip. I returned to see him still working diligently on my vehicle fifteen minutes after closing.

I gave Prince a one-hundred-dollar cash tip that day spontaneously. I don't tell this story to exalt myself as some amazing giver or extravagant tipper. I actually suck at giving most of the time—although I am a consistently generous tipper due largely to my experience working at the car wash.

I tell this story to illustrate an incident in which the desire to fully express thankfulness for a unique service resulted in a unique and special exchange of money. The C-note was a thank-you note. That C-note was spiritual. The C-note was an earthly symbol of the spiritual connectivity that exists in acts of thankful expression. The transaction was a sacrament.

All transactions are sacraments. Because **Failure Rule #3:** *Money Is Spiritual* is true.

LOVE MEANING, NOT MONEY

"If money is your hope for independence you will never have it. The only real security that a man will have in this world is a reserve of knowledge, experience, and ability."

—HENRY FORD, INVENTOR

> **LESSON:** Pursue and value both money and meaning as you seek to marry them, but only love meaning, not money.

Money is not the root of all evil—the *love* of money is.

Because money is not a worthy object of worship and love. But it *is* a worthy tool. If understood and used correctly, it is a tool loaded with immense spiritual power, as **Failure Rule #3:** *Money Is Spiritual* demonstrates for us each time money is used appropriately. When you choose to use the tool of money inappropriately, you step outside of its spiritual power *and into the failure space of monetary idolatry*. Please don't do that.

Because the worship of money is a tired, sad, unsatisfying tune. Don't sing it. It'll leave you empty. It will deposit your soul into a cold failure bucket of spiritual bankruptcy. Don't count on money to set you free from the true burdens of life. If you do, as Henry Ford warned, you will fail to achieve true independence. Avoid failure and find the freedom in viewing your money as spiritual.

> ### A QUICK NOTE ON HENRY FORD
>
> I struggled with whether I should leave Henry Ford in this chapter. Ford was obviously an amazing inventor and an iconic historical figure of American industrialism, but he was also tarnished with a history of overt anti-Semitism. Ford blamed "bankers" and "Jews" for all the cultural elements of society he found distasteful. As a banker married to a Jewish woman, I find Ford's bigotry especially appalling. I ultimately decided to leave his reference in because his relevance to this chapter upholds despite the complexity of his legacy. Like many others discussed throughout this book, my references do not equal a wholesale endorsement of everything someone believes, has said, or has done.

Instead, let the making, earning and growing of your money be nothing but the byproduct of the relentless pursuit of your *calling journey* in accordance with the whisperings of your *internal spirit voice*.

Making money as a singular goal is a fragile, unsustainable, motivational fuel source. It will burn quickly, produce little strength, and be easily cannibalized by the hardships, roadblocks, and challenges that lie before it.

I know several people who did really well for themselves and achieved financial independence. Some of them have achieved this midlife and no longer need to work. Yet as they built their paths to financial independence, they did not adequately nourish pursuits and passions that would provide sustainable ongoing meaning to fill their days in a financially independent life. Aside from the meaning of family life, many of them became depressed, aimless, and devoid of any focused, driving, active, passionate pursuit—monetized or not.

The truth is that until the 1950s, there was no real recognition of the concept of retirement as we know it today. People instinctively wanted to work as long as they lived. They understood innately that their identity was interconnected to their contributive output in some capacity of work or service. Without such output, identity shrivels. It was only in the second half of the twentieth century that people sought retirement for purposes of leisure. Prior to that, retirement was a regrettable reality relegated only to the disabled.

There is nothing wrong with achieving the financial flexibility to work how and where you choose in a way that provides the most meaning for you, even if it takes the form of unpaid service. I am working toward this type of flexibility myself. But you need pursuits of meaning, even in the confines of what we today call retirement.

Don't pursue a financial independence that is decoupled from an equal pursuit of sustainable meaning. Such a decoupling will fail you. Instead, fill your motivation tank with the clean, sustainable fuel of calling-driven enthusiasm bolstered by a long view of legacy construction. Utilizing defined meaning as a core ingredient of your motivational fuel blend will serve to sustain you as failures, detours, losses, and pivots force themselves upon you.

When you prioritize the sustainability of accessible meaning through your pursuits, you step into what author Simon Sinek calls the *infinite game*. In this game, you eliminate the notion of some date-certain victory moment. Instead, as Sinek would describe it, you *"have no finish line and the goal is to keep the game going as long as possible."*

Having a stable source of meaning from active output will appropriately spiritualize your earning of money. It will place you within the energy of an *infinite game*. It will also aid in continued fulfillment when the pursuit of money in and of itself fails to deliver ongoing fulfillment.

Let the actualization of profit, of maximized salary, and of favorable returns be loosely valued (but valued nonetheless). Such outcomes are nothing but the positive, natural consequence of the dignity and meaning of your mobilized *Portfolio of Pursuits*.

Eschew the love of money and instead love meaning. Leverage meaning to keep your money spiritual.

Because **Failure Rule #3:** *Money Is Spiritual* is inescapable.

LET DESIRE BE YOUR DRIVER

"Desire! That's the one secret of every man's career. Not education. Not being born with hidden talents. Desire."

—BOBBY UNSER, FORMER PRO RACE CAR DRIVER AND AUTHOR

> **LESSON:** Desire is the foremost necessary component for overcoming failure.

Failure metastasizes in the absence of desire. Failure fades, erodes, and disappears when desire is nourished. When desire is nourished, the world pays attention to its tangible fruit—the output it produces. This output attracts reward and places value unto itself—all because of desire's power. This reward is a measured thankfulness for desire's output. This thankfulness is expressed by the exchange of money. This radical exchange, performed with this type of purity, is spiritual. Failure doesn't live within such an exchange. Because **Failure Rule #3: Money Is Spiritual** is set apart.

The primary catalyst of great accomplishments, lasting contributions, and creative offerings is desire. The convergence of all actionable energy begins with the supremacy of desire. Desire is the prime moving spirit that will bring you in alignment with your *calling journey*. You need to harness desire in conjunction with embracing your *internal spirit voice's* nudgings. Marry desire with the attentiveness to your *internal spirit voice* and you will be ushered into the vortex of your *calling journey*.

Desire mobilizes action. This action ultimately stirs to create *something*—a conversation that moves a relationship forward, the first brushstroke of a painting, the first stock purchase of a portfolio, the first inquiry into a business for sale, the first reading of a sacred text, or the first pitch of an innovative idea.

The resulting action from your desire can take many forms. It has the capacity to create a new wrinkle in your life story. Your action could cause a new spark in a key relationship. It could position a new product in the marketplace. It could cause you to develop a new way to serve your employer. Or for an entrepreneur, it could have you delivering a new benefit to your customers.

Many times, the forms that emerge by the resulting actions springing from your catalytic desires will return to you the reciprocity of monetized reward as measured gratitude. What does this mean? This means that your decision to follow desire, your decision to calculate risks as you seek to align with your *calling journey* and your decision to amplify your *internal spirit voice* often results naturally in measurable financial return. Because **Failure Rule #3:** *Money Is Spiritual* endures.

Of course, not *all* desire results in financial return once catalyzed. Many other forms of return exist and are also, like money, spiritual. Deciding to act on a desire must not be siloed to a financial cost/benefit analysis. The intangible returns of mobilized desire are numerous and valuable, and they should always be part of any serious contemplation to chase a desire in earnest.

Former race car driver Bobby Unser won the Indy 500 in three different decades. Bobby was born to a family of race car drivers. Yet it wasn't his being raised in an entrenched environment of racing enthusiasts that Bobby credits his consistent success over time. No, he credits desire. Individually cultivated, persistently maintained, well-nurtured, raw desire.

In his book *Winners Are Driven: A Champion's Guide to Success in Business and Life,* Unser promotes the premise that success begins fundamentally with a burning desire to succeed—whatever the pursuit. Unser explains the strategies that sustained his applied desire over decades of racing.

Desire is not just caught like a fever. It's harnessed, integrated, fueled, monitored, and leveraged for a long-game advantage. Desire needs to convert into an intentional visualizing of an objective. It needs to result in a deliberate posture of mental toughness when temporary failure and defeat corrupt your path. Desire requires flexibility and headroom for reasonable iteration while still maintaining fidelity to some sort of mapped framework for multiyear progress tracking toward a North Star endgame. And maybe most critically, desire is necessary to successfully absorb failure and overcome obstacles on your way toward the checkered flag of your pursuit's aim.

Raw, deep desire has the power to help rebuild and ricochet from the effect of failure's harsh leveling. One of my ex-business partners and longtime close friends harnessed his raw desire to ricochet from the effects of a sharp failure from his past. He had made some judgment errors years ago in the mortgage business prior to the financial crisis of 2008. As those errors came to light and followed him, his life began to unravel. He was indicted and sentenced to federal prison. He lost his ownership position in several businesses. His marriage disintegrated. His home went into foreclosure. His credit was destroyed. His reputation was tarnished. He owed the Internal Revenue Service (IRS). His father was dying. And now he would be saddled with a felony on his record forever.

But in the joint, my friend's desire to rebound and rebuild burned and raged. His desire propelled him to action. This relentless action-oriented mindset would ultimately compound gains toward overcoming the sharp leveling effects of his past failure. While in prison, he would brainstorm and write down dozens of business plans. Instead of sulking in self-pity and despair, his desire caused him to rev up his idea machine. He befriended one of the only other white-collar prisoners in his prison camp. Together, they brainstormed and hatched ideas.

When he was released from jail, he first had to start from zero. He could've succumbed to an acceptance attitude of the placism he felt, but he didn't. Instead, he set about *Third Dooring* his way into the adjacent possible wherever he could with a determined TCB attitude. His first job after being released was working for minimum wage as a clerk at a cheap hotel. He needed something to satiate the probation plan, something to get him even a bit of a foothold in the world—*something* to get his work muscles lubricated. While he manned the desk for peanuts at the dingy hotel, he pursued two big ideas in parallel.

First, he leveraged an old, trusted relationship in the mortgage business with someone who had sympathy and grace for his past mistake. He leveraged this relationship to pursue a partnership in the online lending business—a business he had to leave behind when he left for prison.

Second, he leveraged the contact he made in prison. That contact had a wife on the outside who ran a behavioral health clinic. He encouraged my friend to reach out to her. He believed my friend had the right acumen and skillset to help his wife significantly scale her business. He was right.

By utilizing a sound *Portfolio of Pursuits* approach to rebuilding his business life—and subsequently his personal life—my friend both stood up an online lending firm and scaled the behavioral health clinic significantly within several short years. He also was able to happily remarry while continuing to raise his two children in a 50 percent custody capacity. He and his new wife were able to buy a home. Then they bought a fitness center that she primarily ran. Over time he had acquired more and more equity as partner in the behavioral health clinic. Then it was sold for a seven-figure exit. He went on to take a break from entrepreneurialism and once again rejoined the corporate world. He joined a firm selling offshore call center services in the banking space. Within a few short years he became a top-tier salesperson and was earning a multi-six-figure income.

All of these rebounds my friend experienced occurred while he still carried a felony on his record. While he still had abysmal credit. While he battled business adversaries who were suing him. While he maintained restitution payments. While he mourned the loss of his father. And while navigating the difficult waters of raising children as a divorced dad.

My friend's education, talent, intelligence, personality, and network reach were useless without desire. You can be rich in all of these areas, but without desire you will not get very far. Desire lights up all of these attributes. It brings your talent, education, and personality assets to life. It spurs them to action. It exhausts each one of them until they produce results.

It was desire that rose as the primary power to resurrect my friend's lost life after prison. It was the actions borne from his desire that enabled him to find success in several spaces. That success ultimately empowered him to once again become a profound blessing to others. It helped him reintegrate into his children's lives. It helped him discover joy in his new marriage. It helped him bless countless autistic kids as he meaningfully scaled the footprint of the behavioral health clinic. It helped him supply financial life rafts for countless people in need of short-term credit for emergency relief.

The ferocity of relentless desire overcomes failure. Desire crowds out failure. Desire spurs action. Action produces services, products, and offerings of value. That value returns proportional rewards as material symbols of dispensed gratitude. Because while it's not obvious to most, **Failure Rule #3:** *Money Is Spiritual* is powerful.

GUARD YOUR INNER SELF

"The greatest hazard of all, losing oneself, can occur very quietly in the world, as if it were nothing at all. No other loss can occur so quietly; any other loss—an arm, a leg, five dollars, a wife, etc.—is sure to be noticed."

—SØREN KIERKEGAARD, EXISTENTIAL PHILOSOPHER, POET, SOCIAL CRITIC, AND THEOLOGIAN

> **LESSON:** Guard your inner self first, your spiritual core; then the benefit you deliver to the world will be maximized along with the probability of commensurately maximized financial rewards.

Without the integrity of your inner self fully fortified, you will drift into the failure of lost self-control. You will suffer with a blurred vision of your *calling journey*. You will fall more vulnerable to the failure that awaits you with paths of envy and greed. You will lose the proper view of your pursuits, the economics that underpin them, and the proper purpose of blessing enablement that money ought to hold in your life. Because as you well now understand about **Failure Rule #3**, when rightly esteemed, your *Money Is Spiritual*.

You cannot exercise your free will and, with clarity, decide to listen to your *internal spirit voice* if you haven't tightly guarded your inner self. We live in a world ripe with distractions. We exalt stacked commitment lists. We voluntarily bow down to the technology in our pockets, surrendering bit by bit the sovereignty of our inner selves. We are uptight in moments of visceral experience because we are too concerned with how to capture them for a social media post. We consume and pass calorically empty information voraciously. We willfully accept more stimulation instead of thoughtfully creating more healthy isolation.

We worship at the altar of community and collective connectivity while starving inner connectivity and the integrity of self.

It can be a struggle to balance and reconcile the meaning of our external lives with the stability of our inner lives. If you're an entrepreneur, your business is likely an extension of your inner self. It is likely a reflection of your very self. But it was preceded first by your unexpressed self. You need to carefully learn to separate yourself from your business periodically to center yourself back into your originating self. The sense of self that birthed the idea of your business to begin with. That is where your gravity belongs.

If you are a leader in an organization or of a family, you mustn't allow a stubborn and irrational sense of commitment drown out your very self. You were chosen to lead because of who you are, but the very act of leading can sometimes suffocate the essence that elected you to serve. This means you must schedule significant time by yourself regularly. Those who depend on your leadership depend on your inner self to be clear, calibrated, and hovered above the day-to-day trifles.

Maybe this means you take holidays or retreats entirely by yourself. Or that you take yourself out to dinner once a week. It could mean you rethink the ever intrusive open-door policy you have with your direct reports. Maybe, God forbid, it means that you actually *don't* have to attend every single sports game or dance recital your children perform in. Maybe your love and deep commitment to them manifests in more meaningful ways—*organically*—than in the measurable ways our society blindly lifts to the highest value. In his book *Stillness is the Key*, author Ryan Holiday asserts, "It's not enough to be inclined toward deep thought and sober analysis; a leader must create time and space for it."

How about you? Where is your self eroding? What are the relationships, commitments, unchecked passions, and overextended

commitments that have degraded your necessary time with self? Are you confident that your true self is actually what is manifesting in the world? Or has your self been lost to the conformity of being the person you think your commitments need you to be?

As I write this, I am on day two of a four-day personal retreat. I have been scheduling these getaways roughly once a quarter. I am entirely by myself, camped out for a rustic interlude in an Airbnb nestled on a farm. My wife is home, enjoying her own much-needed time with self. I have no social plans here. I speak rarely throughout the day. I only occasionally look at my phone. It is in part a writing retreat, but in totality it is truly a necessary time for the recalibration of my inner self. It is a deliberate focus on inner life, reflection, connecting with nature and nature's God, rest, and critical thinking. It is a time to eagerly listen for the whisperings of the *internal spirit voice* to guide me properly back into the busyness awaiting me when I return home. Prior to taking these retreats, I observed that my sense of self was at risk of slowly disintegrating over time as life would pull me consistently from multiple directions. Without intentional nurturing, the loss of self, as Kierkegaard points out, can otherwise *"occur very quietly in the world, as if it were nothing at all."*

Sometimes you need to embrace silence and isolation to secure the integrity of your inner self. The sixteenth century Jewish mystical philosopher, the Maharal of Prague, explained the crucial relationship that exists between the physical and the spiritual. Speaking invokes the physical and is a trademark of the physical and the external. Silence is the facilitator of the spiritual and is the condition in which the spiritual can regain control. The Maharal explains that the best thing for our body is for it to be guided by the soul. Quiet allows the spiritual to lead the physical, which allows the spirit to guide the body. This is where you have soul control. This is where you realign with your inner self.

If you don't orient yourself to periodically create a surplus of silence that outweighs the noise of your physical life—including your digital life—then you risk the physical leading the spiritual. This will result in an unhealthy restlessness of your inner self. It will result in a life that is vulnerable to veering off into inauthenticity.

Comedian Jim Norton, a man who once played Quiet Riot's song "Cum On Feel The Noize" on a boombox in a girl's ear on the school bus in an attempt to get her to like him, strategized his career pursuits in such a way to deliberately avoid his loss of inner self. On the *James Altucher Show* podcast, Jim explained that because he was determined to become a full-time comedian—his *Thing Two* dream (See **Failure Rule #4**) that aligned with his true self—he refused to allow himself to be exposed to any other job option that he might risk becoming attached to. Jobs that might cause him to lose his inner self. So instead of seeking out jobs that he might risk becoming comfortably complacent with, he chose dead-end jobs, grueling jobs, or jobs (like driving a forklift) that allowed his mind to be free while doing them. Jim centered his occupational choices around preserving his inner self and its acknowledgment of his *Thing Two* dream (**Failure Rule #4**). It was this very discipline that helped him eventually align with the fullness of his *calling journey* when he became a full-time comedian.

In order to preserve your sense of self, you must pay your dues first to yourself. Not to your company. Not to your family for their reputational approval. And not to society in the interest of a shallow obsession with status or vanity.

Pay your own dues by being guided by rational self-interest. Do this and you will ultimately bless yourself, strengthen your family, project benefit to your company, and positively impact those working around you. Guard your inner self, and those in your orbit will benefit from your self-stewardship. In this guarding, take liberty to choose your own path as much as possible.

If you're an entrepreneur, this is in your DNA. You know no other instinct.

If you're an employee, transform yourself into an entre-employee. Don't buy the lie that your job is to only and simply take orders and follow directions. Do what's required but create more than what is required and carve out unsuspected paths by developing unique patterns of work. Find the problems that no one wants to deal with and solve them. Then let it be known, with traceable specificity, how you pursued and operationalized the solutions. Hunt down new ways to make revenue, either with existing assets and relationships or new ones. Build the case and put the pieces together. And then let it be known. Be ever mindful of this on the clock and hold it close in your reflections off the clock.

If you ride the arc of your work-life story with a goal of skill acquisition, of persuasion perfection, and of persona development, you will maximize your meaning experiences, your earnings, and your relationships. In essence, you will be engaging in a lifelong workshop of professional betterment in which you never stop shaping your story for maximum marketability.

Marry your efforts to the reality that we are moving toward a work world in which idea ownership, ingenuity, and self-initiated endeavors will dominate order taking and direction following. Direction-following and order-taking will more and more be wholly dominated by coding in software, not job descriptions for humans. Automation is ever-increasing and will marginalize those without ideas and passion to poverty, dependency, and emptiness. We are moving into a world in which Naval Ravikant, founder of AngelList.com, explains will mean that, *"The best jobs are not decreed or degreed. They are creative expressions of continuous learning in a free market."* You can't generate meaningful creative expressions that will blossom within a competitive free market without guarding the sanctity of your inner self.

To avoid being a casualty of automation and a victim of the homogenization that comes from narrowly following your job description, you need to rely on an internal locus of control. This means that you prioritize your own self-loyalty, harness your idea-generation skills, and project yourself beyond what is expected. It means you guard your inner self. This is necessary whether you are an entrepreneur, an entre-employee, a *solopreneur*, a struggling creative, or merely a soul interested in an authentic life.

Be loyal first to yourself. Then you can blossom into someone who can uniquely produce the most benefit to your employer, your customers, your partners, or whoever else is critical to your ongoing personal economic ecosystem. As you strengthen and protect your inner self and manifest unique benefit into the world, expect financial thank-you notes to begin returning to you. This may not always happen for each effort or in precise proportion to your output value. But because you now know that **Failure Rule #3: *Money Is Spiritual*** is true, with iteration and modification over time, you will begin to be rewarded with relative proportion to the degree you effectuate unique value in the world.

Avoid the greatest hazard of all. Guard your inner self.

LESSONS FROM A PUNK ROCK SON OF A PREACHER MAN

MARRY MONEY AND MEANING

"Deprived of meaningful work, men and women lose their reason for existence."
—FYODOR DOSTOEVSKY, RUSSIAN NOVELIST, ESSAYIST, AND JOURNALIST

> **LESSON:** Don't decouple meaning from money; instead, aim to marry them.

Applying **Failure Rule #3:** *Money Is Spiritual* to your life is painfully difficult when you cannot find meaning in your work. When you cannot find meaning in your work, your efforts are bland offerings of obedience to an empty mission. You must reject this failure space. If you find yourself steeped in the failure of meaningless work, know that **Failure Rule #3:** *Money Is Spiritual* can *always* be applicable. It may not be obvious, easy, or immediate, but it is always applicable. Meaning is discoverable somewhere within the salary or wages you receive. Because they are thank-you notes. Leverage your knowledge of the truth of **Failure Rule #3:** *Money Is Spiritual* and wrestle, grind, and agonize until you find a way to apply its truth to unearth meaning even from work that appears to be hopelessly empty.

When I was younger, long before I had any real financial responsibility, I swayed toward a thoughtless view of money that elevated my own sense of false self-righteousness. I chose to completely devalue money, material things, and any pursuit therein. And I thought very highly of myself for doing so.

I grew up as a punk-rock son of a preacher man, so this mindset was a natural extension of both sensibilities.

As a preacher's kid, I grew up in a home in which the acquisition of wealth was never held in any real value. Finances were rarely spoken of except to extol the endless virtues of frugality. The family messaging around money aligned with what personal finance guru Ramit Sethi observed about American attitudes toward money: *"In America, the only discussions allowed about money are frugality and guilt."* In our home growing up, bragging rights were eagerly claimed when one scored a great sale, no matter how insignificant the savings truly were on the macro picture. The notion of aggressively seeking strategies to earn money and grow wealth—having a dollarwise vs. a pennywise mentality—was slightly shamed, as the pursuit of wealth acquisition was equated with an undue attachment to material things. A path of aiming at wealth was viewed as a dangerous drift away from any focus on spirituality. There was also a detected undertone that implied that entrepreneurialism was somewhat synonymous with an unhealthy wealth-acquisition mindset. The idea of enduring structured training for a predictable, safe career field was implicitly applauded as the modest and measured path.

As a punk rocker, I was of the opinion that money did nothing but corrupt, taint, and destroy the true and pure human spirit. The rebel punks who rejected an attachment to money outright were the pure ones to me. Love of money was for the yuppies, the assholes who ostracized me because of the subculture I identified with, and the shallow zombies who occupied the upper middle class and above. And I was not sophisticated or wise enough yet to distinguish clearly between the empty love of money and the abundant value in rightly using money.

So with both the punk rock and preacher's kid narratives, I bought the lie.

However, through navigating those lies, I managed to eventually get one thing right.

It became clear that the unbridled pursuit of money for, and only for, the sake of money was a shallow and lonely road. I knew that even if a love of money did not bring harm or malice to anyone, it still rendered its pursuer unsatisfied and yearning for deeper things. Making money without producing meaning is deficient. Dostoyevsky was right. If your work is deprived of meaning, you will lose your reason for existence.

As I grew older and was constantly forced to face the reality that money was a necessity and had to be dealt with, I decided I wanted to master it so it didn't master me. This has proved a daunting and difficult task that has humbled me and taught me much.

Yet the deliberate effort to understand, subordinate, and master my relationship with money brought meaning in and of itself. Money was no longer something to revile or worship—it was something to explore, animate, and leverage to maximize meaning, freedom, and relationships. Because Failure Rule #3: *Money Is Spiritual* **is evident for those who have eyes to see.**

I've constantly grappled with trying to both pursue efforts in line with my passions, my enthusiasm, and my unique talents while still trying to maximize income and sufficiently provide for my family and myself. This struggle is obviously common and not unique to me.

Yet it is exactly this struggle—the struggle to constantly marry money with meaning—that brings me daily challenge, fulfillment, wonder, and life.

You need to welcome this struggle.

Avoid the empty, greedy, deceptively utilitarian road of money worship.

Instead, always find a way to apply the power of Failure Rule #3:

Money Is Spiritual—no matter how hard it may be to do so with the work you find yourself in. Strive to marry money and meaning and pave the way toward a dynamic life of abundance. Else, risk being trapped in the failure of meaningless work—a failure that threatens to cause you to lose a core reason for your existence.

YOU GET WHAT YOU GIVE

"Leisure time is only leisure time when it is earned; otherwise, leisure time devolves into soul-killing lassitude. There's a reason so many new retirees, freed from the treadmill of work, promptly keel over on the golf course: Work fulfills us. It keeps us going."

—BEN SHAPIRO, POLITICAL COMMENTATOR, AUTHOR, AND FORMER ATTORNEY

> **LESSON:** Strive to maintain pursuits of meaning as long as you have the physical and mental capacity to do so, whether you're formally working or have retired from formal work.

Some people don't give an aeronautical fornication about finding meaning in their work. Some people couldn't care less about what impact their work has on the world or what value it brings to others. Some people care only about the bottom line or getting their paycheck. One can survive and maintain with this attitude, maybe for a while, but I think it is difficult for most to thrive with this mindset for the long haul. For most, this attitude ends in the failure of occupational emptiness. Because **Failure Rule #3:** *Money Is Spiritual* is true, when you detach meaning from your work, you despiritualize it. When you do this, meaning, joy, and fulfillment disappear.

It is ultimately difficult to sustain prosperity—let alone derive material meaning from your work—without building strong, good-faith relationships. It is difficult to retain meaning and prosperity without treating others fairly. And it's rare for prosperity to continue meaningfully without striving to provide a competitive product or service that upholds value across time.

You get what you give.

You reap what you sow.

And if you're sowing subpar services or products, if you're treating employees and customers unfairly, or if you're engaging in unethical behavior, sustaining prosperity likely becomes improbable.

And when prosperity still remains devoid of meaning or ethics, often times internal dissatisfaction lies firmly just below the surface. This emptiness becomes an itch you can't scratch. Assets, income, and profit or not.

Those who subordinate meaning to the raw pursuit of money chase an almost unattainable satisfaction goal. I know many people who are still trying to scratch that itch. Millions in assets but empty relationship buckets surround them. Comfort, luxury, and opulence environ them, but their hearts remain cold, rigid, and selfish. Early or accidental retirements and no undergirding of meaning framework to collapse into and set their hearts on fire. Hollowness emerges as their most prominent trademark.

So what is worth chasing? How do you determine which pursuits couple meaning with money?

Only you can answer this.

I've chased and discovered meaning wherever I could find it within an ever-evolving, dynamic *Portfolio of Pursuits*.

I want to be free of forgettable work and shallow relationships at work. I want to minimize, delegate, off-board, and eliminate doing any work that is reflexively and easily replaceable. Because the more my work is replaceable, the more I am too. I want to effectuate impact in all that I do in such a way as to inspire others to do their best work.

I want others to be enabled to carve their own path, cultivate more autonomy, and influence within their work footprint, and view work as an integral part of their purposed existence. **Because Failure Rule #3: *Money Is Spiritual* underpins all work, you must find a way to view all work as an integral part of your purposed existence.** As Ben Shapiro points out in this chapter's anchor quote, work fulfills us and keeps us going. Leisure has a short shelf life for fulfilling us. Too much of it and it quickly devolves into "soul-killing lassitude."

When a universal concept that has existed throughout recorded time and within multiple cultures, religions, and people groups does not prove to be discoverable in Hebrew, it is because it was deemed by ancient Jews to have not existed. The concept of retirement does not exist in Hebrew. In Hebrew, people are expected to contribute to society so long as they have the physical and mental capacity to do so.

To maintain sufficient meaning in your life, you need to also have no concept of retirement. Find a way to cultivate pursuits of meaning as long as you have a body and mind to do so. Because you get what you give. So give yourself to pursuits from which you can get as much meaning as possible. Do this whether you have retired from your career or formal work or not. Do this whether you can monetize your pursuits or not. You may not always need money, but you were designed to always need pursuits of meaning.

Meaning is there to be found in your work when you decide to view it as an integral part of your purposed existence. But this takes work. You have to step back and discover the best wire frame to place your work picture in. How you learn to see your work determines how much meaning you will be able to extract from it. The decision to thoughtfully approach your work is an act of giving to it. Receiving meaning from your interaction with your work is an act of getting.

You get what you give. So focus on how you can more fully give yourself to the various work manifestations of your life.

Sometimes you may find yourself saddled with work that you just don't know how to give yourself to. This is not uncommon. Remind yourself that you can get meaning from *all* work. Because the transformative energy contained in **Failure Rule #3:** *Money Is Spiritual* is always applicable. It may not be easy to apply, but it is always available and applicable. And meaning is always there to be found in all work, even if in low quantity. When it's not obvious how you can give yourself to your work, or whether it has meaning for you to get from it, you must decide to first approach your work with dispassionate excellence. Do this consistently over time, and you increase the probability that meaning will begin to emerge.

Sometimes, in order to avoid or mitigate failure and maximize the marriage of meaning with your work, you need to leverage one pursuit—or several—in order to enable or achieve a primary pursuit. Sometimes this means you need to embrace a dispassionate pursuit in order to mobilize a passionate one that can deliver the most meaning to you over time.

I call this the *Thing One and Thing Two Dependency*. It is a sound strategy for failure prevention if you can build it well. This is what you will learn about as you read on and are introduced to **Failure Rule #4**.

UNDERSTAND FAILURE RULE #3

MONEY IS SPIRITUAL

Rabbi Daniel Lapin says that everybody needs a rabbi. Because he may be right, heed his words and understand money's true power. Understand **Failure Rule #3**: *Money Is Spiritual*—if you view it correctly. If you employ it with wisdom.

Money carries immense powers and capabilities to enable spiritual exchanges of value for virtuous acts of service and the production, distribution, marketing, and sale of goods. When this ideal dynamic is at work, blessings, prosperity, and win-win sacramental transactions occur. When this happens, magic is possible. Magic that has the power to lift people out of failure and hard times, *sacred transaction by sacred transaction*.

When money is viewed and used improperly it is stripped of its inherent spiritual potential. When this is in play, the poisonous failures of envy and greed have fertile soil in which to grow. So check yourself and view money properly before you wreck yourself and succumb to the spiritually bankrupt temptations of envy and greed. Check yourself by maintaining a diligent mental and spiritual diet of thanksgiving. Because you now know full well the wisdom in the words Rev. Billy Graham spoke: *envy and greed starve on a steady diet of thanksgiving*.

As you fend off impulses to slide into envy or greed, remember to value each one of your transactions as sacraments. Make sure you fully understand that transactions, when engaged in properly, are earthly expressions of the spiritual connectivity that exists in exchanges of measured thankfulness. Like the spontaneous hundred-dollar tip I gave my man Prince at White Glove Car Wash, out of elevated thankfulness for his impeccable detailing services on my vehicle.

Because *Money Is Spiritual* and **Failure Rule** #3 upholds, you need to pursue and value both money and meaning in parallel. Seek to marry them as much as is possible and guard yourself against the love of money as you focus on your love of meaning. This will help you avoid the failure of being externally attached to money instead of being internally attached to meaning. This will keep you focused on the true security found in your work—your unique stack of special knowledge, honed experience, and nuanced ability. As inventor Henry Ford explained.

As you learn to see money more as spiritual and as an instrumental tool for navigating out of failure, don't forget that desire is the foremost necessary component for overcoming failure. Let it be your driver, like former pro race car driver Bobby Unser would urge you to do. As you do this, you will likely find that the forms that emerge by the resulting actions springing from your catalytic desires will return to you the reciprocity of monetized reward as measured gratitude. Remember the story of my friend, the ex-con, whose desire blazed strong within him after he was released from prison. His desire's fire helped him rebuild a rich, new, beautiful life out of the ashes of his failures.

As you fan the flames of your desire and learn to harness the spiritual power of money, do not neglect to guard your inner self. Else you will lose your very self, which Soren Kierkegaard warned is the greatest hazard of all. If you allow the integrity of your inner self to disintegrate, you will experience the failure of losing your self-control. This often leads to a skewed view of your pursuits, the economics that underpin them, and the ideal use of money as a blessing enabler that ought to guide your actions. Because *Money Is Spiritual*—which **Failure Rule** #3 will always remind you.

Never decouple meaning from money, or you risk despiritualizing your money and robbing yourself of knowing its full power and blessing. Struggle to keep meaning and money married with all of your strength as much as is possible. Don't worship or revile money. Leverage it to optimize your meaning, your sense of freedom, and the richness of your relationships. Finding a way to extract some level of meaning from your money and your work will keep it spiritual. Doing this will help keep you from losing your *"reason for existence,"* as Fyodor Dostoyevsky wrote.

Remember what John Stossel explained—that no transaction is involuntary (unless it is maybe with the IRS or the mafia under some extortion-driven duress). Transactions are sacraments because generally they happen only if both sides at least believe that they will win by engaging in it. So because **Failure Rule #3: *Money Is Spiritual*** ultimately makes the world go round, give each transaction an earnest attempt at delivering value that allows the other side to win as much as you.

And don't abandon your understanding of **Failure Rule #3: *Money Is Spiritual*** just because you've retired from a formal career. Remember that the concept of retirement doesn't exist in Hebrew for a reason—because, as Ben Shapiro articulated, *"leisure time devolves into soul-killing lassitude."* So avoid the failure of falling into soul-killing lassitude. Strive to maintain pursuits of meaning as long as you have the physical and mental capacity to do so, whether you're formally working or have retired from formal work.

Be in tune with your *internal spirit voice*. Avoid the failure traps of envy, greed, and excessive leisure. Marry meaning with money.

Understand **Failure Rule #3: *Money Is Spiritual.***

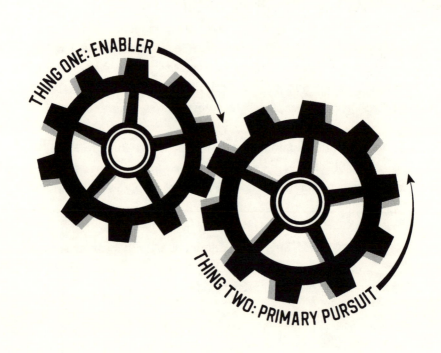

FAILURE RULE #4

BUILD YOUR THING ONE AND THING TWO DEPENDENCY (FAILURE PREVENTION)

"The failures that we have are sometimes expensive educations."
—ASHTON KUTCHER, ACTOR, PRODUCER, AND ENTREPRENEUR

> **PRINCIPLE:** Failure only rules *after* it first sucks. Because failure sucks while also being ultimately inevitable in some form, it is ideal to try and avoid as much of it as possible. Failure prevention and preparation go hand in hand. Prevent what you can to minimize the suck so you can reserve your energy to optimize the extracted value from the failure you cannot avoid. Building thoughtful enabler pursuits *(Thing One)* to sustain and empower you as you chart your plans toward your highest value primary dream pursuit *(Thing Two)* will mitigate the failure that punctuates your *calling journey* path.

THE THING ONE AND THING TWO DEPENDENCY

STRATEGIC FAILURE PREVENTION

"If you can quote the rules, then you can obey them."
—TONY SOPRANO, FICTIONAL MOB BOSS PLAYED
BY LATE ACTOR JAMES GANDOLFINI

> **LESSON:** Carefully building and managing strategic enabler pursuits *(Thing One)* can minimize failure and empower you as you scheme toward your highest value primary-dream pursuit *(Thing Two)*.

The most important, self-evident Failure Rule is simply this: *try to avoid failure as much as is possible*. You need to learn to obey this rule, like Tony's quote above commands. Of course, it is not always possible, but sometimes it is. Why do you want to avoid failure as much as possible? Remember what you learned in the introduction: failure sucks *first* before it can possibly rule. No one wants to fail on purpose, or all the time, or really at all, for that matter. Or at least they shouldn't. However, some form of failure *is* inevitable, and **The 5 Rules of Failure** exist to help you make the most of it when it does happen *and* to reasonably prevent it when you can.

One strategy that can help prevent unnecessary failure is what I call the **Thing One and Thing Two Dependency**. Now I know this sounds like some sort of weird Cat-in-the-Hat-inspired name for a concept. Rest assured it is not. No, when you read the concept name, think more of a slightly disheveled Tony Soprano in his white bathrobe, lighting his first cigar of the day, waving his hands around with quintessential Italian American flailing, while explaining the **Thing One and Thing Two Dependency** concept with a strong Jersey accent: *"First, you build a* **Thing One** *enabler; then you keep working toward your* **Thing Two** *dream. Capisce?"* Can you picture that? Now subtract the nefarious notion of mob criminality being involved while retaining that image and the swagger-tinged sound of Tony Soprano's oratory flourish in your head. Okay, now keep reading.

Developing a strategy to enable your North Star dream with the strong undergirding of a stable, developed, enabler pursuit can help you avoid, or strongly mitigate, failure and the chaos it brings. It will also help you avoid the failure of unnecessarily delaying your *Thing Two* dream actualization, or worse—never working toward it at all. The failure of never escaping the recurring trap of saying at each week's end, "Thank God it's Friday," only to say, "Oh shit, it's Monday," several days later.

This is what the **Thing One and Thing Two Dependency** is all about. Your enabler pursuit is your **Thing One**. Your aspirational dream—which carries the most weight within your *calling journey*—is your **Thing Two**.

THING ONE

THE ENABLER PURSUIT

Thing One: *An enabler pursuit primarily chased as a leveraging mechanism to allow a quickened or steady path toward the fulfillment of a primary pursuit (Thing Two).*

> **LESSON:** Most everyone needs a low-meaning *Thing One* pursuit to sustain them while working toward their *Thing Two* dream realization.

Your *Thing One pursuit* is less about meaning (although, as you've learned, *all* pursuits and work possess some discoverable meaning) and more about building the belts and suspenders necessary to set you free to sustainably engage in your primary pursuit, or your *Thing Two*.

Your *Thing One* is an enabler for your *Thing Two*. It's a path provider, a financial mechanism, and an installed undergirding. Your *Thing One* is the piece of your *Portfolio of Pursuits* that provides runway, revenue, and income redundancy in order to enable and sustain your attachment to your primary pursuit, your *Thing Two*.

There are many manifestations of the *Thing One* enabler pursuit that can be stood up, but there are two distinct models that most *Thing One* pursuits fit into. These are the *Thing One Virtual Model* and the *Thing One Active Model*.

THE *THING ONE VIRTUAL MODEL*

Thing One Virtual Model: *An application of a Thing One enabler that primarily uses portals and partners to generate passive or semi-passive income without excessive time commitments, physical location dependency, or overhead expense burdens.*

Thing One could be many different things for many different people. But in the digital age we live in, one of the most efficient models for building a *Thing One* enabler pursuit is the *virtual model*.

The *Thing One Virtual Model* is an income source that you own, shepherd, and monitor virtually through partners and portals. The *Thing One Virtual Model's* highest attribute is that it carries passive, or at least semi-passive, income potential. It gives you the freedom to be a digital nomad and manage the income stream from wherever you and your device are. It ideally has few or no employees. Instead, it relies on partners, vendors, and platforms. It is a common model used by side hustlers, *solopreneurs,* creatives, and ascending octopi building their *Portfolio of Pursuits.*

When I exited the online lending space as a licensed lender and migrated into the lead-generation space that served lenders, my business operated on the *Thing One Virtual Model*. I had core business partners I shared equity with. I had one 1099 partner who handled vendor and buyer relationships. I had technology vendors whose software-as-a-service (SaaS) platforms automated key pieces of the business.

The *Thing One Virtual Model* runs primarily on partners and portals. It does not require an office, impose the burden of managing employees, cause one to be tied to any particular working hours, or carry the overhead risk of leases and payroll expenses.

The *Thing One Virtual Model* is nimble, remote, scalable, and structured to be passively managed. I spent less than five hours per week maintaining my lead-generation business. Had it not been affected by regulatory headwinds, it would've been the perfect long-term *Thing*

One to financially enable my primary pursuit, or **Thing Two**—which for me is a portfolio that includes writing, related media, productization pursuits, and managing a portfolio of diverse **Thing One** enablers.

My record labels were, at one time, a full-time active endeavor. Back then they were my **Thing Two**, my primary pursuit. While I still carry significant passion for that pursuit, it is no longer primary. It is no longer my **Thing Two**. It has instead evolved into a steady, long-term piece of my developing **Thing One Virtual Model** infrastructure that churns quietly in the background. It requires only light attention and maintenance. During times of reprieve from active releasing of records, it runs passively through the belts and suspenders of portals and partners. It is one thread of enabling **Thing One** support for my aspirational **Thing Two** vision.

Any mechanism to make money consistently online through content creation, affiliate marketing, IP rights exploitation, e-commerce, or similar methods could fall under the **Thing One Virtual Model**. This could be monetizing YouTube videos, copyrighting music or books, driving marketing as an affiliate, becoming an Amazon seller, or launching products—physical or informational—on your own website. There are many ways. They all carry real risk and require thorough research and trial and error. They are not automatic or easy, but they are viable, and there are many, many options.

My son has been paying his cell phone bill from the time he was twelve by monetizing graphic art templates online. He made them once and then paid his cell bill for years off the passive, albeit nominal, residual income. While his only **Thing Two** was finding a way to pay his cell phone bill without clocking in anywhere, he still found a **Thing One** to pay for it using the **Thing One Virtual Model**.

Think of ways you might be able to create or add value online, and explore how you might stand up the *Thing One Virtual Model* as you build your plan to chase down your *Thing Two*, or primary pursuit.

THE *THING ONE ACTIVE MODEL*

Thing One Active Model: *An application of a Thing One enabler that primarily uses more consuming and traditional methods of generating income, characterized by heavy time commitments, often bound by physical location limitations, and carrying more significant overhead expense burdens.*

The *Thing One Active Model* comprises more consuming and traditional methods of earning and maintaining income while strategically chasing a *Thing Two*, or a primary pursuit, in parallel.

The *Thing One Active Model* requires more attention commitment, and hands-on time engagement, than the *Thing One Virtual Model*. It's a longer-tail enabler that also requires patience—a slower crawl toward your *Thing Two*. It requires more sweat equity, more grit, and more stress. It is typically a dispassionate effort, although it doesn't need to be. While it involves a deeper investment at many levels, many still have chosen to take this route. And through creative entrepreneurial juggling and bootstrapped ingenuity, they have, over time, reached their *Thing Two* goals.

THE THING TWO ACCOMPLISHMENT ENABLED BY THE THING ONE ACTIVE MODEL

"Except for my family and faith, there is no cause more important to me than fighting cancer...I have committed the rest of my life to doing all I can to support clinical and research efforts to eliminate this disease."

—JON HUNTSMAN SR., ENTREPRENEUR, BILLIONAIRE, PHILANTHROPIST, AND CANCER SURVIVOR

LESSON: Although it is a longer road, the *Thing One Active Model* can enable amazing *Thing Two* accomplishments.

One application of **The Thing One Active Model** is the creation of a business for the sole pragmatic, dispassionate purpose of generating profit to direct toward a future, often distant, **Thing Two** primary pursuit ambition. This is usually exclusive to the entrepreneurial sort.

The late Jon Huntsman Sr. was a billionaire and an extraordinary entrepreneur. His **Thing Two** was his relentless driving passion to mobilize the world toward the discovery of a cure for cancer. Huntsman employed **Failure Rule #4: Build Your Thing One and Thing Two Dependency** successfully to hold alignment with his mysterious *calling journey*. In this, he was able to prevent the failure of never reaching his **Thing Two** accomplishment.

The Huntsman Cancer Institute, Jon's legacy-defining accomplishment, is one of the major cancer research centers in America. It is a state-of-the-art cancer specialty hospital that has a primary goal of accelerating the work toward a cancer cure through human genetics. The Huntsman family and his close associates donated more than $656 million toward cancer research. These donations were paid-forward thank-you notes that funneled into a free market, out into the world, and upward as an act of service to Huntsman's relationship with God. Every dollar was purposed intentionally toward a reach for future worldwide healing. The donations were a scaled example of the power of **Failure Rule #3: Money Is Spiritual**.

Huntsman could not have built the Huntsman Cancer Institute without a *Thing One* enabler.

Huntsman did not come from money. He grew up poor. His dad was a teacher. His mother, a homemaker. Huntsman made his way as a businessman and entrepreneur in a disciplined, self-directed fashion. His entrepreneurial blossoming most significantly began when he formed the Huntsman Corporation, a global manufacturer and marketer of specialty chemicals.

The Huntsman Corporation had food on its mind—fast food, to be precise. Huntsman saw the need for better packaging in the emerging fast-food industry. When I humbly entered the world in 1974, something much more useful was also born that year—the McDonald's "clamshell container" used for its iconic Big Macs. This invention, along with the first plastic forks, spoons, and bowls, all originated from Jon Huntsman Sr. and the Huntsman Corporation.

The wealth Huntsman accumulated through the Huntsman Corporation and his subsequent business endeavors was a giant enabler toward his *Thing Two* primary pursuit. It was this long-tail, full-time *Thing One Active Model* utilization that ultimately led to the creation of his *Thing Two* accomplishment.

Leveraging the power of money's spiritual capacity, Jon Huntsman Sr. achieved his *Thing Two* dream. He built an empire—his actively maintained, long-tail *Thing One* enabler—and redirected his passion, focus, and wealth from his *Thing One* to his long-ambitioned *Thing Two*.

EMBRACE SACRIFICE AND BE CREATIVE AS YOU BUILD YOUR THING ONE ENABLER PURSUIT(S)

"Great achievement is usually born of great sacrifice and is never the result of selfishness."

—NAPOLEON HILL, AUTHOR OF *SUCCESS THROUGH A POSITIVE MENTAL ATTITUDE*

> **LESSON:** Consider all viable *Thing One* pursuit options and combinations as possible mechanisms to achieve your *Thing Two* dream realization; be creative and be open to unusual sacrifice.

Chris Wrenn, founder of Bridge Nine Records, had to rely on the *Thing One Active Model* to springboard the early momentum of his now worldwide iconic brand. Wrenn's creative approach to **Failure Rule #4: Build Your Thing One and Thing Two Dependency** helped him avoid failure with his record label and maintain the charge of his *calling journey's* path.

Today, Wrenn's record label has released over 250 recordings and has hosted some of the biggest names in the global punk rock and hardcore music scene. Acts such as H2O, Agnostic Front, Strike Anywhere, and Terror. Bridge Nine Records has managed to persevere for over twenty-five years in the ever-tumultuous independent music industry. Today, the company stands strong as a full-time operation with a staff of five music lovers. In 1995, Bridge Nine Records started as nothing but a hobby by an avid hardcore music fan in the Boston area.

But it wasn't all upward and onward for Wrenn in the early years. The dream of scaling his record label needed help. Wrenn created that help by using the profits from a *Thing One* endeavor that fit the *Active Model*. Wrenn understood what Curt Schilling admitted when he said, *"I guess I hate the Yankees now,"* after he became a Red Sox player: Red Sox fans unequivocally hate the Yankees. Hence, Wrenn's *Thing One* endeavor was the creation of *Yankees Suck* merchandise. Wrenn printed batches and batches of stickers, T-shirts, and other merchandise all hailing the suckitude of the New York Yankees. He then hustled Red Sox fans to buy the merch with their hard-earned cash. Wrenn recalls in an interview on noecho.com:

> Most of the early Bridge Nine releases, from our 7th through about our 70th, were underwritten in a large part by Red Sox fans. In our first five years, from 1995 till 1999, I released just five records, which was all that I could afford at the time. Over the next five, after I started selling outspoken bumper stickers and t-shirts to Red Sox fans as they left the games, I was able to release seventy more. It was the financial kick-start that I needed and wasn't going to find anywhere else at the time. Banks were not giving out loans to people trying to release records for hardcore bands, especially when that person was working at a record store for eight dollars an hour.

Wrenn's passion was his primary pursuit of building up Bridge Nine Records to be a global powerhouse in the hardcore punk music scene— his *Thing Two* dream. Like many entrepreneurs, Wrenn realized quickly he needed the enablement of a profitable *Thing One* to help him achieve his *Thing Two*. For Wrenn, it was the utilization of the *Thing One Active Model* in the form of *Yankees Suck* merch sales.

Be open and creative to all possible *Thing One* enablers that can bolster your path toward your *Thing Two* dream. Don't ever be so

blinded by the purity attached to your *Thing Two* ambition that you overlook a pragmatic, low-meaning *Thing One* pursuit that might best enable your *Thing Two* dream. Your *Thing One* doesn't need to have passion and high meaning. It just needs to work.

Just like *Yankees Suck*.

* * *

Some of the most effective *Thing One* enablers require unusual sacrifice.

I once knew two brothers who inherently knew what the Godfather of PMA, Napoleon Hill, preached: *great achievement is usually born of great sacrifice*. These two brothers had no home for many years. Like Metallica sings about in "Wherever I May Roam," the road became their brides. They both abandoned any notion of a home—and the attendant burden of associated living expenses—to labor daily selling merchandise at Disney on Ice events all across the country. The road was their home. And Disney on Ice footed the bill for all their food, lodging, and travel expenses. It was the perfect *Thing One Active Model* to enable their future *Thing Two* dreams. It was wrought with sacrifice but ripe with expense-free living that produced substantial self-raised capital.

Busy soccer moms clamoring at the vendor truck with their excited young daughters at their heels. Ready to spend cash to memorialize their Disney experience. Princesses. Fairy tales. Useless swag. They sold it to them. Every day, for years. This was their life. This was how they embraced **Failure Rule #4: *Build Your Thing One and Thing Two Dependency***. This is how they prevented the failure of never launching or realizing their *Thing Two* dreams.

Stemming from a Shia Muslim Lebanese immigrant family steeped in adversity, the two brothers were raised to overcome any circumstance in pursuit of a better life. Respect for unusual sacrifice was in their blood. For them, that better life would only come through business ownership. But starting a business—or multiple businesses—takes cash and time. Disney on Ice took time—years—but it enabled them to raise the seed money they needed to ignite their dreams.

After several years of dispassionately eschewing an attachment to any home and enjoying expense-free living, the two brothers were sitting on a significant pile of startup cash. Finally, they began implementing their dreams in the Midwest city they lived in. Cigar lounges, nightclubs, gyms, and gas stations all became part of their diverse brick-and-mortar retail portfolio. For decades now, they've captured market share for the fuel, workout, dancing, and fine tobacco needs for much of the city.

With multiple partners and strong familial support, they built their own *Thing Two* empire. Brick by brick. Disney on Ice dollar over Disney on Ice dollar. The fruits of their disciplined use of the *Thing One Active Model* fueled their *Thing Two* dream realities.

Be creative as you design your *Thing One* enabler pursuit(s), like Chris Wrenn did by creating *Yankees Suck* merchandise. Accept that the meaning from your *Thing One* pursuit is often future-oriented. But know that there is inherent meaning in the story you're building because of the dependency between your *Thing One* enabler and your *Thing Two* dream. Because that's the extra value found in **Failure Rule #4: Build Your Thing One and Thing Two Dependency.** Like the two brothers I once knew, don't be afraid to make unusual sacrifices as you stand up a *Thing One* enabler that has more power to bring your *Thing Two* dream into fruition with increased speed and strength.

SOMETIMES IT'S SIMPLE

W-2 JOB AS THE THING ONE ACTIVE ENABLER

"Everybody wants things for free. You've got to put in the work. You've got to grind."

—CONOR MCGREGOR, MMA FIGHTER AND FORMER UFC LIGHTWEIGHT CHAMPION

> **LESSON:** The most common *Thing One* enabler is holding down a simple day job while you side hustle your *Thing Two* dream forward over time.

You don't always need to be cleverly creative, inventive, or circumventing to invoke **Failure Rule #4:** *Build Your Thing One and Thing Two Dependency.*

Sometimes, you don't need to invent hamburger cartons, fuel hatred for the Yankees with Red Sox fans, or nomadically travel with Disney on Ice to enable your *Thing Two* dream.

Sometimes it is much simpler—although not easy—to prevent the failure of not actualizing your *Thing Two* dream.

Sometimes you just need to hold down a good, stable job and side hustle your *Thing Two* dream into reality over time, inch by inch. Sometimes you've just got to put in the work the old-fashioned way. Sometimes, like Conor McGregor explains, you've just got to grind.

While often not as quick or as powerful, the most common **Thing One Active** enabler is the traditional day job. Hold it down and nurture your **Thing Two** dream in the cracks of the day and in your off-hours. This is how you avoid the failure that podcaster Joe Rogan asserts many people suffer from—*living a life of quiet desperation* (borrowed from Henry David Thoreau). You do this by diligently watering, fertilizing, and giving due attention to your **Thing Two** dream development. Do this with discipline and consistency, but don't let it jeopardize your devotion to your nine-to-five—it's your enabler after all. *And you need it.*

Endless examples apply here. Going to nursing school at night or online while you bang down your nine-to-five diligently. Saving money from your day job to seed a business in a way that poses less risk to your immediate income needs. Retaining a day job while pushing a purchased business into the black—by taking no income from the business and leveraging employees and managers. Starting a side hustle with an e-commerce business. Launching a podcast on the weekends. The possibilities are numerous.

If you don't have a *Thing One* strategy, whether virtual or active, your *Thing Two* actualization is likely at risk. Your *Thing Two* dream will not only be at risk of failures along the way, but failures to launch, and failures to optimize.

I'm utilizing both models. I have several **Thing One Virtual** pursuits that I'm building to sustain a long-tail future **Thing Two**. However, on the aggregate, the development of these virtual **Thing Ones** collectively fit within my long-term **Thing Two** pursuit. There's an intrinsic bleed-in—managing a portfolio of **Thing One Virtual** enablers is part of my **Thing Two** dream.

I also have a meaningful and sufficiently lucrative **Thing One Active** pursuit in my day job as a banker. This powerful enabler, in conjunction with my *Thing One Virtual* enablers, will continue to help me build tremendous knowledge capital and accumulated wealth over time to impact an eventual lifestyle form-fitted to my *Thing Two* dream.

Whatever fits your appetite and is within your reach for standing up one, or many, *Thing One* enablers, start doing it. The establishment of a proper *Thing One* enabler will spiritualize the pursuit and achievement of your *Thing Two* dream with increased meaning. The experience of successfully establishing a *Thing One* enabler, in and of itself, will cement meaning within you. While *Thing One* enablers typically carry far less meaning than *Thing Two* dreams, the very dependency between the two can sometimes amount to immeasurable, compounded meaning. Because you will never forget the enablers that deliberately bring you to your *Thing Two* reality. Because appropriating Failure Rule #4: *Build Your Thing One and Thing Two Dependency* yields multiple benefits.

THING TWO

YOUR PRIORITY PURSUIT

Thing Two: *A primary pursuit that carries the most anticipated meaning and often cannot be quickly fulfilled without the leveraging assistance of an enabler pursuit (Thing One).*

> **LESSON:** All pursuits carry the potential for meaning, but a *Thing Two* dream pursuit represents the highest conception of an attempt to marry money and meaning.

Failure Rule #4: *Build Your Thing One and Thing Two Dependency* is useful precisely because your *Thing Two* accomplishment is the most valuable piece of your *calling journey*. Your *Thing One* is a valuable failure prevention tool, but it is still just an enabler mobilized in service of your *Thing Two* dream, which represents the highest meaning of your path.

As you may have sensed in the *Thing One* examples I've detailed, excitement, entrepreneurial adventure, and true marked accomplishment can just as much be the hallmarks of a *Thing One* enabling pursuit as they can be for a North Star *Thing Two* primary pursuit. In and of themselves, these *Thing One* enablers may only seem to carry low meaning. Yet because they are connected to a *Thing Two* dream's dependency on them, these *Thing One* enablers serve to contribute to a rich *calling journey* narrative pregnant with multilayered meaning.

The value that develops through the establishment of *Thing One* enablers compounds and culminates into the maximized value and meaning of a *Thing Two* pursuit.

Think about the three examples I detailed. Jon Huntsman Sr.'s cancer institute was his benevolent gift to the world, all generated from the entrepreneurial rigor he exerted by building the Huntsman Corporation. Chris Wrenn has helped bring passionate soundtracks of struggle and strength to the world because he was willing to siphon profits—what many might say is throwing good money after bad—from his Yankees Suck hustle toward his Bridge Nine Records dream. Wrenn's Yankees Suck hustle tales compounded the meaning and narrative of Bridge Nine Records. The two brothers forever have a powerful narrative to attach to the legacy of their brick-and-mortar empire in their Disney on Ice enablement origin story. In all of these examples, the *Thing One* enabler back stories became part of the fabric of the eventual *Thing Two* legacies.

All this being true, however valuable the *Thing One* enabler experiences become, the *Thing Two* primary pursuit still carries the highest significantly distinct attributes as compared to *Thing One* enablers.

The *Thing Two* attributes are the highest conception of one's goal to marry money and meaning.

CALLING ALIGNMENT AND THE DIVINITY OF PURPOSE

THE THING TWO CORE ATTRIBUTES

"I felt the pain of discipline was less than that of regret
Lifted one foot from the grave when the purpose showed its face
And when the skies crashed down upon me
I looked for someone by my side
You were there, when no one else was
You showed me what's born doesn't always die
The Divinity of Purpose."

—JAMEY JASTA, FRONT MAN FOR HATEBREED, FROM THE SONG "DIVINITY OF PURPOSE"

> **LESSON:** If your *Thing Two* doesn't have a constant, driving tug, it may not truly be your *Thing Two* pursuit.

Before you wrap your arms around what **Failure Rule #4: Build Your Thing One and Thing Two Dependency** will look like for you, you need to clearly identify exactly what your **Thing Two** dream even is. You will know this by what pulls you the most.

Along the ever-evolving trail of my *calling journey,* as I've conceptualized what my **Thing Two** dream looks like, failure has often crashed down upon me like the collapsing of a broken sky. In these times, I felt like no one was by my side. There seemed to be no one who understood the reason risks were taken. No one who understood the attributes of my ultimate *Thing Two* pursuit—that illuminating lighthouse over the horizon calling me to bugger on day after day with passion and resilience. Through these times of devastation and reinvention, as Jamey Jasta describes in the lyrics quoted above, it was always the burning, ethereal sense of being driven by a great *Divinity of Purpose* that carried me through.

It is the ever-presence of a driving, relentless, nagging—still yet unsatiated—*Divinity of Purpose*** pulling you into the tumult of your mysterious *****calling journey*** of meaning that is the core attribute of your *****Thing Two*** primary pursuit.**

If what you believe is your *Thing Two* doesn't pull you into it and instead you have to exhaustively energize yourself to push toward it, then it is likely not your *Thing Two*. Your *Thing Two* will beckon you, stalk you, infest your dreams by night, color your visions by day, and tug at the divine fire in your heart to continually follow it. While your *Thing Two* may not be a singular destination, it will have a continuity of interdependent destinations that populate your distinct *calling journey*. And if you resist the pulling of the *Divinity of Purpose*, you will feel lost like a rudderless boat.

Your submission into the pull of *Divinity of Purpose* **toward your** *Thing Two* **dream will graft you into the unfolding of the very essence of who you were born to become. Yet even the submission into that pull—that tireless tug—requires discipline. Else, laziness and passivity will allow you to rationalize resisting the pull.**

Retired Navy SEAL, triathlete, and public speaker David Goggins discussed this sensibility on the *Rich Roll Podcast*. Goggins explained that he had always had this voice in his head (*internal spirit voice*) urging him to utilize his free will to make choices that would maximize his impact. Goggins recognized this voice as a divine one. This voice buoyed his strength and aided him in redirecting his path out of a backdrop of poverty, racism, abuse, and obesity. Goggins was pulled by the *Divinity of Purpose* into the **Thing Two** North Star of his *calling journey*. He intimated to *Rich Roll* how he would imagine what his life might look like had he made easier, different decisions and never struggled out of obesity, underachievement, and the painful emotional skin of his upbringing. He would then visualize arriving at the pearly gates and God laying before him a story board of what his life could have been had he chosen the hard way. What his life could have been if he had made difficult decisions that ultimately would inspire, bless, and catalyze change in others. Goggins decided he wanted to live that story forthrightly so that God would never have to shame him with a highlight reel of what could have been. His story of maximizing his potential can be found in his bestselling memoir *Can't Hurt Me*.

You must consistently fall into the pulling current of the *Divinity of Purpose*. Your commitment to becoming the self of your calling must be a disciplined, guarded effort. You have to fight to protect your time toward actualizing your **Thing Two** dream. It cannot be a mere whimsical, discretionary dabbling. You must envision large, physical brackets in the prism of your mind that surround your **Thing Two** vision, protecting it from the competing influences in your life. Those competitor forces that swarm around you seeking to defy their rightful subordination.

When your allotted times arrive and you feel the lure of household demands, of passive entertainment pleasures, of real-life worries, and of the encroaching expectations of others, you need to remember your brackets. You need to remember that the pain of discipline is less than that of regret. Your regular times, set aside to develop your *Thing Two* dream, must be protected. Don't let the labor and stamina you have given to your *Thing One* enabler(s) go to waste. Complete the charge of Failure Rule #4: *Build Your Thing One and Thing Two Dependency* **and honor the sacredness of your set aside times to develop your *Thing Two* dream.**

When your **Thing Two** dream shows itself and burns inside you with the *Divinity of Purpose*, harness discipline and submit to its supremacy.

Protect dedicated times to fall into your *calling journey*. Let the *Divinity of Purpose* pull you toward the eventual reality of your **Thing Two** manifestation.

FROM THE ASHES OF FAILURE TO THE CLARITY OF CALLING

"All you need in life is a tremendous sex drive and a great ego...brains don't mean shit."

—CAPTAIN TONY TARRACINO, SALOONKEEPER, GUNRUNNER, BOAT CAPTAIN, AND FORMER MAYOR OF KEY WEST, FLORIDA

> **LESSON:** It is when failure leaves you in a state of disassembly that your *Thing Two* pursuit often becomes the clearest.

Sometimes you don't feel the full power of your *Thing Two*'s tug on you until you are stripped by failure's purification. It is in these times that **Failure Rule #1:** *Failure Purifies* introduces you to the *Thing Two* dream you need to own as you decide to accept **Failure Rule #4:** *Build Your Thing One and Thing Two Dependency*.

There are many examples of **Failure Rule #1** introducing people to the full pull of their *Thing Two* dream. Here are a few.

The late legendary Tony Tarracino, known as Captain Tony, was not one to be pegged as a scholar. He certainly had brains, despite his quote above, but not of the formally curated variety. Captain Tony's resume epitomized an adventurer's detoured route through an eccentric life—saloonkeeper, boat captain, storyteller, friend of Ernest Hemingway and Jimmy Buffett, gambler, gunrunner, mafia target, *and, most notably*, mayor of Key West, Florida.

It is this last one that I find most interesting. In an age in which credentialing is overvalued and raw adherence to the off-road path guided by the *Divinity of Purpose* is often discarded, Captain Tony's electoral accomplishment should be a lesson to us all to be skeptical of the perceived gatekeepers, of irrational credential-worship, and of archaic guild reverence.

Captain Tony dropped out of school in the ninth grade to make his way by illegally selling whiskey during prohibition. His life continued in that vein with him leveraging his wild adventurous spirit, street smarts, and eventually, his crusty Captain's ego to eventually become known as the conscience of Key West. As mayor, Captain Tony sought to *"limit Key West's growth and to keep its reputation as a refuge for eccentrics and renegades."*

Captain Tony was purified by a string of failures in his life that brought him to an inflection point in which the full pull of his **Thing Two** destiny became clear—mustering the courage to run for mayor of Key West, Florida despite having a wildly colorful and different resume than his opponents.

An old friend of mine went through a divorce many years ago and found himself in a position to pursue his **Thing Two** while confidently ignoring his lack of prerequisites. I'm not sure if it was his tremendous sex drive or great ego, but maybe it was something like that.

His marriage was a short-lived, ill-matched union. The institution itself was anathema to my friend's calling pull. He ignored the pull of his *Divinity of Purpose*, tried marriage, and squirmed uncomfortably within its confines for about a year before the marriage disintegrated into a natural parting of ways.

As the divorce reality took root, my friend was able to more poignantly feel the tug of his long-sensed *Divinity of Purpose*. That purpose was to be a warrior. To be nomadic. To gallivant around the world risking his life to ward off threats. To bring necessary violence in the cover of night, in far off lands, so that we could immerse ourselves in relative luxury and peace in the comfort of our beds.

After his divorce, he had space to give in to the pull of his *Divinity of Purpose*. He had the opportunity to deliberately bend his ear to its relentless whisper. It was a whisper that he finally realized he had to obey if he was to avoid future regret.

His marital failure prompted a full, transparent inventory of his deepest desires. **Failure Rule #1:** *Failure Purifies* imposed itself upon him. But instead of wallowing in self-pity or excessive regret, my friend saw opportunity through listening to his *internal spirit voice*. He allowed **Failure Rule** #1 to introduce him to the full pull of his **Thing Two** dream. He then made plans to align his next steps with its pull.

After having not seen him in years, he described this pivotal period in his life as he and I sat belly-up to an Irish bar drinking beer and eating shepherd's pie. He described how he oriented his life in accordance with his *Divinity of Purpose*—that relentless internal pulling inside that urges you to dive into the tumult of your mysterious *calling journey* of meaning. The *Divinity of Purpose*—the core attribute of a **Thing Two** primary pursuit.

The most empowering, deliberate reinvention step he took to fold into his **Thing Two** reality was to enroll in a variety of training schools to prepare him to work for a private security firm. He was one of the only non-ex-military trainees in the schools. He didn't have the most essential assumed prerequisites that would predict success. In Captain Tony's words, my friend didn't have the brains or specific experience-informed knowledge to statistically succeed. Much like Captain Tony's run for mayor of Key West, Florida, was perceived.

No one thought my friend would survive these schools with no military background. But he ignored the odds, listened to the increasingly loud *internal spirit voice* that led him there, and ultimately passed all of his training with flying colors. In my friend's case, the prerequisite of military-experienced brains didn't mean shit.

Fast forwarding several years, he went on to work for SCG International, a firm that provides security for governments, law enforcement, military units, and corporate entities. He went on to assist soldiers in pre-deployment, help fight international piracy, and supports intelligence and security contracts the world over.

When I met with him, he expressed how satisfying it was for him to be living his **Thing Two** dream. He expressed deep gratitude for the hardships that he walked through because they forced him to soul-search his way into his North Star new reality.

He excitedly explained that he hadn't slept in the same place twice in over a year. He had traversed all over the Middle East for the majority of that year and had been globetrotting throughout the world in prior years. To him, this was part and parcel to who he always knew he was. He had never found the circumstantial space or motivational alignment to become that person until he was confronted with the confusion space of his divorce. He had always felt nomadic, restless, and bound for endless adventure. In the failure space of his divorce, he was able to embrace the *Divinity of Purpose* and actualize this core part of his **Thing Two** Being. His nomadic, adventurous propensity was now satiated day in and day out, from one conflict to another, and from one continent to another.

If you find yourself in a space of confusion, disassembly, and apparent failure, embrace stillness and try to feel the pull of the *Divinity of Purpose* **deep within. Loosen your resistance to its strenuous tug and let yourself be pulled into its clarity. Let failure purify you. Let Failure Rule #1 help you see your** *Thing Two* **dream with full 4K clarity. Find the pivotal next step that will allow you to fall into the**

pull of the *Divinity of Purpose* carrying you toward your *Thing Two* destiny—even if it is littered with surmountable tumult.

And then you, too, like my friend and Captain Tony, can crash into your *calling journey* as you leave behind the ashes of failure's purification.

THING TWO IS YOUR UNIQUE SOUL OUTPUT

"Art is the most intense form of individualism that the world has known."
—OSCAR WILDE, IRISH POET AND PLAYWRIGHT

> **LESSON:** Shape your *Thing Two* pursuit to resemble an amalgamation of your interests, experience, skills, and style in a way that is distinctly unique to you.

Your ***Thing Two*** dream will pull you. That pull may not be fully apparent until you collide with purifying failure. Whenever it becomes apparent, you will know its authenticity if it resembles the most unique representation of all that you are and are evolving to become. It is then your job to embrace it, submit to it, and shape it naturally as your *calling journey* sails on.

Because while the core attributes of a ***Thing Two*** primary pursuit are alignment with your *calling journey* and a connection to the pulling *internal spirit voice*'s expression of your *Divinity of Purpose*, another very important attribute is the production of unique soul output.

This means that your ***Thing Two*** primary pursuit is distinctly marked by every ingredient that makes up the stew of you. It is a one-of-a-kind cornucopia of your collective experiences, business and personal, all fashioned within your ***Thing Two*** approach. It is what

Naval Ravikant calls "specific knowledge"—knowledge that only you possess in the way that you possess it.

Think of the unique *Thing One* enabler stories that are grafted into the *Thing Two* tapestry of Jon Huntsman's Cancer center, of Chris Wrenn's Bridge Nine Records ethos story, and of the two brothers and their regional retail portfolio. Their offroad personal and business stories make their *Thing Two* accomplishments a distinct output of their souls. Their stories in and of themselves become, in the spirit of Oscar Wilde's quote above, art that heralds their intense individuality.

Your *Thing Two* pursuit will likely have branding, titling, imagery, narratives, and cross-pollinated resume color attached to it that is a coagulation of all that you are, all that you have been, and all that you wish to become. Your *Thing Two* is an offspring, a carrier of your DNA, and an offering to the world that is intricately woven in the womb of your unique experiences. Your *Thing Two* output is the culminated ingredients of your life, your perspectives, your values, and your imagination mixed into one legacy-building special sauce.

While my *Thing Two* is a *Portfolio of Pursuits* with a diversity of output goals, one of those output goals is writing books. I aspire to write a variety of books in different genres—spy thrillers, business psychology/self-help, rock bios, financial thrillers, and more.

My aforementioned first spy thriller, BLAZE: *Operation Persian Trinity*, was a unique output of my soul. The book is best described, as author Brad Thor would call it, as "faction"—which means you don't know where the facts end and the fiction begins. The book was informed by the facts of numerous news articles, books, and periodicals, but also by the facts of my life experience.

Blending my unique story, my evolving personal worldviews, and my curated humor into the dialogue, character development, and plotlines resulted in an output uniquely produced by my soul.

The novel blends the tension of the three Abrahamic religions, and their respective eschatology, with Irish-centric humor. It joins the beauty of religious soul searching with the grit of real-world vulgarity. It serves as a danger warning of the cultish nature of the apocalyptic Twelver Shia theology driving Iran's foreign policy. It highlights the anti-racist history of the skinhead movement germinated by Black, Jamaican immigrants to Britain who were apolitical, working-class lovers of music and fashion. This was all woven together in a world of geopolitical espionage and guided with literary pepperings of the punk rock ethos. All of this is an amalgamation of interests that produced output unique to my soul.

Your **Thing Two** should be an imprint as unique to you as the characters of a great novel. Your **Thing Two** should be as unmistakably unique as the trademark attributes of fictional assassin Mitch Rapp, from Vince Flynn's novels, who was known for ignoring CIA protocol in his pursuit of doing the right thing to eliminate enemy threats. It should be as memorable as the trademark imagery of British spy Alex Hawke, in Ted Bell's novels, pensively battling his demons over a glass of Gosling's Rum. It should be as uniquely intersected as Israeli spy Gabriel Allon, in Daniel Silva's novels, who balanced the duality between the beauty he gave to the world as an art restorer and the anguish he ingested from years of killing terrorists.

As you listen to your *internal spirit voice* and give in to the tug of the *Divinity of Purpose* toward your **Thing Two** dream, be mindful of all the ingredients you need to mix into its manifestation. Make your **Thing Two** your distinctly unique soul output. Let your **Thing Two** be an artistic representation of your intense individuality.

SOMETIMES YOU NEED TO BURN THE CANDLE AT BOTH ENDS

"I'm somewhere out there
Burning the candle at both ends
It's the way of the road
Do what ya gotta do to roll along
And I can't think of a better way"

—THE KOFFIN KATS, FROM THE SONG "THE WAY OF THE ROAD"

> **LESSON:** At times you will need to burn the candle at both ends as your *Thing Two* pursuit pulls you into its calling path. You need to welcome this.

The Koffin Kats are a psychobilly band from the motor city of Detroit, Michigan. Psychobilly is a punk subgenre that mixes rockabilly with punk—think Sid Vicious collaborating with Elvis. The Koffin Kat's music, while rooted in psychobilly, harnesses other punk and rock flavors to create their own special sound. Their image is also a distinct stamping of their unique soul output. When one thinks of The Koffin Kats, imagery of a stand-up bass, mohawks, hot rods, tattoos, sleeveless denim jackets, and partying on the road quickly jumps to mind.

The Koffin Kats have lived their **Thing Two** dream. Early on, they abandoned any tethering to normal life, slavery to bills, and monotonous nine-to-five jobs. For a long time, they have all had to supplement their income with creative side work, but it's all been subordinate to The Koffin Kats for the majority of their career. Now, they have converted many of their previous side hustles into permanent income sources while still maintaining the business of The Koffin Kats.

For many years before COVID-19, they were only home for two months out of the year. And that was just so they could record another album and hit the road for the next ten months supporting it. They all maintained cheap housing so that their at-home overhead expense burdens were manageable while they traversed the globe rocking one club after another.

The Koffin Kats function as a well-managed business. As noted in the lyrics quoted above, they are the embodiment of a "burn the candle at both ends" work ethic—a sensibility so associated with The Koffin Kats that a fan got a tattoo with a candle burning at both ends surrounded by The Koffin Kats logo and the band's recognizable iconography. They bootstrapped their own networks of contacts, tribal legion of fans, merchandise line, printing press shop, and content creation strategy—all to support the entity they birthed with their own unique personalities, work ethic, and musical talent. Every aspect of the existence and maintenance of The Koffin Kats is unique soul output stemming from the founding members—Eric, Vic, and Tommy. No one gave them a job. No one created a framework for them to follow. They organized themselves with ingenuity and have given the world immortal content that will outlive them. I released two records for The Koffin Kats on my label Sailor's Grave Records and am proud to have helped them bring some of their music to the world.

Whatever your *Thing Two* is or looks like it might become, do not be discouraged that there is no clean, safe, existing framework to help you. Don't be disheartened that there is no readily accessible blueprint and no prescriptive step-by-step instruction manual for you to leverage to make your *Thing Two* dream happen with turnkey ease.

Let the *Divinity of Purpose* guide you to your own special path construction. Find your own unique **Thing One** enablers, build your own precise **Thing Two** dream, and submit to it with all that you are until it becomes a reality bearing your own unique soul output.

Abiding by **Failure Rule #4:** *Build Your Thing One and Thing Two Dependency* isn't easy. Sometimes you'll have to burn the candle at both ends—and like it. Like The Koffin Kats did.

THING TWO IS DEMOCRATIZED

"The gatekeepers must change."
—PRINCE, LATE MUSICIAN, SINGER, ACTOR, DANCER, AND CHANGER OF HIS NAME TO A SYMBOL

> **LESSON:** The information age has created a democratization of access and reach that can uniquely enable *Thing Two* dreams like never before in history.

While abiding by **Failure Rule #4:** *Build Your Thing One and Thing Two Dependency* isn't easy, it is yet easier than it has ever been before, thanks to the advantages of living in the information age. Standing up a failure prevention strategy with a *Thing One* enabler powered by the automation and leverage of the digital world can help you strengthen the efficacy of your *Thing One* enabler. Building your *Thing Two* dream by the power of that same automation and leverage can help you reach your *Thing Two* accomplishment more quickly and with greater scale. Take advantage of the democratization the information age has produced.

The age of control and certainty for the world's gatekeepers is receding. Gatekeepers still exist, and as old ones are eradicated, new ones emerge, but the world is moving toward an ever-increasing, horizontally democratized landscape of opportunity paths.

Old gatekeepers struggle to find new value to remain relevant in their tastemaker roles. The dinosaur media is struggling to hang on to their nostalgic past and are losing ground daily to the ubiquity of new media.

Still, new platforms that have served to crush old gatekeepers—Amazon, Spotify, YouTube, Uber—are themselves now creating gatekeeping with bots, third-party content filters such as Disqus, and the demonetization practices of the new cancel culture.

Yet even with all of the new hyper-intermediation firmly in play, the net effect of the massive disintermediation that has taken place in the digital age has still left the world in the most democratized state for gatekeeper circumvention.

With the net increase of the democratization of opportunities to connect to customers and audiences directly, the paths to actualizing your *Thing Two* dreams is easier than it ever has been. E.L. James didn't need a gatekeeper to publish *Fifty Shades of Grey*. The entire Soundcloud rap genre—a scene that includes artists such as Lil Peep, 6ix9ine, and Lil Yachty—emerged in a gatekeeper-free environment. Disintermediation has allowed creatives to bring their art to the world—and monetize it—without the approval of rigid tastemakers.

Not only is the hold traditional gatekeepers held being challenged and minimized, but there is a widening of alt-gatekeepers emerging that are disrupting the old-world notions of credentialing.

Specialty gatekeepers are coloring outside the lines to curate opportunities distinct to people whose talents and ambitions have not fit neatly into homogenized higher-education experiences.

Peter Thiel, renowned investor and co-founder of PayPal, Palantir, and the Founders Fund has been quoted saying:

> My only claim is that not all talented people should go to college and not all talented people should do the exact same thing.

Thiel has commented that he had a generally good experience in college. Yet after he experienced years of being an entrepreneur exposed to contrarian thought and divergent individuals who succeeded with unorthodox career steps, his thinking around college and credentialing evolved. With this backdrop, he decided to erect his own alt-gatekeeping enabler—the Thiel Foundation. With a simple mission statement to *"support science, technology, and long-term thinking about the future,"* the Thiel Foundation is the realization of Peter's goal to enable and quicken the paths of those who either weren't well-guided by higher education or who were better served by a wholly detoured path to follow.

Broken out into a three-pronged program triage, the Thiel Foundation serves multiple enabling purposes. Its *Thiel Fellowship* track offers a two-year program, accompanied by a $100,000 grant, for young people who drop out of school to "build new things." The goal of the *Breakout Labs* track is to get behind companies engaging in radical envelope-pushing science with structured support mechanisms and funding. And the *Imitatio* track is entirely focused on supporting immortal written word content that furthers publications that build on Rene Girard's mimetic theory. Girard's mimetic theory proposes that human desire is never autonomous but collectively cultivated. This theory highlights the problematic nature of imperfect mediators, of subliminal envy messaging, and of broken gatekeeping models that govern society's power structures.

Tucker Max, public speaker and author of *New York Times* bestselling book *I Hope They Serve Beer in Hell*, developed his own alt-gatekeeping creation. His alt-gatekeeping creation counters the traditional gatekeepers of the book publishing world and gives authors a more structured self-publishing path. Tucker's creation is his company Scribe Media. Originally named Book in a Box, Scribe Media helps authors write, shape, publish, and market their books from soup to nuts. This includes book coaching, guided authoring, in-person workshopping, full-blown ghostwriting, multipronged marketing, branding, and all of the other accoutrements necessary for launching a book—editing, art design, typesetting, distribution facilitation, and more.

With an internet-enabled world that decouples one's dependency on location-based learning, the possibilities for new and alternative credentialing are endless. Surgically approached learning and carefully curated portfolios of specialty credentials is now more attainable than ever. Code Academy, an online curriculum for aspiring programmers to learn how to code, is one such example. Adding coding skills to one's resume—regardless of whether one's main role is IT-related or resides in a line of business—is always a strong, desirable differentiator in the eyes of hiring managers and employers. It is also a strong skill for tech-minded entrepreneurs and *solopreneurs*. With low-barrier pricing and a high-value endgame, one can enhance their skills and resume while logging in at home in their underwear and gain a skill to help them build their *Thing Two* dream.

Another democratized element of the information age that can streamline the operations of a *Thing Two* dream, is the immediacy and digitization of payments. The world is moving toward fast, frictionless digital payments. While many payment modalities still have latency of one or more settlement days, with the prominence of Venmo, PayPal, and other peer-to-peer payment schemes, money can now be sent and received instantly. And subsequent money movement to one's bank account from their digital wallet can also now be instant through The Clearing House's Real Time Payments network and through a push-to-debit card option using the Visa Direct program on credit card network rails. This helps to democratize a variety of both *Thing One* enablers and *Thing Two* dreams—from marketplace payouts and e-commerce payments to gig economy payouts and payment acceptance for freelance work.

If your *Thing Two* is an e-commerce business, there are a plethora of frictionless fulfillment companies that accompanied the birth of e-commerce available to help operationalize your dream. Physical warehouse space is no longer necessary. It is also no longer necessary to tie up time or hiring dollars managing the grind of picking, pulling, and packing orders. And it is no longer required for you to handle payment acceptance management for the daily order volume flowing through an e-commerce site. Fulfillment companies can handle all of these functions for you. Whether it's using Fulfillment by Amazon (FBA), Teespring, Printful, or the many other similar companies, the premium paid to professional fulfillment companies can help build your *Thing Two* while you maintain your *Thing One* enabler. Or it can simply help you focus on higher priority elements of developing your *Thing Two*.

In the early years of building my record labels I held down a day job and attended to the many responsibilities of having a young family. Having a competent fulfillment company—like Merch Now in Albany, New York—handle all the daily orders in the background was a huge advantage. The premium paid was well worth the convenience. They processed all orders while I simply received a monthly check and statement for what was sold and shipped. If I had to nightly do the manual work of processing the orders, my *Thing Two* would have developed much more slowly.

Outsource where it is reasonable and take advantage of the democratization enabled by the information age.

The information age has also democratized the lending landscape with the birth of non-bank online lenders. While most controversially associated with small dollar short-term lending (more commonly known by the stigma-heavy moniker of Payday Lending), the non-bank lending space is also rich with business and personal loan options that can help enable and grow your *Thing Two* dream. Lending Club, Prosper, SoFi, Kabbage, Biz2Credit, and OnDeck are some top-of-mind examples.

Debt is like fire. It can burn and destroy or warm and sustain. It has both burned me and enabled me. Over time I've learned to respect and manage it with reverence when I decide to use it. If you're building your *Thing Two* dream and you need financing, you may find difficulty in getting unsecure financing from traditional lenders. Non-bank lenders take risks that traditional banks do not. You will pay for their risk-taking, but many lenders still offer term loan rates that are lower than credit cards but higher than traditional bank loans. If used wisely and strategically, such loans, democratized by the birth of non-bank online lenders, can help enable the growth of your *Thing Two* dream.

The world is changing dynamically in favor of those looking for off-road paths to build their *Thing Two* dream. This bodes well for you if you embrace Failure Rule #4: *Build Your Thing One and Thing Two Dependency.* Harness an abundance mentality and use the democratized environment that the information age has created to push your North Star *Thing Two* into an eventual reality.

THING TWO ACHIEVEMENT

ANYONE CAN DO IT

"Commit, within financial reason, to action instead of theory. Learn to confront the challenges of the real world, rather than resort to the protective womb of academia. You can control most of the risks, and you can't imagine the rewards."

—TIM FERRISS, ENTREPRENEUR, AUTHOR, AND PODCASTER

> **LESSON:** Anyone can couple action with reasonable risks to pursue their *Thing Two* dream; it is repeating this coupling as a practice that will drive *Thing Two* achievability.

Failure Rule #4: *Build Your Thing One and Thing Two Dependency* does not restrict its effectiveness to a select amount of people. No, it is there for anyone to engage with. You just have to believe in its truth and follow through with your plans to construct it.

When I was exploring how to best find my way into the book space after finishing my first spy thriller, I attended the annual *Thriller Fest* conference in New York City. It was a fruitful time of sitting in on seminars led by great authors, such as Steve Berry (*Kaiser's Web, Warsaw Protocol*), Michael Connelly (*Bosch, The Lincoln Lawyer*), and David Morrell (*Rambo*). I learned much and met many established and aspiring authors who traversed, or were traversing, from the ordinary shelter of a theoretical idea to the actioned production of ideas birthed into reality.

After one of the sessions, I was waiting for an elevator to open so I could retreat to my hotel room for a break. When the elevator door opened, a vaguely familiar face was staring at me from within. I instantly knew that I had known this man but couldn't quickly place how or from where. He looked at me with the same realization.

Within a few minutes of confronting each other with our mutual realization, we figured out how we knew each other. Twenty years prior, we had both worked out at the same gym in West Chester, Pennsylvania. I was training for a bodybuilding competition, and he, being a former Golden Gloves boxer, was training to maintain shape for the ring.

His name is John Dixon. We hadn't known each other that well back then, but well enough to have had good conversations about training, writing, and life. In addition to being a boxer, John had been a youth services case worker and then a middle school English teacher for many years. He had a heart for at-risk kids with rough lives who needed hope and imagination to move forward. This sensibility led him to write a series of young adult adventure novels informed by his collective work experiences and love for fighting.

John was an ordinary guy who used the *Thing One* enablers of his resume composite—boxing, at-risk youth counseling, and teaching—to funnel into his extraordinary *Thing Two* dream: writing powerful young adult novels. His path exemplified the general democratized nature of *Thing Two* achievability—*anyone can do it*.

In our conversation John informed me that he had just inked a deal with Simon & Schuster to publish his young adult novel, *Phoenix Island*. Additionally, a deal was struck to adapt the novel to a television show, which became *Intelligence* starring Josh Holloway on CBS. John invited me to the launch party for the show. It was wonderful being among all his family and friends in a rented-out hall to watch the advance premiere of the pilot episode.

With the advances he secured for both the novel and the TV show, John, within financial reason, took the *reasonable risk* of leaving the safety of the protective academic womb of his teaching job. He then coupled this risk with the *action* of committing to diving headfirst into the volatility that is being a full-time writer. He's since released *Devil's Pocket*, the sequel to *Phoenix Island*, and is reaping the multitude of rewards that come with living his **Thing Two** dream.

I once saw a copy of *Devil's Pocket* for sale in a bookstore in the US Virgin Island of St. John as I was vacationing. I noticed it after purchasing some wicked strong Vietnamese coffee. I picked up the paperback copy, thought of my friend John's great story, and smiled inside for the rest of the beautiful morning.

Be like my friend John. Leave the theory-drenched cocoon of academic paralysis and the self-guarded prison of unrealized dreams. Instead, take reasonable risks and commit to action to fall into the pull of your **Thing Two** dream. So you can achieve it.

DON'T SKIP FAILURE RULE #4

BUILD YOUR THING ONE AND THING TWO DEPENDENCY

Failure prevention can never be perfected. Failures—whether they originate from personal misjudgments or are externally wrought by circumstantial hardships—will come. And when they come, they can teach you and make you stronger if you step outside of them and view them through the right lens.

But Ashton Kutcher is right. Your failures—the avoidable kind—are expensive, punishing educators. You would be wise to quote the self-evident Failure Rule: *Try to avoid failure as much as is possible*—and in the spirit of Tony Soprano's statement, *obey it*.

You should also obey **Failure Rule #4**: *Build Your Thing One and Thing Two Dependency*.

Define the conditions and characteristics of your North Star ***Thing Two*** dream. Future-scope your personally curated best authentic life. Do this with specificity, but also with curious flexibility. Your ***Thing Two*** dream can be malleable and can often become better with unexpected shaping and modification over time.

As you chase the beaming lighthouse illuminated in the distant horizon, work to build stabilizing *Thing One* enablers that help you get there with as little failure as possible. You cannot simply ignore the realities, responsibilities, and grind of the present because you're dedicated to the favorability of your *Thing Two* future life. Bear the burdens you need to bear. Bear them with integrity, work ethic, and the pride of thorough contribution.

Find the right *Thing One* enablers that fit your life. They could fall into the *Virtual Model* or the *Active Model,* or both, but find them. And build them. Find mentors to inspire your journey. They could be virtual mentors you've never met or people you have: people like Jon Huntsman, Chris Wrenn, and the two Disney on Ice brothers.

Never ignore the tugging of the *Divinity of Purpose*—the core attribute of a *Thing Two* primary pursuit. If you ignore it, it will eventually make you sick some way or another. Instead, find a way to safely submit to its pull and fall into the joyful tumult of your mysterious *calling journey* of meaning. Like my warrior friend who never sleeps in the same place twice and does what others won't in the cover of the night so we get to live like others often cannot—with the freedom to pursue our own happiness.

While you're doing your best to follow the self-evident Failure Rule of prevention, take inventory of all of your soul-defining interests and values. Make sure to mix all of those ingredients into the batter of your *Thing Two* dream cake. Bake that cake over time with dedicated and protected efforts. Then be motivated by the unique soul output you are creating. Like the outlaw psychobilly rockers from the Motor City who gave themselves their own job with a music career that is wholly distinct to the Koffin Kats.

If you become discouraged as you struggle to find and build the right *Thing One* enablers, do not forget the privilege of living in the information age. Remember all the tools and gifts this age has produced that have democratized the curation of your long-tail *Thing Two* dream. You may feel ordinary now, but you can still develop and obtain an extraordinary *Thing Two* life. Like my friend John Dixon did after years of teaching middle school English class before his ideas became published novels and a CBS television show.

Sometimes you need to follow some rules.

Don't skip **Failure Rule #4:** *Build Your Thing One and Thing Two Dependency.*

FAILURE RULE #5

YOU ARE NOT YOUR FAILURES (IMPRESSION MANAGEMENT)

"The best solution is to be kind and good while ignoring the opinions of others."
—LEO TOLSTOY, AUTHOR OF WAR AND PEACE

PRINCIPLE: Never let the failure events you experience define you. You must detach yourself from the optics of your failures. Sometimes your failures may cause division around you. Others may disapprove or even hate you. Prepare to accept this with peace, knowing your identity is not tied to your failures. Convert these rejections into amplified motivation as you move forward. Through this, make sure to be kind and good to those who judge you even as you decisively ignore their opinions. Guard your idealism and choose objective responses to your failure events. If your failure confronts you with a tragic moral choice, learn how to choose wisely and own your decision with peace—regardless of outcome. Process your failures with healthy humor and stay unmistakably authentic. Harness the creative reshaping power of chaos when your failure moments push you into rock bottom. Then submit with faith to the new streams the rocks at the bottom push you into.

DETACH FROM THE OPTICS OF FAILURE

"Don't let the noise of others' opinions drown out your own voice."
—STEVE JOBS, FOUNDER OF APPLE, BUSINESS MAGNATE,
INDUSTRIAL DESIGNER, INVESTOR, MISFIT, AND TROUBLEMAKER

> **LESSON:** When failure strikes, you cannot let the impression it makes on others affect you; be kind and good as you ignore the low-resolution opinions of others.

Do not attach yourself to the optics of failure. You are not your circumstances. You are what you decide to do about your circumstances. Your life and your pursuits do not hold their value by whether it—or they—"worked out" but rather by how *you* worked things out regardless of outcomes.

Jettison any irrational considerations of the opinions of others if they stop at the external. When others fail to see the heart of who you are and what you are supposed to do, you need to push aside their opinions.

Never forget **Failure Rule #5:** *You Are Not Your Failures.*

Actor Dwayne "The Rock" Johnson knew this in 1995. He chose to see beyond his circumstances and to detach from the optics of his current state of being broke. He recalls:

> I had seven bucks in my pocket and knew two things: I'm broke as hell and one day I won't be.

Anyone not living in a complete media-starved bubble knows that he was right. Through grit, multiple reinventions, and the consistent grind of developing a *Portfolio of Pursuits* mindset, The Rock has become the opposite of broke and the antithesis of failure.

The Rock's determination and eventual success wasn't just tethered to the discipline of detaching from his current circumstances to see a different future. Along the way, The Rock also maintained an obstinate, healthy adherence to being authentic. In an MTV award speech in 2019, he recalled what it was like when he first got to Hollywood. Everyone had an opinion on who he should be—and none of those options were rooted in advising him to be himself. He's half-Black, half-Samoan, built like a biblical giant, and comes from the low-brow world of professional wrestling. Nobody knew what the hell to do with him. They wanted to shape him. *Develop* him. *Groom* him. *Change* him.

The barrage of identity deconstruction advice never stopped—"Well, you gotta be a certain way. You gotta drop some weight. You gotta be somebody different. You gotta stop working out. You gotta stop calling yourself The Rock." But Dwayne Johnson *is* The Rock. The Rock *is* built like a brick shithouse. And The Rock already has a way of Being. So instead of compromising, he ignored the impressions of others and remained authentic. He wasn't going to allow himself to be a product of the Hollywood environment. Instead, he was going to make it a product of him:

> I made a choice, and the choice was, I wasn't gonna conform to Hollywood. Hollywood was gonna conform to me.

As you see beyond stuck circumstances and bootstrap yourself toward your *Thing Two* dream, do not compromise your authenticity. If being your authentic self is a stumbling block, you may have a misaligned *Thing Two* dream. Remember the words that Jesus said:

"For what will it profit a man if he gains the whole world and forfeits his soul?"

My best friend works in the cigar industry. At one inflection point in his career, he decided to go on some interviews to see what else was out there. He had been wildly successful in his sales career specifically due to the unique authenticity of his personality. From his language to his clothing. From his intentional rejection of corporate speak to his creative outside-the-box approach to dealmaking.

So as he kicked the tires on some other opportunities, he deliberately decided that he would not dampen, hide, or mute any of his controversial personality traits. One company advanced him forward into four interviews within a week's time. Each interview was conducted with video calls on Zoom. The first interview he wore a Mötley Crüe T-shirt visible underneath his blue blazer. The second, a Misfits T-shirt. The third, a Van Halen T-shirt. The fourth, a Ramones T-shirt. He wore an array of eccentric bracelets. He swore liberally but naturally. He talked loudly. He held back no opinions and let his unvarnished self be present. And of course, he smoked a cigar on every video call.

The company had never seen anyone like him. They could see, feel, and hear the vibrancy of his magnetic, unique personality with full strength. Instead of disqualifying him, it attracted the prospective employer to him.

My friend never took that job, but he was offered it—quickly and with favorable terms and compensation. What it confirmed to him, though, was that he must always be his authentic self. It taught him that compromising his authenticity would not only diminish the integrity of his Being but also cause him to miss out on the true opportunity matches that might be out there for him.

If you're feeling like the very act of being your authentic self is placing you in positions of failure, then you need to step back and reassess where you ought to place yourself instead. Listen to your *internal spirit voice,* and work to find out where your authentic self can prosperously amplify.

I was in existential pain when I decided to shut down my fitness center. It was a euthanized dream. An abandoned pursuit—sacrificed strategically to sustain other dreams and pursuits. It was one tentacle sliced from the octopus of my *Portfolio of Pursuits*. I would survive and thrive. I knew this. But I needed to mourn.

I was talking with a friend during this time and was seeking some understanding and support for the emotions I was cycling through in the purging of this pursuit. He was as supportive as he could be but still only saw the event through the lens of shameful failure. To him, *it had to be my fault somehow*. Not just in terms of having blind spots in the execution. Not just in terms of any failure in performing thorough due diligence. Not just in having the audacity to pursue the unknown in a world in which no one can ever accurately predict precise outcomes. But in his instinctive view, it was a failed idea wholly to begin with. *"Next time you'll think harder before doing something crazy like that. Next time you won't do something with so much risk."* For him, this was all logical and obvious because *he would never even think of doing something like it*. For him, *the meaning of a pursuit was always subordinate to a fidelity to predictable safety and failure avoidance.*

You cannot listen to those who are stuck in this mindset.

For those in your life who won't detach from the optics of failure, you need to detach from their opinions. It's best to instead follow Tolstoy's advice and *"be kind and good while ignoring the opinions of others."* Find others in your tribe. Those who've failed and kept going. Watch them, listen to them, and humbly position yourself as their mentee whenever possible.

If you unwisely become preoccupied with the opinions and imagined perceptions of others—*most notably those of family*—you will risk the possibility of your story being written by others, at your expense, for the benefit of their feelings and satisfaction, all the while neglecting yours.

Alt-medicine advocate and author Deepak Chopra expresses it this way:

> What other people think of you is not your business. If you start to make that business your business, you will be offended for the rest of your life.

Heed Deepak's advice and mind your business. Don't allow the thoughts other people may have of you to be integrated into the business of your self-worth and decision-making. Instead, choose to merely see their opinions as ideas to objectively consider. Else, you will be forever irritable and perennially offended. Why live that way when you can simply be kind while ignoring the misaligned opinions of others?

For many of us, it's the voices—real or imagined—of our family that most skew, interrupt, and obfuscate the clarion call of our *internal spirit voice*. Many people desire favorability, acceptance, approval, and praise from their family for their decisions—and ultimately their way of Being. But we are all built like stones, not bricks. We are individual creations, with our own special cracks, grooves, nooks, crannies, fault lines, ornamental beauty, and pockmarks. Are we to shoehorn the decisions we make about who we are becoming into a plagiarized brick-shaped mold that duplicates the aggregate mold of our parents? Or one that mirrors the collective opinions and choices of our family? If we do, we muzzle our *internal spirit voice* and betray the very core of who we are—*a mysterious soul, formed in a secret place of spiritual essence, knitted together in the depths of our mother's womb.*

Psychoanalyst and bestselling author Dr. Jordan Peterson talks about how individuality is truly reached when you're respectfully free from fear of judgment by your parents. This doesn't mean that you ought not absorb, internalize, and emulate the beliefs and attributes of your parents that align with your conscience and personality. I certainly hope that my children do. But they—and you—need to be discerning. Dr. Peterson asserts:

> One of the times in your life when you actually realize that you're an individual is when you go and ask your parents something and you realize that they don't actually know more about what you should do than you do. And that sucks.

Much like the first sting of fresh failure, this does suck. But after this realization sucks, it rules. It rules because as you rise into the comfortable skin of your unique individuality and authenticity, you become strong. That strength will be the foundation that carries you into an adventurous life of seeking alignment with the glorious tumult of your *calling journey*.

Failure throws out the old sheet of paper and gives you a glorious blank sheet for you to begin drafting the next chapter of your journey with color and enthusiasm. You cannot draft that next chapter if you're hung up on the optics of your failure. You cannot draft that next chapter if you're hung up on the opinions—known or anticipated—of others. Your strategy for impression management needs to be completely derelict—don't manage it all.

Seth Godin, author of *Purple Cow: Transform Your Business by Being Remarkable*, explains his observation of this hang-up this way:

> We don't choose to be remarkable because we're worried about criticism. We hesitate to create innovative movies, launch new human resource initiatives, design a menu that makes diners take notice or give an audacious sermon because we're worried, deep down, that someone will hate it and call us on it.

Learn to accept that people may not like what you do, create, or choose. Learn to be okay with the idea that people may hate you. We're all very different. If you're doing anything bold or interesting, someone somewhere is bound to hate you. Smile. It's okay. Sometimes it's even fun.

Detach from the optics of your failures. Outline the next chapter of your life with audacity. Be kind and good as you ignore the opinions of others. Don't try to manage the impressions you might make.

Tattoo **Failure Rule** #5 on your soul: *You Are Not Your Failures*.

REJECTION IS FUEL

"I take rejection as someone blowing a bugle in my ear to wake me up and get going, rather than retreat."

—SYLVESTER STALLONE, ACTOR

> **LESSON:** Use rejection as fuel to energize your fire inside to burn into a brighter, more powerful flame.

Rejection is fuel. Count on it. Anticipate it. Know it well and let it inform the courageousness and consistency of your efforts. With each rejection, leverage what you learn to strengthen and grow your idea muscles. Don't resent those who reject you. Analyze the disposition from which each rejection springs with as much of an objective mind as you can muster. Do this knowing that just as **Failure Rule #5: *You Are Not Your Failures*** is true despite how you feel, facing rejection is a necessary part of learning the value of your failures—regardless of whether you like it or not.

Because sometimes you need to accept rejection as a call to change. Like a bugle blowing in your ear.

After my first spy thriller, *BLAZE: Operation Persian Trinity*, was released, some of the criticism from my editor was echoed in feedback from readers. I had assimilated much of my editor's critique into my rewrites but failed to do the hard work on some of the major structural change suggestions he made. This was a mistake. In hindsight, I should've slowed down and more thoughtfully considered his suggestions.

But ultimately the cumulative rejection of some of the elements of my writing served as constructive fuel. As I set out to frame the pacing, plot, and various storylines, and character constructs for my second novel, CALIPH: *Ottoman Rising*, I harkened back to the advice I failed to assimilate when writing BLAZE. I metabolized the rejection of portions of my first novel's structure as fuel. That fuel led to a sophomore effort with immensely more focused pacing, stronger dramatic sequencing, better character development coordination, and a more balanced blend of action scenes and expository passages.

Dr. Jordan Peterson, author of 12 *Rules for Life*, asserts that the *"willingness to be a fool is the precursor to transformation."*

One of Long Island's best singer-songwriters ever, pianist Billy Joel, once lamented, *"I really wish I was less of a thinking man and more of a fool not afraid of rejection."*

I don't think we need to choose between these two viewpoints. You can be a thinking person *and* approach your pursuits with the wide-eyed adventurism of a fool's sensibility. Sometimes, to see yourself as a fool *is* an act of thinking. Approach your pursuits with as much analysis, preparation, and craft development as you can. Then, move forward—like a fool—with the full knowledge that you have gaps, both known and unknown, that may result in rejection and failure along the way. Then metabolize that rejection as fuel to help you refine your path toward your *Thing Two* dream.

Be a thinking person. Be willing to be a fool. And don't fear rejection. Let rejection land on you like the disruptive, intrusive sound of a bugle blowing in your ear.

Take inventory of your motivations and your skills. Balance them against the rejection noise fed back to you. Seek to understand the context from which this noise arises, and you will better understand your own path. You'll more clearly see the next necessary pivot in your calling after you process each necessary rejection.

Sometimes you need to reject rejection and strengthen your resolve.

My ex-business partner in the online lending business vacillated between overly praising my performance with undue exaltation and overly criticizing my performance with unmerited assassination of my competency. I saw through both extremes and held fast to my own balanced assessment of my work product, competency, and growth trajectory. Yet there was no denying that on the criticism end of the scale, I had to wrestle with how to assimilate his absurd rejections. These rejections were transparent psychological bullying tactics he used to effectuate certain power moves, but they had to be metabolized nonetheless. Metabolizing these rejections was more complicated because he was a real mentor of mine. I truly admired and sought to emulate so many of his valuable attributes—and still do today. That backdrop made my thoughtful rejections of his rejection tactics manyfold more difficult.

Unlike my eventual acceptance of my editor's rejection of portions of my writing, in which I changed my approach, the criticism of my ex-partner was invalidated as I moved to the next chapter in my *calling journey*. It did not take long into my career in banking, specifically the payments space, to realize that my competency had been undervalued in my previous role as partner in the online lending firm. Over the following years, I would intermittently hear the barking voice of my ex-partner in my head as I would reach milestones of achievement and recognition. I would smile inside and gratefully reflect on my decision to burn that rejection as fuel to invalidate the messaging of the old criticisms.

Author J.K. Rowling was stuck in the terror of poverty and joblessness after returning to England from Portugal following her divorce. She had to wrestle with the shame of living off state benefits to do what she needed to do to take care of her and her daughter. She was penniless and couldn't find work. They were cramped in a small apartment. Rowling tumbled into a deep depression. She recalled those days in a 2008 Harvard University commencement speech this way:

> An exceptionally short-lived marriage had imploded, and I was jobless, a lone parent, and as poor as it is possible to be in modern Britain, without being homeless...By every usual standard, I was the biggest failure I knew.

Have you ever felt like the biggest failure you knew? Have you ever felt like no one could possibly understand the cascading failures of your life that had distilled within one single season of your journey on this earth? I have. And in those times, I leverage the stories of those who have also felt the weight of that despair. And I harness inspiration from their tenacity to get through and out of those times.

Rowling didn't let this rejected state of being stop her from cultivating the start-and-stop dream of finishing her manuscript for *Harry Potter and the Philosopher's Stone*. Rowling felt rejected by her marriage's failure, by the job market, by her own ability to monetize her skills and take care of her daughter, and by Being itself. Yet she channeled that rejection as fuel to escape into the world of *Harry Potter*. She would spend her days with her daughter sleeping in the pram next to her, hunkered down in cafes finishing the manuscript that was only three chapters deep when she arrived in England after her divorce. She continued in her Harvard speech to explain:

> Failure meant a stripping away of the inessential. I stopped pretending to myself that I was anything other than what I was and began to direct all my energy to finishing the only work that mattered to me. Had I really succeeded at anything else, I might never have found the determination to succeed in the one area where I truly belonged. I was set free because my greatest fear had been realized, and I was still alive, and I still had a daughter whom I adored, and I had an old typewriter, and a big idea. And so rock bottom became a solid foundation on which I rebuilt my life.

When you're in the grips of overwhelming failure, you need healthy escape routes. You need something in your life that takes you out of the abyss of your circumstances, temporarily but regularly, so you can restore your reserves. This will help you deal with your failures and try to find a way forward.

Writing *Harry Potter* was both Rowling's escape mechanism *and* her way forward. The empty space and time failure afforded her, coupled with the fuel of a comprehensive rejection by life itself, birthed one of the most enchanting narratives depicting the dichotomy of good and evil that ever charmed the world's imagination. She traversed from being dependent on the state to being the first person to ever earn one billion dollars by writing books.

If there is no rejection, there is no discovery. The burnt fuel of metabolized rejection amplifies the electric moment of a success finally realized. Bolstered by ashes of processed rejection in your rearview, the thrill of achieved success is multiplied when it graces you with its mysterious, and often temporary and ambiguous, presence.

You must constantly stretch yourself, enhance your vulnerability and put yourself on display to align with your unfolding *calling journey*. Rejections are pit stops along the way that give you an opportunity to evaluate your efforts. To correct your efforts if it's prudent. Or to confirm your resolved Being and path forward when it ought.

Cowards don't lose; they just never win. Cowards fear failure. Cowards bow to the god of security and stability. Cowards fear rejection.

Be a thinking person while also approaching your pursuits with the wonder of a fool. Metabolize rejection as fuel. This is how you manage the feedback of others on the impressions your work has made.

Like Stallone, be energized by the bugle sound of rejection blowing in your ear as you move through each season of your tumultuous *calling journey.*

READY, FIRE, AIM

OWN YOUR DECISIONS

"My life is ready, fire, aim, and it is one of adventure."
—JESSE ITZLER, OWNER OF THE NBA'S ATLANTA HAWKS, ENTREPRENEUR, AUTHOR, AND RAPPER

Irish Diplomacy: *The art of telling someone to go to hell and having them look forward to the trip.*

> **LESSON:** Don't wait for perfect conditions before acting in accordance with your *internal spirit voice*; own your decisions, and reject the notion that good decisions must always produce predictably good outcomes.

Knowing **Failure Rule #5:** *You Are Not Your Failures* is real and that perfect pre-conditions for launching a pursuit do not ever exist, don't be afraid of firing before you've achieved perfect aim.

Wisdom seeks counsel with a thoughtful, wide-net approach. Read. Consult. Study all the information accessible. Listen to those who have gone before. But when all the data at hand has been gathered, it will be you who channels the vortex of input to effectuate the right decision. You can't deliberate forever.

At the end of the day, or the end of your *calling journey*, it is *you* who needs to own your decisions.

This often means that you will have to reject the opinions of someone close to you, someone you love and respect, and someone whom you wish understood the decision you are convicted to make. Many times, it can be someone who has genuinely empathized with you and has shared in much of the pain that you've experienced from previous failures and rejections.

In the TV show, *Ramy*, starring millennial Muslim comedian Ramy Youssef, Ramy, playing himself, is struggling with direction in his life. He's wrestling with a kind of early twenties coming-of-age struggle in which he's trying to recognize what his *calling journey* is. He wants to identify what his dreams really are. He wants to carve out some sort of viable path to pursue them. He's trying to scope out his *Thing Two* pursuit.

The problem is that this is all completely foreign to the career messaging he's been raised to ingest. His Egyptian immigrant parents are entirely focused on the lower elements of the hierarchy of needs—food, water, safety, security, warmth, rest. The first two layers of the pyramid. Ramy, growing up in America, has a different lens through which he sees his priorities and future. He is focused on how he can leapfrog to the higher layers of the hierarchy of needs pyramid. He is seeking self-actualization, accomplishment, and some prestige that aligns with his *internal spirit voice*. As he is discussing his desire to follow his dreams with his parents in one of the episodes, his dad rebukes him and warns, "That's how white people talk." For Ramy's dad, following your dreams was irrelevant; securing provisions within the lower layers of the hierarchy of needs was the only thing that mattered.

Like Ramy, if there is a chasm between your parents' view of your *Thing Two* dream development and your conviction of your vision, then you need to respectfully ignore their opinions. Find a *Thing One* enabler to help with the lower levels of the hierarchy of needs and push into the tumultuous journey of actualizing your *Thing Two* dream. Do this, and you can own your decisions with satisfaction, regardless of the outcomes.

I have a kitschy plaque on the wall in my bedroom with the definition of Irish diplomacy. It reminds me that sometimes I need to employ this as part of my impression management strategy. Of course, the act of engaging in Irish diplomacy itself requires you to be nice in *"telling someone to go to hell"* in such a way that they look forward to the trip. Which really means you're not telling them to go to hell at all. You're really just, once again, following Tolstoy's advice and *"being kind and good while ignoring the opinions of others."* Whether you think of it as Irish diplomacy or as following Tolstoy's advice, as you progress into your *Thing Two* pursuit, there will likely be times when you have to adopt some semblance of this attitude. Often with family or someone close to you.

I am a strong proponent that there are times when one must move forward with a ready, fire, aim approach. Walking this back with a bit of a qualifier, I would say that maybe it's not *totally* aimless. It's just not a clear target. It's more of a compass guiding you. The traceable route of the map will emerge as you iterate intelligently along the way. So, more precisely, it looks like *ready, strongly approximate your aim, fire, and sharpen your aim in flight.*

Perfect aim is the enemy of forward movement. It's the bad friend of incurring opportunity cost.

Whether it's been in starting a business, buying a business, contemplating a marriage, purchasing a home, choosing a job, investing, or getting a tattoo, I've found that if you know yourself well and process all the information at hand at the point of decision, you will be comfortable owning that decision forever. Regardless of how or if it works out in the end. This is because I know that any failures that I face are simply events. Since I know well **Failure Rule #5: *You Are Not Your Failures*,** I do not tie these events to my identity or self-esteem.

Jesse Itzler does a lot of firing. The idea that his calling would somehow be contained in one pursuit clearly does not resonate with Jesse. Instead, he's constantly found the adjacent possible and iterated a wildly diverse, fun, and successful career. He aims after he fires. He fires at multiple things in parallel. He has a *Portfolio of Pursuits* mentality.

After graduating college, Jesse signed a record deal and released his first rap album under the name Jesse Jaymes. He went on to co-write songs with Tone-Loc, land a single on the Billboard Hot 100 chart, and write the New York Knicks' theme song. But he didn't confine himself to music. He lurched into the adjacent possible—those related intersecting opportunities that sat naturally to the side of his current pursuits. He started Alphabet City Sports Records. The label intersected Jesse's love of music with his love of basketball. He mixed classic arena songs with highlights of historical play-by-play calls for teams such as the Wizards, the Mavericks, and the Lakers. But even this was only one thread in the tapestry of his *Portfolio of Pursuits*. Jesse is an octopus with many tentacles. He went on to co-found Marquis Jet, one of the largest private jet card companies in the world. He became a partner in Zico Coconut Water. And ultimately Jesse became the owner of the NBA's Atlanta Hawks. Jesse Itzler didn't wait for perfect aim. He didn't focus on just one thing. He embraced a life of ready, fire, aim and discovered a world of endless, diverse, entrepreneurial adventure.

Remember *wabi-sabi* in the Definition of Terms? As I write this, I'm sitting on my balcony in South Philadelphia smoking a cigar, listening to Steel Pulse, and staring at a view of the Delaware river. It's a pretty river to look at, but in my view, it's bookended by two decrepit buildings that typify urban decay. The contrast between the river view and the decayed buildings is *wabi-sabi*. It's beautiful in its imperfection. Rocker and Van Halen alumni, David Lee Roth, described *wabi-sabi* this way on the *Joe Rogan Experience* podcast, *"It's perfect because it's a little fucked up."* Comedian Louis C.K. used to deliberately make sure that every set on a TV show he was working on had some element that was a little off. A little imperfect. A little fucked up. A little *wabi-sabi*. For Louis, *wabi-sabi* was the essence of life, art, and beauty.

Be prepared to expect, accept, and appreciate some *wabi-sabi* as you embrace some version of the *ready, fire, aim* approach to your pursuits.

Because good decisions do not always lead to clean and direct outcomes that are recognizably good.

Don't be afraid to launch your pursuits with a *ready, strongly approximate your aim, fire, and sharpen your aim-in-flight* approach. Embrace the love of *wabi-sabi* in your life. Don't be married to perfect conditions as a prerequisite to moving forward, or you'll be in the waiting room of life forever, clinging to some bullshit notion of safety.

Act on your own internal convictions and listen to the pulsating whispers of your *internal spirit voice*. Gather as much information as you can. Consult those you respect—both those you know and virtual mentors through books and other media. Soul search. Let an idea ruminate appropriately. Pray on it if you're of the persuasion.

But when the vortex of data is finally channeled and the next affordable steps in your *Thing Two* pursuit are clear, then you need to act. Approximate your aim and fire. Move with swiftness and audacity as you refine your aim in flight. Then own your decisions with fulfillment. Regardless of the outcomes.

Because even if you find some failure in your outcomes, they don't define who you are.

Regardless of your outcomes, you can take refuge in the freeing truth of **Failure Rule #5**: *You Are Not Your Failures.*

KNOW WHEN TO BYPASS PERMISSION

"Real entrepreneurs have what I call the three Ps (and, trust me, none of them stands for 'permission'). Real entrepreneurs have a 'passion' for what they're doing, a 'problem' that needs to be solved, and a 'purpose' that drives them forward."

—MICHAEL DELL, FOUNDER OF DELL TECHNOLOGIES, BILLIONAIRE, AND PHILANTHROPIST

> **LESSON:** When your *internal spirit voice* is in clear opposition to the external feedback loops that surround you, you need to bypass permission and act.

Don't let placism control your sense of agency on the front end of contemplating a pursuit. No matter the real or perceived failure state you find yourself in, if your *internal spirit voice* is clearly guiding you to a pursuit decision, then you need to listen and act. Consider thoughtful input but don't seek unnecessary permission. Don't look to those who see you only through a prism of placism to validate your decision. Because the truth of **Failure Rule #5: *You Are Not Your Failures*** exists to free you from such artificial constrictions.

As I mentioned before, the dream of starting my own record label had been growing inside me long before I acted. I knew that many of my friends and family, all of whom loved me very much, would never understand or green light my pursuit with a vote of confidence.

It was too abstract, too outside the realm of what they would ever see themselves doing. And when the dream hatched, I literally had zero business experience, let alone specific experience in the music industry.

And remember, I was unemployed.

So predictable resistance to the idea would have been reasonable.

But I knew deep inside that it was the first significant pursuit that would be part of the overall tapestry of my life's work and my unfolding *calling journey*. As Michael Dell describes above, it was the *purpose* driving me forward—the *Divinity of Purpose*.

So I didn't ask permission. I just executed.

In his song "Get Got," country singer Toby Keith describes a laundry list of pithy gems of wisdom that emanate from a fictional old man delivering life's guidance to a young man. It's veritable front-porch wisdom put to song. The old everyman prophet gives advice on how to handle a jam with a job, a woman, and decision-making. And on this last one, decision-making, the directive whispered from the porch is, "*Don't mix whiskey with decision/Ask forgiveness, not permission.*"

I concur with most of the old man's wisdom in the song. When one finds themselves in a hole, they should stop digging. And one should always drink upstream from their cattle. But with this specific lyrical phrase, I only agree with one piece—the bit about not asking permission. There are times when one needs to harness the power of the *Divinity of Purpose*, approximate their aim, and fire toward their *Thing Two* dream without asking any explicit permission from those closest to them.

Results are important. Gathering input is important. Yet if you're comfortable with the full range of potential outcomes, if you've digested all relevant input available, and you are still generating negative impressions around your decision, you need to just move forward. Bypass permission.

The rest of the lyrical phrase I would respectfully discard. You don't need to ask forgiveness when you bypass permission. Further, sometimes mixing a little whiskey with your decisions can be quite good for slowing you down and helping you land on the right approach.

So I didn't seek a permission slip when I dove in and created my first record label. It is the one "P" I did not consider. I was consumed with the other three Ps. I had *passion* for the music and the message. I felt *purpose* in pushing my dream into reality in order to help bring new art into the world. And I needed to work to solve the *problem* of the meaning deficit in my work life. Launching Thorp Records gave me all three of the Ps that Michael Dell identifies in his quote above—while deliberately ignoring the fourth P of permission.

Circumstances and pieces came together bit by bit. Determined ambition met Providence—like the *Carl Moment*—and the dream began taking visible shape.

I knew my path was questioned and criticized along the way. I knew that failures and trials would come. I was okay with that, and you have to be too. This is how you pursue your authentic self.

Businessman, motivational speaker, and former stockbroker Chris Gardner knew when to bypass permission. He was broke and getting broker, selling medical technology—bone density scanners. His wife was less than supportive of his idea to chase after a dream of becoming a stockbroker. She could only see the hole of their current circumstances. She saw him as the one with the shovel who couldn't stop digging, like the line from the Toby Keith song. In her view, Chris *was* his failures.

But Chris Gardner bypassed her permission and saw a different future for himself. Chris understood **Failure Rule #5: *You Are Not Your Failures*.** He refused to believe that he couldn't be like the stockbrokers with the natural smiles and nice cars that he would observe when he hustled around San Francisco trying to sell his bone density scanners.

They told him all he needed was to be good at math and be good with people. And he believed them.

Sales kept declining; his wife left him, and Chris found himself homeless while taking care of his young son. Yet in this unbelievably difficult set of circumstances, Chris followed the promptings of the *Divinity of Purpose* pulsating inside. He kept chasing his dream to lift himself off the streets by becoming a stockbroker. There was no one close to him who would encourage him in this idea. It would have sounded too fantastical, too unrealistic.

In the movie *Pursuit of Happyness,* based on Chris's memoir, there is a scene in which actor Will Smith, playing Chris, is playing basketball with his son. As his son is practicing his shot, Will Smith begins to advise him that he'll probably just be about as good as he was at basketball when he was young. He elaborates:

> That's kind of the way it works, ya know, and I was below average. So you'll probably ultimately rank somewhere around there. So ya know, you'll excel at a lot of things, but not this, so I don't want you out here shooting this ball around all day and night.

Instantly his son's entire demeanor is deflated. He crumbles into a disinterested participant. His father somehow thought it was okay to prescribe mediocrity to cure the boy's enthusiasm for shooting hoops. But it wasn't. His son begins packing up the ball, ready to pack it all in for good. He lost his drive. **Mediocrity is not attractive.**

Then Will Smith, as Gardner, realizes what he had done. He had treated his son precisely the way his wife had treated him. After several seconds of emotional silence, he pivots and delivers a new message to his son:

> Hey. Don't ever let somebody tell you that you can't do something. Not even me. All right? You got a dream, you gotta protect it. People can't do something themselves, they wanna tell you that you can't do it. You want something, go get it. Period.

Many parents really don't care at all about their kids' dreams. They just want their kids to be safe. To be self-reliant. To not have problems, letdowns, and failures. To not ever have to move into their basement when things don't work out.

This is an understandable and a natural instinct, but if you're a parent you need to guard against this. My daughter has been diligently and skillfully practicing and performing ballet since a very young age. Most of her upbringing has been largely consumed with and oriented toward this passion. The passion is real. Her talent is real. The dreams connected to this passion are real.

As a parent, I have to delicately balance my support of her *Thing Two* dream of building a future around this passion with equally encouraging her to build balance around this dream with *Thing One* enablers and a *Portfolio of Pursuits* mindset.

Because nothing is safe. Especially the pursuit of our dreams.

Don't tell someone they can't do something just because you couldn't. Don't try to moderate someone else's dream because you don't understand it. Fan the flames of the dreams held by those you love. And remind them that dreams don't become a reality in a vacuum. They need strong, sometimes diverse enablers to guide them into existence. Remind them that dreams are not safe. Sometimes they don't ever happen. Yet affirm that they should chase them anyway while advising them that they need to also build a *Portfolio of Pursuits*. They need to be like an octopus, with many tentacles to keep them going when others are severed.

I have a friend who was homeless in his early twenties. There was never a movie made about him. He didn't write a book or appear on *The Oprah Winfrey Show*. Yet, like Chris Gardner, he also had to listen to his *internal spirit voice* and bypass permission to move forward in his life.

His mother struggled her way through nursing school as a single parent with three children. She never had any money. When she graduated nursing school, her life began changing. She lost weight. She met a man. He had money. They got married. Somehow, in that whirlwind of change, my friend fell through the family cracks. His paths were not supported. He ended up homeless.

Yet my friend didn't grovel back to his mother and his new stepdad asking for help or a permission slip on how he should best reorganize his life. He slept in a park by night and worked at McDonald's by day. He eventually saved up enough money to begin attending community college—homeless all the while. He studied each evening at the public library. He leaned on his straight-edge hardcore ethos, his reliance on the nonattachment principles of eastern philosophical thought, and the gritty work ethic of a young, tattooed punk kid.

Eventually, he was able to afford to rent a room from the parents of a friend. Over time, he graduated school, moved out totally on his own, settled out west, and built a stable career in human resources. And he now has a good relationship with his mother and the rest of his family.

He never let failure or placism lower him into a victim mentality. He wrote his own permission slips every step of the way. He believed in the spirit of **Failure Rule #5:** *You Are Not Your Failures*.

Be kind and good while ignoring the impressions you make on others. When you operate with a soul-informed, internal decision-making engine, you can simply bypass permission and move forward.

Your life, authentically lived, will ultimately leave the impressions it ought on those who are right to receive them.

BANKRUPTCY BLUES

PROTECT IDEALISM, REJECT CYNICISM

"There is only one way to avoid criticism: Do nothing, say nothing, and be nothing."

—ARISTOTLE, PHILOSOPHER

> **LESSON:** You must protect your idealism in the midst of failure; reject any cynicism that may cause you to lose sight of your *Thing Two* dream.

It is extremely difficult to believe in **Failure Rule #5:** *You Are Not Your Failures* under the crushing weight of certain failures. But this is when you have to be most aware of the power of your idealism. And most wary of the destructive forces of opportunistic cynicism.

In 2007, failure came crashing down on me with a fury.

The ramifications of the transition from physical product dependence to digital download delivery in the music industry came rapidly. The entire retail landscape transformed in short order. Sales dropped. Physical returns and their attendant fees hit record labels hard. Chain stores that carried large portions of sales for labels filed Chapter 11 bankruptcy and then eventually closed down altogether.

I was underwater and couldn't find a lifeboat to hook on to.

I had to eliminate expenses, chase new income, and shed debt. I let go of the publicist, the office space, the web designer, and the part-time help. I tried everything. But eventually I had to engage in the nuclear option. I had to declare personal bankruptcy to properly reorient my life. I had to push the reset button in order to reinvent and move forward on multiple levels.

When this type of failure hits, you question every decision that contributed to bringing you to the space of ultimate devastation. Your *internal spirit voice* is audible, but it sounds confused, hard to interpret, and difficult to trust. Especially if it was the adherence to that voice that actually steered you into the vortex of steaming failure.

My record labels were worth nothing at this unique inflection point. There was nothing to sell—I tried. At the time, I had no idea that due to the long-tail shift that would come in the digitization of music, that the underlying IP rights would ever hold real, lasting value. In that time, my present circumstances clouded me with emptiness and blackness. I felt devoid of any tangible hope. As you read about in the introduction.

Yet once this blackness passed, I began to notice an inner peace about the cleansing that I was walking through. Although garbled, I could still hear my *internal spirit voice*. I knew that regardless of the failure I found myself mired in, that all the decisions I had made were important to my ongoing *calling journey*. The money was always merely the fuel to keep the passion going anyhow. I had only run out of that fuel, not the power of my gritty, raw, driving passion.

After the numbing debilitation of the initial failure strike subsided, I began to see light, reinvented futures, and the value of the efforts that brought me to the point-in-time failure event.

The ashes of failure began to fall beside me like incinerated fuel. **Failure Rule #1:** *Failure Purifies* was in full operation. As author Janet Fitch noted, *"The phoenix must burn to emerge."* My spirit began to rise with the power of a phoenix. I was going to move forward. *Differently*—with new wine skins. *Better*—with a deeper value for nonattachment. *Stronger*—with a wider vision-casting muscle to propel my diehard entrepreneurial spirit.

At the time, there were several people in my life who had confessed to having viewed me as a role model. They had admired and tried to emulate my grit. They knew I built my record labels by sleeping only four hours per night for the first four years. They saw the successes that punctuated over time. They saw the unbridled tenacity in me. They had taken steps in their own lives to replicate that spirit.

But when failure struck, these friends admitted that they no longer viewed me the same way. How could they? It didn't work out for me after all, right?

The late comedian George Carlin said that if you scratch any cynic, *"you will find a disappointed idealist."* These friends lost their enthusiastic idealism by watching me go through failure. They went on to abandon any of their own pursuits that didn't have safety as its highest attribute. The whispering of their *internal spirit voices* was fully suffocated to death by their disappointment in my failure moment. They had no interest in risking an outcome that might even remotely resemble the failure that I had to confront, conquer, and rise from.

The criticism did not "confront me," as the landlady in George Thorogood's song "One Bourbon, One Scotch, One Beer" would say. Even in the midst of the failure of bankruptcy, I did not seek safety as my highest value. Instead, I emerged stronger and more able to confront the calculated risks I purposed to continue taking.

Oscar Wilde was quoted as saying that *"a cynic is a man who knows the price of everything, and the value of nothing."* I knew the price of my failure *and* I knew its value. I didn't become jaded. Cynicism never took root. And my idealism was now colored with the empowerment of bone-deep pain.

If you prioritize safety and the avoidance of criticism as your highest values, then you will never do anything, say anything, or be anything of high impact. You need to reject the instinct to elevate a fidelity to safety and the avoidance of criticism.

Baseball legend Jackie Robinson once remarked that if you're going to spend your whole life in the grandstand just watching what goes on, *"you're wasting your life."* Don't resign to sitting idly in the spectator seats while others bravely follow the *Divinity of Purpose* into the mystery of their tumultuous *calling journey*. Don't waste your life.

Whatever failure befalls you, find a way to retain your idealism. You need to reject the inner cynicism of negative self-talk and the external cynicism of those around you. Leverage the wisdom that can be found in your failure. Internalize the powerful truth of Failure Rule #5: *You Are Not Your Failures* with all of your Being.

Comedian Stephen Colbert offered his own observations of cynicism:

> Cynicism masquerades as wisdom, but it is the farthest thing from it. Because cynics don't learn anything. Because cynicism is a self-imposed blindness, a rejection of the world because we are afraid it will hurt us or disappoint us. Cynics always say no. But saying yes begins things. Saying yes is how things grow. Saying yes leads to knowledge.

Don't view your failures or the failures of others as an excuse to never say yes. Don't sit on the sidelines, wait, and point at those who encounter failure in a difficult pursuit. Instead, ignore cynicism and protect your idealism even in the midst of devastating failure.

Use the regenerative power of **Failure Rule #5:** *You Are Not Your Failures* to help you maintain the chase toward your *Thing Two* dream. And always be kind and good while ignoring the cynicism and criticism of others.

WHEN YOU HIT A ROCK, LET IT PUSH YOU INTO A NEW STREAM

"Rock bottom became the solid foundation on which I rebuilt my life."
—J.K. ROWLING, AUTHOR OF HARRY POTTER

> **LESSON:** When you hit rocks along your *calling journey* path, submit to this inertia and fall into the new streams the rocks pull you into.

As you fail you will hit rocks. Some small. Some large. Some encrusted firmly at the bottom-most part of one of your *calling journey's* streams. Sometimes you will hit multiple rocks in quick succession. But all of these rocks, while they may hurt and disrupt your flow, will push you into a new stream. While they will represent failure moments, these moments will not define you—because **Failure Rule #5: *You Are Not Your Failures*** is reliable. When you hit these rocks, you must learn to embrace the new streams it pushes you into with a curious discovery mindset.

Recall again the lessons of J.K. Rowling's experience. When Rowling's marriage failed, she hit a rock. That rock pushed her into a new stream. She moved back to Britain from Portugal, leaving the life she had with her ex-husband behind in the lapping waters of the rearview stream.

Once in Britain, she hit yet another rock—she was broke, unemployed, and caring for her daughter. While struggling with the emotions of living off of the state, this season in her life pushed her into yet a new stream—one that had been quietly waiting to pull her into it. It was that manuscript. The one for which she had only written three chapters so far and hadn't touched in many months.

The rocks she had hit in life pushed her into a new life stream that allowed her breathing room to refocus on writing *Harry Potter*—the imaginary world she escaped into as a mechanism to grapple with the mysteries of death. It was this stream—the actualization of her gift of writing—that reignited the embracing of her *calling journey*. But she had to hit several rocks on her way to this reignition. Rowling fell to rock bottom incrementally. She hit multiple rocks in quick succession. It was from this rock-bottom foundation that her life was rebuilt into the flourishing of her *Thing Two* dream.

Sometimes you need to hit rocks to guide you into the stream of your *calling journey*. Don't reject the rebuke these rocks seem to impose on you. Accept them with faith as you surrender into the new streams they push you into.

After I hit the hard, large bulging rock of going through a personal bankruptcy, I continued to hit hard, stifling rocks repeatedly with a frequent cadence over the following years.

The toxic debt was discharged, but so was my income and my full-time involvement in a space that I had been working in for seven years. I embraced reinvention on multiple levels, but I was rebuilding from rock bottom. And there was more than one rock to encounter on the way up from that bottom—just as Rowling discovered.

I was still cleaning up the rubble of my life as I enthusiastically clung to idealism in building my financial planning practice. But this was yet another business with no guaranteed salary. It was kill or be killed. Every day required me to pull deep inside to harness the reserves of rugged individualism and drive that I had built up throughout my entire work life.

After two years I had managed to build a slightly below-average client portfolio at best. Most practices took over five years to reach a point of stability. I just didn't have the time to get there. The global financial crisis had hit, and things got worse. The auto belt was contracting. As went Detroit, so went Toledo. Clients were pulling money. And I couldn't pay my mortgage.

I worked harder during this time than ever. Appointments all day and most nights. But none of it was bearing enough fruit. Sales cycles were long. Times were wildly uncertain. And people were not willing to make decisions in this environment.

Eventually, the hard rock of mortgage default pushed me into new streams. It had been over a year. Something had to change. Instead of holding onto the rock and clinging to some hope of changing my current circumstances, I simply let go. I deliberately surrendered myself to the strong currents that were pulling me into new streams.

I began to spend less time on my financial planning practice. I pivoted energy toward resurrecting my record labels with new investment. I pulled the trigger on beginning to write my first novel. And I boldly followed through with the difficult decision to abandon our home. I just packed up the family and left Ohio. We moved back to Pennsylvania, where all of our family was, with nothing lined up. All three of these streams were pulling me as I hit the rock of mortgage default. And all three of them, in time, served to pull me into a better life that was unimaginable at the time—because I surrendered into them.

Entrepreneur Sara Blakely hit several small rocks in her life. These tiny rocks nudged her into new streams that aligned with her *calling journey*. Sara was on the path to becoming an attorney. But this path was blocked early on when she scored very low on the Law School Admission Test. This early warning sign was one of the rocks that Sara hit. It pushed her into new streams—none of which appeared to be in alignment with her *calling journey* at the time, if she had even identified what that was yet.

The first stream was to accept a job at Walt Disney World. This didn't last long. After three months, she was pulled into a new stream. The new stream was to go work for Danka selling fax machines door to door. Nothing in this job appeared to have anything to do with a *calling journey* for a dynamic, creative woman with an entrepreneurial instinct. She was a salesperson for technology that was drifting toward being obsolete. Yet she excelled at it and rose to become a national sales trainer.

Sometimes our *calling journey* pulls us into it strangely. Like my *Carl Moment*. This is what happened for Sara.

While she was hustling in the thick Florida heat, from office building to office building, pimping Danka's fax machines, Sara got increasingly dissatisfied with the appearance of the seamed foot of her pantyhose as she wore open-toed shoes. She did, however, like the way that the control-top model eliminated panty lines and made her body appear tighter and firmer.

So on one occasion when she attended a private party, she decided to experiment with the pantyhose by cutting off the feet. She wore them to the event under a new pair of slacks. She discovered that the pantyhose continuously rolled up her legs, but she still achieved the desired aesthetic result—she wore open-toed shoes without the eyesore of the seamed foot of the pantyhose.

This annoying, nagging trait of the pantyhose she wore was a small, jagged rock that pushed her into the roaring waters of her *calling journey* stream. It was the imperfection of her pantyhose that bridged her from being a fax machine salesperson to a female entrepreneurial role model.

Sara set out to solve the pantyhose problem with only the five thousand dollars she had in savings. It was the high value currency of her big idea that propelled her, not the limited value of her seed money.

She deployed that limited seed money to research and developed her new pantyhose idea. Then, she went out to sell that idea without any validation of the viability of her idea. Eschewing any permission slip, she drove to North Carolina, the epicenter of America's hosiery mills. She overcame rejection after rejection as she presented her idea to mill owner after mill owner. They were used to only dealing with established companies, not some random fax machine salesperson with an unproven idea. She went home, still, without any validation or interest in her idea.

Two weeks later she got a call. One of the male mill owners she presented her idea to decided not to rely on his own reactionary male opinion of a product designed for women. So he presented the idea to his three daughters. The feedback from them was overwhelmingly positive. The male owner listened to his daughters and offered to support Sara's idea. Over the course of the next year or so, a prototype was developed, a patent was filed, and Sara charged $150 to her credit card to trademark the name *Spanx*.

Sara bootstrapped her way into meetings with multiple national retailers, such as Neiman Marcus, Bloomingdale's, and Saks. Orders followed. Then she got Oprah's attention by sending a gift basket full of products. Oprah went on to name Spanx one of her favorite things in November 2000. By 2012, Sara was featured on the cover of *Forbes* magazine as being the youngest self-made female billionaire in the world.

Don't hold onto the rocks you hit along the wild ride of your *calling journey.* **Know when to surrender into the new streams that emerge to pull you into them. Don't judge a rock or a stream on its face—surrender to the stream with an open mind as to where it may take you. Detach your emotions from the pain inflicted by the rock. In that pain, remember the truth in Failure Rule #5:** *You Are Not Your Failures.* **Let that truth fill you with courage as you allow the new stream to carry you forth.**

J.K. Rowling had no idea that the pain of her divorce would set into motion a series of events that would enable her to finish a novel that would mesmerize the world. Sara Blakely's broken law school dreams and pantyhose problems never announced to her with certainty that they would push her into being the youngest self-made female billionaire in the world.

Let go of the rocks you hit and fall into the streams they push you into. Embrace the inertia of the new streams. Stay aligned with the tumultuous mystery of your *calling journey*.

THE NECESSITY OF SHAME

FOOD STAMPS SUCK AND GRATITUDE RULES

"I am for doing good to the poor, but...I think the best way of doing good to the poor, is not making them easy in poverty, but leading or driving them out of it."

—BENJAMIN FRANKLIN, FOUNDING FATHER, INVENTOR, AND PROPONENT OF EXERCISING NAKED

> **LESSON:** Should you ever fall into dependency, embrace healthy shame and gratitude simultaneously; then leverage both sensibilities to motivate your fight back to self-reliance.

There is room within the reality of **Failure Rule #5: You Are Not Your Failures** to feel healthy shame when it's necessary. If the shame originates from the health of your own conscience, ambition, and determination. And if the shame travels with an equal counterweight of genuine gratitude.

No one likes the feeling of not being able to fully hold their own. No one likes the feeling of not being able to personally meet all the ends needed to take care of their family. Or at least no one should. In times like this, constructive shame has its necessity.

The personal bankruptcy and the strategic mortgage default weren't the only sharp rocks I ran into. During this time, while working harder than ever, I eventually resigned to accepting public assistance for food. I had months without any income. I burned through all resources. I needed to feed my family. I resisted this for as long as I could.

I abhor the thoughtless abuse of government benefits. It should not be glorified or encouraged. Nor should it be advertised to make those who may qualify aware it exists. If you need it, you know it.

We were blessed to have many wonderful, generous people in our lives who helped with financial gifts during this time. Family, friends, and the church helped. Even in this, I felt deep, appropriate shame. I knew I needed to learn how to receive because it is, in and of itself, a gift to the giver to graciously receive with gratitude. I did that. But I still retained the necessity of shame.

This shame was powerful. This shame motivated me.

I believe in order for government to do less, free people need to do more. I want government to do less. Government should only regretfully fill the gaps left by the failures of free people to charitably help those around them. But in my circumstances, the gap was wide. The available charity was scarce. My income, variable as it was, continued shrinking. New opportunities were nowhere to be quickly found. Those who had helped me didn't have the means to help to the extent that was needed. So, I reluctantly allowed the government to help fill in the gaps.

I remember being petrified and paranoid when I would go to the grocery store. I feared that someone I knew would see me pulling out my EBT card—the modern access device that has replaced food stamps—when I would use it to buy food.

I remember, in between financial planning appointments with clients, going to the government building to fill out my assistance paperwork. I was the only one in a suit. I don't say this to contrast myself with others who were there in some condescending way. I actually hate wearing a suit. But it just made me stand out. It made me feel so conflicted inside. Here I was, still hustling every day and most nights, putting my suit on, and trying to make a living. But everything kept circling the drain, no matter how hard I tried to prevent it. My work ethic was in furious conflict with the shame of my circumstances. This drove me to keep fighting.

Ben Franklin was right. The best way to drive yourself out of poverty is to consciously feel and embrace the discomfort of your poverty. You must feel every ounce of shame that your situation produces. You must hate your life to reclaim your life. The best way for the poor to help themselves is to not allow themselves to feel any ease in their poverty.

Economist and philosopher Adam Smith said that *"entitlement is such a cancer because it is void of gratitude."* He is right. If you ignore the healthy shame that ought to accompany the receiving of public assistance, your attitude is cancerous. If you're receiving assistance and you actually view yourself as being entitled to it, your attitude is cancerous. If you find yourself in this horrible position, you need to embrace the truth that food stamps suck and gratitude rules. To have gratitude in this position, you need to embrace the necessary shame of your predicament. You need to leverage the discomfort of that shame to pursue self-reliance once again with a relentless ferocity.

However, if you find yourself in these circumstances, the only type of shame you need to recognize is the kind that emanates from within. Pay no mind to the impressions you make on others. Because **Failure Rule #5: *You Are Not Your Failures*** is true, you must ignore when others signal distaste, project low-resolution judgment, and succumb to short-sighted conclusion-jumping. Remember Stephanie Land? She knows this. Just as I had felt, she also felt the burning stares from shoppers at the grocery store when she would use her EBT card to access her government assistance to pay for food. She ignored the shallow judgment she felt being telegraphed by others, but she paid attention to the healthy shame and discomfort inside. The placism she endured motivated her. The shame and discomfort she experienced drove her to write cathartically about her struggles as a hard-working single mom on assistance. Those writings became the book *Maid: Hard Work, Low Pay and a Mother's Will to Survive*. It reached number three on the *New York Times* bestseller list in 2019. Stephanie's powerful story even got President Barack Obama's attention who hailed the book as *"a description of the tightrope many families walk just to get by, and a reminder of the dignity of all work."*

If you've found yourself dependent on the government or other people, you need to internalize your shame. Use your shame as fuel to drive yourself into a new direction, out of dependency. Don't let the deceptive hooks of the entitlement mentality anesthetize your ambition, your ingenuity, and your determination to nimbly reinvent yourself.

Roger Miret is the singer for the seminal New York hardcore punk band, Agnostic Front. He also has a solo career for which my record label, Sailor's Grave Records, released one of his albums entitled *My Riot*. In 2017, the documentary *Agnostic Front: The Godfathers of Hardcore*, appeared on Showtime. The documentary shines a light on the tumultuous *calling journey* of meaning that Roger has had in over thirty years of maintaining his *Thing Two* dream by touring the world and singing for Agnostic Front.

In 1986 Agnostic Front released a song on its second album, *Cause For Alarm*, entitled "Public Assistance." The lyrics were written by Peter Steele of Carnivore and Type-O-Negative. The song was a harsh criticism of welfare abuse. With a backdrop of fast, furious guitars led by barking vocals, the song indicts the entitlement mentality:

"You spend your life on welfare lines
Or looking for handouts
Why don't you go find a job?
You birth more kids to up your checks
So you can buy more drugs
Cash in food stamps and get drunk."

Miret, a working-class Cuban-born immigrant who struggled immensely with drugs and poverty himself, received a barrage of criticism for the song's lyrics within the punk rock scene and the media. Eighties talk show host Phil Donahue spoke out against it. Punk legend and front man for the Dead Kennedys Jello Biafra condemned it. It was heralded as racist. Even with Roger having a tattoo on his neck that reads "100% LATINO," his band was mislabeled as being a white supremacist band. Roger explained the song this way in an interview with *SLUG* magazine:

> I believe everyone should have public assistance that needs it; I have had public assistance myself, but where the song came from was when Vinnie and me both tried to get public assistance to go to the doctor. I was given care because I was Hispanic and he was turned down just because he was white. I just thought that was wrong. So we wrote this song about how screwed up that was, and the people that didn't get it called us racists for it.

Forever holding fast to his own beliefs, Roger never stopped singing the song. In 2016, at the Punk Rock Bowling Festival in Asbury Park, New Jersey, I watched Agnostic Front storm the stage singing "Public Assistance" with the same conviction and visceral aggression with which they had sung it thirty years prior. I was so struck by this performance that I described my experience and the context of this song being played for thirty years with the same conviction—despite the controversy—on an appearance I made on the *Wilkow Majority* radio show on Sirius XM in 2018.

Yet while the lyrics to "Public Assistance" clearly eviscerated the ingratitude of an entitlement mentality, as he explains in the *SLUG* magazine interview, Roger was not against accepting public assistance when used as a hand-up and received with a gratitude mentality. In his book *My Riot: Agnostic Front, Grit, Guts & Glory*, Roger recalls the pain of growing up in poverty. On many occasions with no food to eat, Roger and his dad would go to the park and set traps to capture pigeons. They'd lure them with crackers. Then they would capture them in their self-made contraptions of metal nets, which were made from twisted clothing hangers. After the pigeons were caught, Roger recalls:

> My mom cut off their heads, cleaned them and boiled them to disinfect them and remove the feathers. Then we had pigeon soup.

Roger recalls elsewhere in his book:

> We lived on welfare. We had food stamps and federal assistance because my mom was twenty years old and raising three kids by herself. She was embarrassed about taking money from the government, but we needed it.

Roger was able, through hard personal experience, to cultivate a view of public assistance that delineated between a thoughtless abuse earmarked by an entitlement mentality and a humble use of assistance that, coupled with the healthy power of self-generated shame, motivates one to get off of it. Roger goes on in his book to conclude:

> Say what you will about how corrupt and intrusive the government is, but we wouldn't have gotten by without the welfare system.

If you find yourself in the clutches of poverty and dependency, you need to embrace healthy shame while protecting your idealism. Feel the discomfort and unease of your life deeply and let that drive you with tenacity to claw your way back into self-reliance. Let the void of this lonely space trigger your imagination. Fantasize about your *Thing Two* dream. Like J.K. Rowling reimmersing herself into the theatre of her mind, where Harry Potter lived, to birth new art while she was entrenched in the lonely corridor of state dependency. Scheme your way into successfully building realistic *Thing One* enablers. *Hustle. Fight. Reinvent.*

It is in the disdain for your negative circumstances that you will discover the empowerment to escape them. And as you work your way to escaping poverty, exercise your gratitude muscle as much as possible.

The radical actions I had to take—abandoning my home in Ohio and moving the family to Pennsylvania with nothing but hope of a new day—were acts of fortitude in response to the writhing discomfort I felt in the grips of poverty. As time went on and these actions bore the fruit of renewed self-reliance and eventual abundance and prosperity, my gratitude muscle had become fortified with unbelievable strength.

I thank God every day for every tiny pleasure, every accessible privilege, and every blessing in my life. The life I have now—rich with meaningful work, intimate relationships, and strong financial prosperity—was entirely foreign, inconceivable, and seemingly unachievable years ago when I was nestled in rock-bottom poverty. I will never take it for granted. And I know it could be stripped away at any time by a wide array of events or the unique convergence of negative circumstances. Because nothing is safe.

If you find yourself in the grips of dependency, embrace the necessity of healthy shame while still understanding Failure Rule #5: *You Are Not Your Failures*. Leverage that shame as motivation to fight your way out of despondency. Be thankful and humble, and find joy—even in the midst of the terror produced by poverty-stained fear. Because being on food stamps truly does suck. And embracing gratitude under all circumstances truly does rule.

LEARN TO ACCEPT TRAGIC MORAL CHOICE

"Sometimes we have to choose between, not a good option and a bad option, but between two terrible options. I have been in this situation before when making decisions for my dad with his worsening dementia...Sometimes we have to pick the 'least worst option.'"

—VIKI KIND, MA, AUTHOR OF *THE CAREGIVER'S PATH FOR COMPASSIONATE DECISION MAKING*

> **LESSON:** Ready your mind for the time when you must choose the least bad option between two terrible options and then peacefully live with your choice.

Viki Kind is right. There are times in life when you must choose between two terrible options. The very conundrum presented in these times *feels* like failure, and your instincts may urge you to attach this feeling to your identity despite the truth of **Failure Rule #5: You Are Not Your Failures.** You must reject this feeling and instead wrestle with the reality that sometimes you don't have a good choice, and you don't have the choice to not choose at all. Instead, you are confronted with a tragic moral choice—a rigid binary option menu in which both choices suck. You then have to try to determine which option will suck less. And then you have to resolve to live with that decision with peace.

For Viki Kind, she had to evaluate what the least bad option was as she struggled to manage end-of-life care for her father, who suffered from a deteriorating condition of dementia. This is a very common example of a time in life in which tragic moral choice presents itself. This example extends also to animal lovers. When one has a pet encountering escalating end-of-life issues, contemplating a cost/benefit analysis seems cold, but it's just not that simple. The choice between potentially artificially extending a pet's life with a high probability of increased, but slightly delayed, diminishment is never easy. The number of variables at play that are uniquely different from situation to situation make such a choice between the least bad options very difficult. These types of choices stretch us morally. Yet the outcome is definitively tragic, regardless of your choice.

There is no real winning in tragic moral choice. Only less losing if you choose wisely. And then there is the process of loss management as you reorient your life and move forward.

Tragic moral choice also occurs in high-stakes political decisions. How many times have you heard someone say they voted for the lesser of two evils? How many times have you heard those people being judged by those who say that the lesser of two evils is still evil? Again, it's never that simple. The phrase "lesser of two evils" is often applied when evil is really not even in the mix—just two poor choices, according to one's opinion. And when one chooses not to choose at all in such a circumstance, they are still choosing. Their inaction still has an effect on the outcomes of the choice at hand.

You can't simply run from tragic moral choice when it presents itself. It will force you to have a say whether you like it or not.

During the Arab Spring of 2010, some political pundits argued that it would have been better to have kept Mubarak in power in Egypt—brutal and unpalatable as he was—than it would be to displace him with Morsi. They argued that Mubarak was the lesser of the two evils. Whether you agree with this opinion or not, this predicament is a clear example of tragic moral choice. Life will eventually bring you some version of tragic moral choice. You need to learn how to view it, make decisions within its limitations, and accept your choice with integrity and peace—even while acknowledging the imperfection of your decision-making abilities. And as you accept your tragic choice with peace, you must also accept the feeling of failure that accompanies it with a distinct detachment from your self-opinion. Because **Failure Rule #5: *You Are Not Your Failures*** is a necessary truth of life to internalize.

It was within a year after the Arab Spring, in which the people of Egypt faced a difficult tragic moral choice, that I was forced to deal with a tragic moral choice of my own. My business partner and I owned and operated an online lending shop with an office right next to a fitness center that we also owned and operated. The fitness center was purchased by the online lending business and was being supported by it as it was being rehabilitated. But the rehabilitation was too slow; the online lending shop was beginning to have trouble, and my partner was sentenced to prison for a mistake he had made in the mortgage business years prior. I was left running both businesses by myself. I was left to manage the tension that existed on the investor relations front. I was left to step back and evaluate what paths made sense to move forward. There were no good choices, only the choice between two terrible choices.

In this situation of tragic moral choice, I determined that shutting down the fitness center was the least bad option. There were approximately 900 members of the fitness center. Given the financial constraints of the circumstances, there was no path to appropriately compensate those members whose paid-up memberships would be severed. There was no way to avoid defaulting on a large commercial lease for the space. Yet shutting it down was still the least bad option.

The day that I pulled the plug on the gym was one of the most difficult days of my business life. My best friend, who was working with me at the online lending office at the time, stood by my side through it all. That evening, we went to what we called our "Camp David," named after the presidential country residence. It was a beautiful waterfront property on the Elk River in Maryland owned by my friend's father-in-law. We were given permission to spend the night there. I was in pain and deeply appreciated such a sheltering place of respite. I sought my exile on the Elk River. It involved lots of sorrow, bourbon, cigars, and emotional late-night conversation with a trusted friend.

The voicemail on my phone was full that evening. It was congested with threats, hate, and all varieties of vitriol. It was a mix of employees I had to let go, personal trainers who lost their 1099 gigs, and longtime members who wanted my head for closing what they thought would be their home gym for years to come. Each message filled me with sadness. Each message stung. And I understood the anger in each voice I heard. But I had made my decision. There was no damage control to be applied at this inflection point. I had to engage in impression management with a deliberate dereliction—by not managing it all.

I had to accept being hated and move forward.

The other choice would have been to allow the fitness center to cannibalize the already unsteady health of the online lending company. The other choice would have been to allow the fitness center to cause my primary income to be destroyed and my reputation with investors to become irreparable. The other choice would have caused an equal number of employees working for the online lending business to ultimately lose their jobs. If I had made that choice, it would also have eventually produced a fatal blow to the gym.

So I made the right decision. I made the best decision when confronted with an unavoidable tragic moral choice. I sought to do the least harm to the smallest number of people—amid circumstances where someone would be hurt regardless of what I chose. Any CEO who has initiated a reduction-in-force effort in order to save a company understands this type of difficult decision.

When tragic moral choice enters your life, you need to learn how to confront it head on. You need to objectively evaluate your two terrible options and resolve to find the least bad option. And you must reject coupling the feelings of failure that surround making such a decision with your self-worth. Because it will have been largely inevitable that the failure choice of facing two terrible options would confront you at some point, in some form. Because sometimes the best decision still leaves gaps, flaws, and collateral damage that cannot be avoided. And **Failure Rule #5:** *You Are Not Your Failures* will be there to give you proper perspective in that moment—so long as it is locked within you.

Learning to accept—and peacefully live with—your decision in the face of tragic moral choice is the height of difficulty. So prepare yourself before it visits you. Because chances are, at some point it will.

LANDMINE

"Every morning I jump out of bed and step on a landmine. The landmine is me. After the explosion, I spend the rest of the day putting the pieces together."
—RAY BRADBURY, AUTHOR OF *THE ILLUSTRATED MAN* AND *FAHRENHEIT 451*

LESSON: If your very Being feels like a landmine, know that you have the power to organize the chaos of each explosion you cause to shape new order that will synch you with your *calling journey.*

Many people awaken each day in a messy state of disarray that feels predisposed to failure. Many wake struggling to knit their minds together to face the day with cohesion. Because on some level all of our very lives are landmines laced with failure explosions ready to go off.

Yet **Failure Rule #5:** *You Are Not Your Failures* is true particularly when you are a hot mess. And its truth can help you pick up the pieces of each explosion you set off—large and small—day in and day out.

Actor Dwayne "The Rock" Johnson advises that you should strive to be the person that *"when your feet touch the floor in the morning the devil says, 'Aw shit, they're up.'"*

Some days I feel this way. But most days I wake up, slowly peel myself out of bed, desperately trying to remember what my day is supposed to look like. Then, I set foot on the crookedly placed area rug beside my bed and step on the landmine that is me. As Bradbury describes above,

I then spend the rest of the day putting all the pieces of that explosion back together again.

Most days, I wake up in an indiscriminate fog, struggling to shake off weird and often frightening dreams. I wake trying to decouple myself from a tornado of ambition, fear, insecurity, and irrational ego.

I am a landmine.

On right-focused mornings, I get my day started slowly by deliberately diving right into the tornado of thoughts and feelings that need to be confronted. The landmine has already exploded before I even get caffeinated. My first act of confronting the chaos of this daily explosion—the act of wakening to consciousness—is to try to tick off areas of gratitude in my mind. I reflect and I pray. Then I envision the overarching areas of my day that I want to shape and make an impact on. First and foremost, I make sure that I am ready to greet my wife each morning with a smile and tone of voice that she deserves to be greeted with. This is my first act of taming the beast that is me. Of stamping out the chaos created by the landmine that is simply me just waking up.

My second act of taming the chaos that lays waiting for me each morning is dealing with the mess collected in the kitchen sink. Dr. Jordan Peterson advises that one ought first to clean their room to kick-start their journey of chaos-taming. I suck at cleaning my room, and I hate it. So I do dishes.

Doing the dishes is my centering activity. It is the first accomplishment of the day. As I scrub and tame the cluttered chaos left by the previous evening's meal, I physically feel my body calm into an organized rhythm. My mind begins to ease into focus on what lies in the day ahead. I drink black coffee while I do it. The combination of the caffeine surge and the creation of kitchen sink order grounds me in the chaos-taming mindset I need to make it a great day.

Then I push forward into my workday, inspired by the chaos around

me. I'm inspired to ignite creativity and use it to shape chaos into order, to effectuate productized work output, to enhance significant relationships, and to enjoy the habitable newness that comes from birthing creation from disorder.

When my first marriage began to truly unravel, I embraced the creative, reshaping power of chaos.

My ex-wife had confessed she didn't love me many months prior. She said she wanted to work on the marriage and didn't want to give up. I stopped wearing my wedding ring during this time. I told her I'd begin wearing it again if she came to love me and could commit to our marriage definitively. She tried working on our marriage but admitted later, in a definitive outburst, that she was faking it.

It was during this strange marital wind-down period that my work life experienced some upheaval. The core stable piece of my income had gone away when I exited my position in the online lending partnership. I had replaced most of it with consulting income. I had other income too. We were by no means in any sort of immediate financial crisis. The income was high, but it was variable, and sustainability was an issue.

With me not having an office to go to each day, I was home. This upset the long-cultivated balance of separation my ex-wife enjoyed and I innocuously accepted and allowed. I worked all day and most nights. She took care of the kids, spent a lot of time in the gym, and governed every aspect of the home. This balance of separation was inherently unhealthy and was indicative of a dis-unified marriage. We both should have worked to untangle this, but we failed. When this balance was ultimately upset, it produced the optics and emotions of chaos.

My ex-wife leveraged this chaos to justify what she had long wanted to do, which was leave the marriage. She needed a compelling set of circumstances to pull the trigger, and this was it.

I chose to leverage the chaos differently. I decided that I could no longer cast pearls upon swine. There was nothing more I could do to try to save the marriage. The good faith efforts were not bilateral. I wished they were because I didn't want the divorce, but that was the reality. And I accepted it.

With that acceptance, I decided to confront the chaos with creativity and reshape it into a variety of new threads. This is when my online lead-generation company was born. It is when my banking career in the payments space was born. It is one of the periods in which my record labels were reignited with a vigorous stimulus plan. It is when I completed my first thriller novel and actively dove into that space by attending Thriller Fest in New York City.

The power of my chaotic circumstances drove me into a wonderful, creative reshaping of my work life and artistic output.

Journalist and high-school dropout Tim Pool's career was born in the sweaty chaos of the Occupy Wall Street protests of 2011. Tim had no college degree and no credentials. He grew up in a lower-middle-class household on the south side of Chicago. He had not finished his high school education, let alone acquired any higher education. He left high school at age fourteen.

He went to the Occupy Wall Street protests with the goal of capturing some meaningful unique moments in history. He livestreamed his experience with video and aerial drones. He let his viewers live chat with him while he did this, and he allowed their input to guide where he would position his shooting of the protests. The aerial drone he used was a toy remote-controlled Parrot AR Drone that he modified with software for livestreaming. He called this system DroneStream.

His footage attracted mass attention. No one had done this the way that he had. His drive and ingenuity—all catalyzed while he slept in the dirt amid the chaos of the protests—made a dent in journalism history. His footage was ultimately used as evidence leading to the acquittal of photographer Alexander Arbuckle, who was swept up and arrested by the NYPD during the protests. Pool's footage proved that the arresting officer lied under oath.

Pool confronted the chaos of his own bottom-floor career status by documenting the external chaos of the Occupy Wall Street protests with a bold, innovative act of unprecedented journalism. This ultimately blossomed into a multi-threaded career, including working for Vice Media and Fusion TV. He went on to be nominated as a *Time* 100 personality in March 2012. Pool leveraged the creative, reshaping power of chaos to ignite his *Thing Two* dream of performing unmistakable journalism.

Pool spoke a little bit about the ethos that drove him during an appearance on the Joe Rogan podcast. Pool and Rogan were discussing the flaws in the rigid notion that upper mobility was unachievable. While they both acknowledged that there would never be an equal set of cards dealt for everyone to launch their pursuits, they both agreed that one of the main ingredients of success was perseverance. They discussed that sometimes the motivation that birthed the perseverance that led to success was having been dealt a bad set of cards. Rogan asserted it this way: *"There's some benefit in being born with a shitty hand of cards."* As they continued to discuss, Pool shared how he was contacted often by people asking him how they could do what he did. He would walk them through the steps—many tedious and difficult—and most of them would reply with a litany of excuses for why they couldn't do that. They simply weren't willing to sacrifice their comforts to pursue the meaning that Pool pursued. Their current hand of cards was simply not shitty enough to motivate them.

When you find yourself amid the chaos of messy circumstances that appear like a hand of shitty cards, step back and look at them differently. Knowing Failure Rule #5: *You Are Not Your Failures* is true, remember that you are also not your messy circumstances. Use your creativity to find the reshaping opportunities within the chaotic cards you've been dealt. Use your ingenuity, and then, with applied perseverance, use the power of chaos to mold your life and circumstances into something new, different, and better than you may have previously conceived.

Your life—and your very Being—may be a landmine, just like mine is. But that doesn't mean you don't have the power to put the pieces together after each explosion with forward-enabling creativity. Day in and day out.

ACCEPT DIVISION IN FAILURE AND STAY GREAT

"The best art divides the audience: half love it and half hate it."
—RICK RUBIN, LEGENDARY RECORD PRODUCER

> **LESSON:** Sometimes you need to accept, even induce, division to forge forward with integrity as your authentic self as an entrepreneur or a creative.

As an *entrepreneur, creative, or person living out your authentic Being* in the world, you must understand that sometimes divisiveness is necessary. Sometimes division is healthy. Yet still, division will color your immediate circumstances with the failure optics of discord, schism, and uncertainty. And while it often colors circumstances with temporary failure, know that over the arc of time **Failure Rule #5: *You Are Not Your Failures*** will strategically place you outside of those colorings in those distinct moments when division is both necessary and healthy.

Division as a status is a dirty word. Divisive as a character assignment is an even dirtier branding. As a culture, we generally value those who unite. We value those who promote inclusion, not those who cause division.

Although unity and inclusion are important (and ideal) aspirations, they cannot be the highest values of one seeking an authentic life. Nor can they be the highest values of effective leaders. They cannot be the highest values of one seeking to adhere to the whispering of their *internal spirit voice*.

Sometimes, along the dusty, winding road of your *calling journey,* **you need to accept unavoidable division. Sometimes, you need to peacefully accept—even at times with a sense of accomplishment—when your actions, your art, your decisions, and your Being itself serves to divide.**

Aristotle was right about asserting that if one seeks to only avoid criticism then they will be destined to a life where they essentially *"do nothing, say nothing, and be nothing."* The same is true for one who only seeks to avoid being divisive. The artist who only fashions their work in alignment with the trends of the moment. The writer who avoids controversial topics and politically incorrect themes out of fear that their work will divide. The politician who waters down all conviction in an attempt to go along to get along. The business leader who is more concerned about how people feel about them than how their decisions shape the company for an optimized, clearly defined future that benefits all aligned employees, clients, customers, and shareholders.

Peacemakers, power brokers, diplomats, and those skilled at corralling stakeholder alignment are valuable. Their role in any family, organization, business, or social circle are of the utmost importance. Yet while this is a high value, it cannot be a higher value than right-decisioning, integrity alignment, and fidelity to soul-heavy authenticity. Sometimes your family members will come against you. Sometimes your employees will despise you. Sometimes portions of your leadership team will try to sabotage your vision. Sometimes your friends will abandon you for simply being your authentic self, evolving as it may be. And in some circumstances, it's imperative that you deliberately make difficult decisions to induce circumstances of division.

Make no mistake, division is *never* **a good goal. Unity, cohesion, harmony, and logical alignment should always be the goal. But blind**

agreeableness is never a good goal either. An excess of agreeableness is a trademark of weak, disrespected, and conflicted leaders. It is a trademark of spineless friends, fickle family members, and immature artists.

You need to be prepared to accept division as a possible, unavoidable result of your decisions, your pursuits, and your way of authentic Being. And in this acceptance, you must forge forward with right-decisioning, authentic living, and bold leadership knowing that you will likely need to contend with necessary divisiveness at some point along your *calling journey.*

The same man who advised *"blessed are the peacemakers"* also soberly posited to His followers, *"Suppose ye that I am come to give peace on earth? I tell you, Nay; but rather division."* (Luke 12:51–53) The same figure, whose name inspired how we named time, addressed the necessary division often created by the passionate. Jesus voiced His preference for a clear, extreme stance over hollow moderation by proclaiming, *"So, because you are lukewarm—neither hot nor cold—I am about to spit you out of my mouth."* (Revelation 3:15–17)

Great leaders divide as much as they inspire and unite. Great ideas destroy as much as they build. Great art agitates as much as it comforts. Legendary music producer, Rick Rubin, has cultivated an impressive client list of diverse artists built on this premise. He knows that lukewarm art is spit out, forgotten, and never becomes perennial. *"The best art divides the audience: half love it and half hate it,"* contends Rubin. This understanding has led him to help develop some of the most distinct, visceral, divisive, and perennial recordings ever.

Slayer. Kid Rock. The Red Hot Chili Peppers. Danzig. Johnny Cash. NWA. The Beastie Boys. Kanye West. Rage Against the Machine. Eminem.

What do all these artists have in common? Every single one of them has made an indelible, divisive mark on culture.

Those who love them, love them passionately, and often for decades or a lifetime. Those who hate them have often been driven to extreme opposition efforts—like aggressive campaigns by oppositional press, targeting by agenda-protective special interest groups, backlash by offended political movements, or outcry by blasphemed religious groups.

Even a quick scanning of the above list of artists elicits a multitude of feelings due to the conflicting ideologies and messaging represented from one to the other. Kid Rock and Rage Against the Machine emerged from two entirely different political and subcultural worlds—both pronounced and provocative. Slayer and Johnny Cash both represent entirely different worldviews on the value of faith and religion. Eminem and Kanye West couldn't be farther apart, as I write this, on their view of the sitting US president. Yet all of these artists have made profound lasting impact. Because great art divides. Because, with Rubin's guidance, these artists all valued authenticity over a fickle aim for unity and wholesale cultural acceptance.

Similarly, great leaders divide. Sure, they still often rightly aim for unity as their ultimate goal, but that never really materializes in reality. As great leaders pursue unity with boldness and authenticity, unavoidable division is still a piece of the natural result of their bold efforts. John McCain and John Kerry did not create an excess of division. Sure, they had fans and foes, like any other presidential candidate, but neither carried a large-scale passionate following. Both were generally nothing burgers in the eyes of voters on both sides. Both were lukewarm and were spit out at the ballot box. Donald Trump and Barack Obama, regardless of how you feel about either one of them, exuded strains of greatness that ignited passionate followings and resulted in unavoidable division. Most either love or hate them.

In my work as a banker, I witnessed the Churchillian decisiveness of a great leader who was not afraid to divide. The bank experienced a transition in its leadership by bringing in a new CEO in a time of trouble. The new CEO came on board with a distinct, well-cultivated, strategic vision for the company. This vision, by extension, applied also to the company culture.

In contrast to the old leadership that allowed deadwood to flourish, disorganized mediocrity to go unchecked, and undisciplined spending to be overlooked, the new CEO sought long-term unity and prosperity by first *dividing*. Everyone was given an opportunity to digest, internalize, and conform to his vision. They were given time. The vision was clear, documented, and constantly reinforced with enthusiasm. Those who stubbornly clung to the old mindset of mediocrity were either spit out by force or smothered into self-selected departure. Those who embraced the vision, leaned in to help achieve it, and were able to shed the old culture's mindset and instead embrace exceptionalism were retained. Those who embraced the new vision were not only merely retained, but they were also duly rewarded proportionately to their merit. The CEO's decision to accept unavoidable, temporary division for the sake of long-term unity and alignment resurrected the organization and restored the stock price. And those who have remained with the organization have never been more fulfilled and inspired.

An entrepreneur must accept the possibility of unavoidable division hand in hand with an acceptance of the possibility of unavoidable failure.

When I walked away from my partnership in the online lending firm—causing the appearance of financial instability—unavoidable division followed. Division within my own family. And division within the social sphere attached to the family.

My marriage, already in a tenuous, splintered state, accelerated to a state of complete division. I resolved to accept this as an unavoidable division resulting from my right-made decision. I accepted this as a condition of temporary pain. I believed the pain would subside over time and that Providence would yield to me a better, more unified future.

This core, painful marital division naturally led to my divorce. My divorce, like many divorces, led to a division of opinions on the event within my family and among my friends. And within my wife's family and among her circle of friends. Neighbors who fell on her side of the divide looked at me with disdain. Others on both sides of the divide voiced their opinions with sympathies and judgments distributed indiscriminately between both my ex-wife and me.

Difficult decisions made within the confines of a clear mind and a good conscience sometimes lead to division. And you need to prepare to accept this division with peace.

Heartland Payment Systems is an independent sales organization in the credit card merchant acquiring payment space. Heartland's founder, Bob Carr, had to accept a similar division in his life. In his early years as an entrepreneur, failures cascaded around him with no redemptive lifeboat available to save him from drowning. In his book *Through the Fires: An American Business Story of Turbulence, Triumph, and Giving Back*, Bob describes his predicament in those early days this way:

> Ambitious business ideas have fallen short. Unpaid bills have piled up. Credit cards have been cancelled. Bill collectors have come after me for house payments.

Much like my own experience, Bob's indivisible entrepreneurial constitution led to marital failure. His wife's support for his authentic nature was dependent on the maintenance of favorable economic and material circumstances. Bob laments the unavoidable division he encountered as follows:

> After I struck out on my own, charging toward an uncertain future, Susan grew disenchanted, and then disapproving. As a fledgling entrepreneur, I worked hard for big success, but often came up empty. In 1975, she finally gave up on me. We separated the following year.

Bob learned to accept this painful division. But he never stopped listening to his *internal spirit voice* that urged him to remain faithful to his entrepreneurial nature. Bob deeply understood the truth of **Failure Rule #5:** *You Are Not Your Failures.* Years later, Bob founded Heartland

Payment Systems, remarried, and grew the company wildly. While he later encountered fierce failure in the form of a colossal data breach (a failure he overcame), the company at one point grew from the sixty-second largest payment processing company to the sixth. Bob's personal net worth, in large part due to his shares in the company, was valued at over $300 million. He had become wealthy beyond his imagination. And he bought and lived in President Woodrow Wilson's house to boot.

If, like Bob, you've worked hard for big success but have come up empty, keep working. Keep listening to your *internal spirit voice*. Keep pursuing the path of your mysterious, tumultuous *calling journey* of meaning. If your actions, decisions, failures, and ideas have resulted in division, learn to accept this as a necessary component of living out your authentic self with integrity.

Live your life *hot*—or you will be spit out into a bland, mediocre, lukewarm existence. Do this or be cursed to a life marked by neither messy failure nor sparkling success. By neither the thrill of big thinking nor the pain of broken dreams.

Like great art, leaders, ideas, and movements, everyday great people also sometimes divide. Accept division as you make difficult decisions. Accept division in your failure. And stay great.

THE POWER OF FAILURE HUMOR

"I told my psychiatrist that everyone hates me. He said I was being ridiculous—everyone hasn't met me yet."

—RODNEY DANGERFIELD, COMEDIAN, DIVORCEE, VICTIM OF ANTI-SEMITIC BULLYING, AND ALUMINUM SIDING SALESMAN

> **LESSON:** Cultivate an insightful, playful, and self-deprecating sense of humor in times of failure and let it ease the tension of your hard times.

If you seriously believe in the freeing power of **Failure Rule #5:** *You Are Not Your Failures,* then you will also freely learn to laugh at your failures. If you know that *You Are Not Your Failures,* your spirit will be seriously lifted as you take your failures less seriously.

My uncle used to constantly snap into Rodney Dangerfield impression mode at every holiday gathering. He had many of Rodney's brilliant off-the-cuff-sounding one-liners down pat. He would deliver them with much of the same self-deprecating, blue-collar swagger that Rodney had perfected. My uncle fits the bill of an archetypal Rodney Dangerfield fan—retired detective, military veteran, working-class salary, blue-collar ethos, divorced twice, and always feeling a day late and a dollar short.

My uncle had been known for driving half-tracks—a vehicle that is half army tank and half truck—in his backyard and through his neighborhood. He would romp around the yard and the neighborhood in the half-track, to the chagrin of his neighbors, while chewing tobacco, throwing M80s and cursing at his dog just for shits and giggles. This is but a glimpse into his irreverent way of living. He was also a huge Rodney Dangerfield fan and regularly impersonated Rodney. Impersonating Rodney wrapped his whole persona together just perfectly.

Yet even in his rough ways, he was always smiling, happy to see people, and eager to give anyone who would listen a comedic update on the misery that he claimed was his life. For years at Thanksgiving, I would ask him how he was doing, and he would always offer the same response. He would swing his neck quickly, get right in my face, exaggerate his facial expression like Rodney, and tell me, *"Kid, you don't wanna know."*

My uncle used failure humor—inspired by Rodney's quintessential failure humor style—as a mechanism to process and minimize the failures in his life. This is an important and powerful skill that can help you lighten the emotional load of failure as you traverse through it.

When my financial planning practice was failing and I couldn't pay the mortgage, I immersed myself in failure humor as a healthy defense mechanism to pull me through the difficulties of that time. I became obsessed with the comedy of Denis Leary. This was several years after the TV show *Rescue Me* on FX was released. Denis Leary's character in that show, Tommy Gavin, resonated with me deeply. He was a post-9/11 alcoholic firefighter in New York City struggling with the reality of his family falling apart. I found myself binging on that show, going back and watching old episodes over and over. I internalized much of the sharp failure humor instincts that drove the show. I began subconsciously adopting them in my own life. This helped me tremendously as I navigated many similar relationship issues that the fictional character of Tommy Gavin struggled with in the show.

I remember talking with my brother on the phone around this time. I was in a low place. Yet when we spoke, I had him laughing hysterically at my ironic self-deprecating, comedic positivity. I had listed off all the horrible circumstances in my life and finished my commentary by advising him my next career move was to figure out how to join the Somali pirates. I told him that if a nine-year-old in flip-flops can man an AK-47 and figure out how to properly rob and pillage, why can't I? Hanging and banging on the high seas seemed like a growth industry to me. My brother couldn't believe that I could joke and make fun of myself in such stressful times.

The power of failure humor strengthened me as I walked through hard times. Sometimes you need to take yourself less seriously in order to seriously put your life back together.

Comedian Bill Burr knows this. He's constantly funneling his own battles with his childhood-driven temper and anger into comedic stand-up masterpieces. His bits not only give him an outlet to make fun of himself, but the process of him converting his issues into humor actually forces him to look at himself and his issues honestly. In an interview on the Joe Rogan podcast, Bill described how he goes to therapy in order to actively work on unraveling the root causes of his reactionary temper outbursts.

Developing an instinct for failure humor can force you to take an overdue high resolution look at yourself, so you can evolve into a better you.

My best friend is a master at failure humor. While he grew up to be a master cigar salesman, humor has always been the sharpest tool in his kit—one that has made him the top salesman for his company year in and year out. He learned this skill early on in life. When we were kids, from six years old all the way through high school, my friend was a target for bullies. He was overweight (back then, but not now), and he is an Arab. These two factors, in a largely white suburban area, did not help him assimilate well into the social fabric. Mostly it was the jocks coming after him. But when we were really young, there was also one skate punk hooligan who gave him hell—*me*. It only took a few months of my picking on him before he made me laugh so hard with every audacious comeback—usually directed at himself—that I couldn't help but want to be his friend. He would literally laugh and revel in every insult flung at him. He truly loved the art of the insult and was happy and honored to have them directed at him. You can't bully someone like that. You just end up their friend. It was this ability to utilize failure humor to his advantage that helped my friend win over bully after bully, year after year, one laugh at a time. Like the time he busted out the Curly shuffle—the wild floor-sweeping dance move originated by Curly of the Three Stooges—in the high school lunchroom, on demand, as instructed by a bully's orders. Days later that bully became the protector bodyguard against any other bullies who dared to mess with my friend.

There is no one who has perfected the use of failure humor more than Rodney Dangerfield. Long before he joked about being in such bad physical shape that his body ought to be donated to science fiction, Rodney Dangerfield was clinically depressed, divorced, and suffering from meaning deficit as a fledgling aluminum siding salesman.

Rodney was bullied when he was younger for being Jewish. He was the constant butt of cruel anti-Semitic jokes. Most of the kids picking on him came from affluent families—a fact that explains a lot about Rodney's failure humor that often focused on contrasting working-class folks with the wealthy upper class. Rodney never had the luck of being born with affluenza. His father, Phil Roy Cohen, was a comic too. He was also a juggler and toured the vaudeville circuit. However, while comedy was clearly in the genes, Rodney never had the privilege of absorbing any of his father's talents firsthand. His father abandoned the family shortly after Rodney was born, leaving Rodney's mother to raise two kids on her own.

To cope with the pain of being tormented by his bully classmates for being Jewish, Rodney began writing jokes. Like my best friend, Rodney figured out early on that sometimes the best way to traverse through the pain of being bullied is to use the power of failure humor. By age seventeen, Rodney was performing on amateur nights at various clubs. By nineteen, he was performing comedy full time.

But real life snuck up behind Rodney and slowly muzzled his *internal spirit voice*. He met singer Joyce Indig, fell in love, and settled down in the garden state to start a family. His full-time comedy pursuit was relegated to the rearview as putting food on the table emerged largely in the windshield forward view. This is when he began selling aluminum siding to make a living.

While Rodney's new life suppressed his *internal spirit voice*, it didn't kill it. His *Thing Two* dream of being a full-time comedian didn't go away. The *internal spirit voice* kept nudging him. His *internal spirit voice* broke through the fog created by the depression he suffered and the marriage issues he came to struggle with.

For a decade or more, he scribbled jokes down between appointments selling aluminum siding and paint. He did this diligently while continually processing the deterioration of his marriage and dealing with his clinical depression. Yet neither the depression, the failing marriage, nor the unfulfilling job managed to fully kill the *Divinity of Purpose* that bubbled up inside of Rodney and called him into a life of comedy. Rodney acted on his belief in **Failure Rule #5: *You Are Not Your Failures*** by resurrecting his pursuit of his *Thing Two* dream.

As Rodney grappled with the failures of his life, his *internal spirit voice* was urging him to embrace comedy. That voice continued to get louder and louder. Rodney eventually listened to it and began doing stand-up at night while still selling aluminum siding by day. His act was fully marked by his distinct brand of failure humor. His jokes were replete with comedic takes on bad marriages, references to absentee parenting, and stereotypes of the downtrodden working man.

Rodney would inadvertently poke at his upbringing when he would tell a story about when he was a child and lost his parents at the beach. He would recall that he asked a policeman, *"Do you think we'll ever find them?"* *"I don't know,"* came the reply. *"There's so many places they could hide."*

He would jab at the topic of bad marriages when he would confess that his wife had cut sex "down to once a month." He would add, *"I'm lucky. Two guys I know she cut out completely."*

In the classic film *Easy Money,* Rodney contrasts the lifestyle of a working-class slob with an upper-class snob. In one scene, the slob, Monty Capuletti (played by Rodney) is being chewed out by the snob—his rich, judgmental mother-in-law. She tells him, "You pollute the air with your smoking. You reek of liquor and God knows what else. You're an ecological menace!" Monty's response? "Yeah? Well, you were the inspiration for twin beds!"

Rodney also had an appreciation for the *wabi-sabi* elements of life. Again, in *Easy Money*, there is a subtle storyline around the walkway at Monty's home that he just never got around to fixing. The tiny failure of Monty's domestic life helped craft a profile of a working-class guy who was less concerned with the maintenance of material things and more concerned with maximizing his experiences with his friends and family—albeit punctuated with the everyday excesses of working-class vice. In this, it was a small piece of *wabi-sabi* embedded in the art of the film. The broken walkway was a perfect additive to the story of Monty Capuletti's life. Monty's life was *wabi-sabi*. It was perfect because it was a little fucked up.

All of Rodney's bits were failure humor at its best. Yet somehow in Rodney's therapeutic indulgence in failure humor, he was still able to think big and pull himself out of the drudgery of colorless living and into the rich color of his *calling journey*. In one scene from the classic film *Back to School*, Thornton Mellon (played by Rodney) is chastising his son for focusing on small things, like organizing his room. Thornton tells his son, "You're always so neat. You're just like your Uncle Vito. We were kids, his room was always in order. His towels lined up neatly... combs, brushes, hair lotions all in the right place. What did it mean? What is he today? He's an attendant in the men's room."

Holding unmerited fidelity to some honor notion attached to selling aluminum siding to hold down a regular guy life was small thinking to

Rodney. To him, it was like keeping your room nice and neat while the chaos of the larger, outside world remained untouched by the magic of his comedic talents. Indeed, to Rodney, selling aluminum siding was like Uncle Vito being an attendant in the men's room. It was a product of small thinking. So after years of selling siding, Rodney finally listened fully to his *internal spirit voice*. He left the safety of his proverbial clean room of small thinking and charged forth with big thinking into the untamed outside world of comedy.

At forty-five, Rodney got his first big break—an appearance on the *Ed Sullivan Show*. By age forty-seven, he was a guest on the Johnny Carson show. It was the first of sixty-three appearances. By age fifty-eight, Rodney had released a comedy album, landed his first starring role in a Hollywood film, and was emerging as a comedy icon for his blue-collar failure humor.

Rodney spent his life wrestling with the impressions of others. He used his gift of failure humor to rise above the anti-Semitic bullying he endured as a kid. He converted the failures and rejections that persisted in his life into brilliant comedy that has blessed and inspired multiple generations of fans.

If you're grappling with the messiness of failures—whether it's being bullied, going through a divorce, or being stuck in a meaningless job—remember Rodney. Take Failure Rule #5: *You Are Not Your Failures* **seriously as you take your failures less seriously. Remember the power of failure humor. Find a way to use it to ease the tension of your life as you work to reshape your life.**

You may feel like you get no respect now, but like Rodney, that doesn't have to stay that way forever.

BE UNMISTAKABLY AUTHENTIC

"You are the final authority on your life. You are the CEO...when you realize that failure does not really matter. The funny thing is that nothing matters as much as you think it does when you realize you are the final authority. So much of what we think matters is based on the opinions of other people... Worrying about what other people think is a jail of our own creation, and the irony of it is those people are in the same jail with us."

—SRINIVAS RAO, PODCASTER AND AUTHOR OF
THE ART OF BEING UNMISTAKABLE

> **LESSON:** You—and only you—are the final earthly authority on the meaning of the failure events of your life.

Part of accepting **Failure Rule #5:** *You Are Not Your Failures* is realizing that you are the only real true earthly judge of your failures anyway.

I'm going to take you back again to the life of Srinivas Rao now. Long before Srini appeared on Netflix's *Indian Matchmaking* in search of a suitable marital match, he had been consistently unveiling the back stories of unmistakable creatives who are great at doing bizarre and unusual things. From bank robbers to billionaires, Srini has been building a repository of fascinating, inspiring, and insightful stories through his podcast *The Unmistakable Creative* for over a decade.

Like many of Srini's podcast guests, he stumbled awkwardly into his *calling journey*. Srini's calling is marked by the true north of his *Thing*

Two dream of being a full-time *solopreneur* creative. He stumbled toward his *Thing Two* in large part by walking through various iterations of failure as a misfit corporate tech employee.

In his book *The Art of Being Unmistakable*, Srini details, with candid vulnerability, his experiences as a misaligned employee struggling with his ability to understand or conform to the expectations of corporate culture. In those days, he had fashioned his life around the external values he had been inculcated with: *building impressive education credentials, achieving a high salary, and creating an impressive persona of accomplishment*. He was sure to develop these both on paper in his resume and socially in the image he projected to others.

Yet as he chased the benchmarks that aligned with these hollow external values, he felt anything but accomplished, inspired, or free. The values he had embraced and the corporate pursuits they caused him to follow left him confronting persistent anxiety. There were many underlying root causes to this condition. He suffered horrible leadership under irrationally abusive bosses. He was reassigned from project to project after investing his passion on them, only to never see them come to fruition by his guided hand. This left him unfulfilled and feeling as if his work product was constantly undervalued and discarded. On top of all of this, his very body rejected his choice to ignore his *internal spirit voice* calling him to the more off-road, entrepreneurial life of a creative. The incongruence between his external life and his *internal spirit voice's* yearning manifested in a chronic case of irritable bowel syndrome.

Srini had conformed to society's linear trajectory expectations of *college → grad school → corporate ladder climbing → happiness*? He fell into the trap of this lie in part because he didn't view himself as someone destined for doing anything great, unique, or remarkable. In *The Art of Being Unmistakable*, he confesses that his greatest sin was that he wasted much of his life because he never believed he was capable of something great.

Like Srini, I believe this condition is ubiquitous. So many people suppress dreams and ideas because of the messages they hear all around them about what is realistic, achievable, and "makes sense" for their lives. The tired, visionless opinions of those around us often choke out our *internal spirit voice*. And when we fight against that current, we often battle the false impressions and unspoken criticism of those around us.

Only you know what the notion of doing something great means to you. For some, it may be that doing something great actually is thriving and carving out an unmistakable path in a corporate environment—I have derived a great deal of fulfillment through pushing this as a large piece of my output life. For Srini, he had to go off-road, abandon the corporate world altogether, and find the amplification of his *internal spirit voice* through his love of surfing. He had fled his corporate life in an act of authentic rebellion to the societal pressure he had succumbed to. Yet in this authentic rebellion, he was finally aligning himself with the *Divinity of Purpose* inside pulling him into the life of a creative. He leveraged his abundant luxury of free time to dig deep. He combined this leveraged luxury with his renewed love of surfing—and the metaphoric value it brought to his *calling journey*—to center him into the *Divinity of Purpose*. When he was out in the ocean with nothing but his board and his thoughts, he could hear his *internal spirit voice* clearly. And he listened to it.

During this transitional time of traversing from corporatism to calling, he struggled through poverty, occupational displacement, and temporarily having to contend with relying on his parents for a place to stay. But after the optics of failure subsided, Srini found traction on the path that would truly set him apart with unique greatness—something he never thought possible when he was mired in corporate malaise. Over time, he has become a prolific podcaster, author of multiple books (including a *Wall Street Journal* bestseller), and a prominent public speaker.

Like Srini, there have been many times when I had to enact radical, dangerous change in my life in order to align with my *internal spirit voice* and stay on the path of my *calling journey*. Like Srini, sometimes these changes induced financial hardship, caused relationship strains, and produced impressions of failure within the perceptions of those around me.

Early on in my career as a banker in the payments space, I ran into a colleague in the stairwell. I had heard that he had, like Srini, enacted radical change in his life because he was convicted to follow his *internal spirit voice*. He had decided to put in his resignation at the bank so he could buy a one-way ticket to Syria to pick up arms and fight alongside the Christian Kurds who were being targeted by ISIS. I asked him about his decision, and he quietly responded with a voice of heartfelt conviction that he had never felt more strongly about anything in his entire life. For him, this radical act of abandoning a known and comfortable life was exactly what his *internal spirit voice* was calling him to do. So he listened to that voice and set into motion an abrupt reorganization of his life.

If you find yourself boldly reorganizing your life with attendant risk to align your actions with the directives of your *internal spirit voice*, remember that you are the CEO of your life. As Srini explains in this chapter's anchor quote, failure does not really matter when you understand that you are the final earthly authority on your life. It does not matter because Failure Rule #5: *You Are Not Your Failures* will help free you. You know the difference between the appearance of failure due to temporary optics and the security of fulfilling success based on soul-driven decisions.

Learn from the unmistakable *calling journey* of Srinivas Rao. Follow your *internal spirit voice* regardless of how many failures and rejections litter that path. Accept **Failure Rule #5:** *You Are Not Your Failures.* Know that you are the earthly CEO of your life—including the failures of your life. Remember that as CEO of your life, you get to decide how to best view your failures—no one else.

EVERY DAY YOU CAN RE-SKETCH YOUR LIFE

"By the time I was thirty, nobody would work with me. I was friendless, I was hopeless, I was suicidal, lost my family—I mean, it was bad. Bottomed out, didn't know what I was going to do."

—GLENN BECK, RADIO PERSONALITY, AUTHOR, ENTREPRENEUR, AND SELF-PROCLAIMED DIVORCED, ALCOHOLIC MORMON

> **LESSON:** Every day you have the opportunity to re-sketch the story of the rest of your life—despite your failures—because Failure Rule #5 is the truth: *You Are Not Your Failures.*

Failure Rule #5: *You Are Not Your Failures* frees you to re-sketch your life after each failure event.

Sometime shortly after 9/11, talk radio host Glenn Beck expressed on the air how all he wanted was a Jack and Coke. He described in detail the Tennessee whiskey pouring over ice and the dash of Coca-Cola splashing perfectly atop the amber liquid. After the attacks, the times were instantly altogether strange. Globally, times were stressful. Personally, times were jarring for those in tune with the coming zeitgeist the terror attacks produced. This new reality vortex made Beck want nothing but a Jack and Coke. You see, Beck's yearning for a stiff drink was a triggered response that harkened him back to his failure days. He hadn't always lived and shined in a state of stability and distinct public recognition. Long before Beck built an alt-media empire and became known as the right's answer to Oprah, he was a dismal hot mess.

Beck was first a deejay who experienced a modicum of success. The success inflated his ego and shattered any sense of humility within him. He confessed that in those days he viewed the Mercedes logo as one of the defining symbols of his life because it represented his twisted idolatry of material achievement and worship of success superiority. I have been driving Cadillacs now for about ten years. I have a beautiful tattoo of a Cadillac symbol on my calf for different reasons. For me, it is a symbol of grit, hustle, and the American bootstrap ethos. I have the word "Hustle" tattooed in script below it. For me, the luxury car symbol of Cadillac is about spirit. In contrast, for Beck at that time, the Mercedes symbol was akin to some insecure mark of upper-class separation. In those days of Mercedes worship, Beck recalls being put together and successful on the outside but an absolute mess on the inside.

Beck's success in his deejay days didn't last forever. Eventually, his addictions, his hidden depression, and the awful way he treated people caught up with him. He recalled that he once fired someone for bringing him the wrong pencil. He dabbled with cocaine use, once describing waking up with blood all over his face wondering what the hell he was doing with his life. He was drunk every day, although he congratulated himself for waiting until five o'clock. For Beck, the alcohol muted his pained spirit and quieted the inner cry of his suicidal depression. He was a happy drunk, he has often explained. He even notes that it was easier for him to be a good father when he was drunk because he could slow down his thoughts and temperament to be more present with his children than when he was sober. But the alcohol could only hide the root cause of his soul crisis for so long. His relationships ended up collapsing. His work deteriorated, and he eventually found himself falling down the success ladder, getting divorced, and contending with near poverty.

Around this time Beck recalled an incident when he was driving over a bridge listening to the grunge band Nirvana on the radio. Depressed, he was trying to muster the courage to just drive off the bridge and end it all. Thankfully, he didn't find that courage. But the depravity inside didn't go away. His life continued to unravel. He found himself living in a dingy apartment. He was near broke and was unable to afford Christmas presents for his kids.

This is when Beck's pivot point began emerging. He was struggling with the gripping feeling *that he was his failures*. He hadn't yet learned **Failure Rule #5:** *You Are Not Your Failures.* As Beck embraced introspection amid his exiled isolation from his family and meaningful work, he vowed to reorganize his life in a way that would allow him to reclaim his severely tarnished good name. He committed himself to change his life, so it was clear from that point on that he was *not* his failures.

There was no fairy dust in Beck's dingy apartment that he sprinkled on himself to make this happen. It took years. One measurable, sustainable change at a time. He had to deconstruct and meticulously discard old thinking so new thinking could thrive. Big pivot moments emerged over time. He met his current wife, Tanya. They both converted to Mormonism. He shifted his broadcast career from music deejay to talk. Strong relationships, both personal and professional, began building again.

Beck had stayed off the drink, found a good woman, discovered his spirituality, and refocused his career. He proved that every day we all have the opportunity to re-sketch our life. He proved that if we do that wisely, we can regain our good name and recreate our life. He proved that *we are not our failures,* **unless we sadly choose to be.**

It was in the empty, hollow space of failure that Glenn began following his *internal spirit voice*. It was in the disheveled mess of failure that he recognized the *Divinity of Purpose* and united with his *calling journey* to seek truth in the world, in himself, and to communicate that widely to willing hearts and minds.

Today, Beck has not only become one of the most prominent right-leaning Libertarian political voices but also a champion of self-empowerment messaging, entrepreneurialism, and Judeo-Christian thought. He was a first mover in the creation of a strictly online streaming network with his channel, *The Blaze*. The channel has hosted shows by well-known political personalities, such as Mark Levin, Steven Crowder, Phil Robertson, Dave Rubin, Andrew Wilkow, Jason Whitlock, and others. Guided by consulting input from Peter Thiel, his approach to creating *The Blaze* was heralded and studied by Silicon Valley tech companies as the model for the future of TV viewing long before that prediction became true with the now-achieved ubiquity of cable cutting. On top of all of this, Beck has had *New York Times* bestselling books in a variety of genres: *world history, political commentary and opinion, dystopian fiction, holiday fiction, political thrillers, and spiritual self-help.*

It is in the last listed genre, spiritual self-help, that Beck co-wrote a book with bestselling author and former psychiatrist Keith Ablow titled *The 7: Seven Wonders that Will Change Your Life*. It is in this book that Beck reveals the failure stories of his life and the principles that helped him make sustainable changes. Beck and Ablow identify seven principles, which they call wonders, that they assert to be key for one to achieve a self-directed radical life transformation.

Glenn Beck learned how to boldly re-sketch his life. With the stains of serial failures now long in his past, his media reach has grown to be vast, controversial, and divisive. Because greatness divides. Regardless of whether Beck leaves you hot or cold, he is indisputably a prime example of someone who followed his *internal spirit voice* to guide him out of rock-bottom failure. His monumental pivot proves the truth of **Failure Rule #5:** ***You Are Not Your Failures.***

DEVELOP BULLDOG TENACITY AND CREATE SOMETHING OUT OF NOTHING

"When I die I want people to look at my tombstone and to say, 'That was a crazy motherfucker who gave a shit. He liked the music, and he wanted to win.'"

—TONY BRUMMEL, FOUNDER OF VICTORY RECORDS

> **LESSON:** You don't need to come from wealth or have a stacked resume, a college degree, or substantial seed money to actualize your *Thing Two* dream; bulldog tenacity and vision can often suffice.

Never forget **Failure Rule #5:** *You Are Not Your Failures.* And never forget that no matter how resourceless you find yourself in your failures, you *can* rise up and create something out of nothing. But you may need to develop some bulldog tenacity to do it.

Eric Weinstein and his brother Bret coined the phrase intellectual dark web (IDW). The phrase refers to an eclectic group of informal, self-rising pundits who transcend tribal thought, identify as being politically homeless, and hold reason and curiosity above partisanship. Eric is also the managing director of Thiel Capital, the investment firm founded by billionaire Peter Thiel. During an appearance on Joe Rogan's podcast (a fellow member of the IDW), Eric explained the concept of *"the corporate end of rebel and the rebel end of corporate."* I found this phrase curious and thought of several music entrepreneurs who might fit into this interesting dichotomy.

Jamey Jasta, singer for Hatebreed, fits well into the corporate end of rebel. He is primarily a rebel singer for a hardcore metal band. Yet, he has embraced mechanisms of corporatism to help his band ascend—becoming the host of the Headbanger's Ball on MTV2, building a network that landed his band a slot on Ozzfest, launching a podcast, starting a record label, and marketing a clothing line. He is rebel first and corporate by necessity.

Tony Brummel, founder of Victory Records, is the rebel end of corporate. He built the largest independent record label, brick by brick, with the strategic mind of any great corporate CEO. But he did it with the heart of an authentic, tenacious rebel who was out to prove what was possible for a guy who never graduated college or received any seed money. Reread the anchor quote with Tony's words at the top of this chapter and you'll get a flavor of the type of rebel spirit who hangs at the end of his corporatism.

Long before our money read *In God We Trust*, it read *Mind Your Business*. Go Google (actually, use Duck Duck Go instead) the Fugio cent. And long before Tony Brummell spent his free time hanging out with his pet goats, affectionately named Angus and Lemmy (nods to AC/DC and Motorhead, respectively), he had been carefully minding his business ever since he left home at age seventeen. Tony's success was born out of sheer passion for hardcore punk and alternative rock music. He followed that passion early on with an unbridled tenacity, embracing a rugged bootstrap ethos that is remarkable. Tony recounts the early startup days in an interview for Absolutepunk.net:

> I think there are a lot of people that lack originality and don't do their own thing. I think what would make things better is if people just stopped worrying about what everybody else was doing and just worried about their own world…I don't have a degree. I've never

had a resume. I don't come from a rich family. I started Victory Records with eight hundred bucks.

Tony has always been an original. With no college degree and eight hundred dollars, he created a large something out of virtually nothing. He carved his own path, minding his business, without worrying about what everybody else was doing. In this, Victory was one of the first hardcore punk labels to embrace the subgenre of emo. Emo is a more melodic, soft derivative of punk with less abrasive vocals and highly personal and emotional lyrics, themes, and visual messaging. Having been built with a strong roster of tough, masculine-centric metallic hardcore acts, such as Hatebreed, Blood for Blood, and Buried Alive, Victory's move to a softer, more nuanced subgenre like emo was seen as a traitorous departure from the original aesthetic of the label. Victory found itself being called the "hair and makeup" label. Tony was seen as selling out.

Yet true to his independent spirit, Tony never let such accusations bother him. He went on to develop groundbreaking emo acts such as Hawthorne Heights, Thursday, and Taking Back Sunday. This elevated Victory into soaring new heights as the dominant label in independent music. Victory has sold over fifteen million albums over the last thirty years and earned six Recording Industry Association of America (RIAA) certified gold albums, six RIAA certified gold singles, and one RIAA certified platinum single.

Tony's story is not a failure story. The lesson in Tony's business life narrative is one of failure prevention by adhering to the *internal spirit voice* and staying on an independent path, despite all criticism. And it's one to remember if you find yourself resourceless amid a failure phase of your journey. For thirty years, right up until Tony sold Victory Records to Concord Records in 2020 for a $34 million exit, he deliberately ignored the impressions of others as he aggressively built an iconic catalog full of perennial hardcore, metal, punk, and emo titles. Tony did this with a relentless, determined drive that is captured perfectly in the label's emblematic logo—a bulldog.

While Tony's accomplishments and ingenuity are unquestionably commendable, some people report a difficult experience in their dealings with Tony. Great entrepreneurs often divide. People either love them or hate them. Think of Steve Jobs. Stories of the divisive nature of his management style are as prevalent as those praising his visionary leadership approach. With Tony, it goes even deeper than just a love-vs.-hate choice. His brazen duality has seemingly caused some to both love *and* hate him simultaneously.

I've had some business experiences with Tony that almost resulted in deals. The deals never closed for a variety of reasons. From these dealings, I have seen the aspects of Tony's approach that may have caused others to find him difficult to work with, although I found them navigable and often playful.

We are all complex, multidimensional Beings with unique mixes of attributes and flaws. For great people, attributes and flaws often both become equally amplified. Winston Churchill is known for being a virtuous hero for his efforts to defeat Nazism and also for being a cold strategist who supported controversial policies toward India. Martin Luther King Jr. is rightly known for being America's best-known catalyst for racial equality while also being remembered for struggling with adultery and other notable personal demons.

While Tony undoubtedly deserves high praise, study, and admiration for his fierce, independent grit, critics would say he also deserves a cautionary glance for his style. Tony has been said to alternately overvalue and undervalue people in a seemingly deliberate attempt to manipulate them into his will for a transaction. For anyone with a self-aware business acumen, this is widely transparent and manageable. For others, less aware, it could lead to the consummation of a less-favorable deal, or worse.

Throughout his thirty-year career, Tony has stirred up a ton of controversy, attracted scorn and envy from competitors, and had near-epic public battles with artists on his own label. He's also been praised by his veteran alumni artists who sign new deals with him and bring their secondary projects to him eagerly. Most are either hot or cold with Tony. Tony's style of loud greatness naturally spits out lukewarm responses.

You don't have to be divisive to be a great entrepreneur, but for some, the two cannot be decoupled. Yet to be a great entrepreneur like Tony, you *will* have to discern when you must amplify your *internal spirit voice* and ignore the white noise of chatter created by the controversial impressions you've left with others.

If you are hovering above a rock-bottom position of failure, remember **Failure Rule #5:** *You Are Not Your Failures.* Remember what Tony was able to do without a resume, wealthy parents, or a college degree—*and with only eight hundred dollars.* Channel the bulldog tenacity of Tony Brummel, and find a way to create something out of the nothing you have found yourself in.

YOU ARE HOW YOU DECIDE TO RESPOND TO FAILURE

"Naked I came from my mother's womb, and naked shall I return. The Lord gave, and the Lord has taken away; blessed be the name of the Lord."

—JOB 1:21

> **LESSON:** You are not your losses or your sufferings, and—as Failure Rule #5 upholds—*You Are Not Your Failures*, but you *are* how you decide to respond to your losses, sufferings, and failures.

As I've traversed through failure after failure in my life, it has always been a quiet recognition of and fidelity to the whisperings of my *internal spirit voice* that has guided me forward with courage. Through the chaos of near-death, and certifiably fatal, business collapses. Through the demoralization of bankruptcy court. Through the necessary shame of poverty and state dependency. And through the betraying sting of a failed marriage. As each of these pieces of my life got taken away, I always heard my *internal spirit voice* comforting me with the truth of Failure Rule #5: *You Are Not Your Failures*.

As you experience things being taken away from you in life, hold Failure Rule #5 close to your heart and top of mind. Repeat this truth to yourself often—*you are not your failures, you are not your failures, you are not your failures*. Say it to yourself over and over and over. Make it a mantra. Impound it in your psyche.

Remember also that you are not the suffering you endure because of your failures. You are not a mere causal reflection of the losses you incur because of your failures. You need to step outside of the shrapnel that explodes from the bomb of your failure events. Detach your identity and self-esteem from the shrapnel. In the midst of devastation, in the sorrow of loss, and in the grip of afflictions that surround your failures, you need to move forward. To do this, you need to mute all the disorder floating in your orbit. You need to muzzle the chatter around you that tries to tell you who you are and what your circumstances add up to.

You need to silence everything but your *internal spirit voice*.

You need to zoom in and hear your *internal spirit voice* because the line from *The Magic Strings of Frankie Presto* is right: *"things get taken away... you will learn to start over many times—or you will be useless."*

Said differently and anciently, *"The Lord gave and the Lord taketh away."*

All you need to do is examine the biblical account of the life of Job to find an example of someone who pressed on through total devastation, swarms of affliction, and every mark of failure that could possibly befall a person. In this, Job ignored the voices of doubt around him—even his very wife's—in order to maintain fidelity to the clarion call of his *internal spirit voice*.

Whether you believe this story to be the word of God, a fairy tale, or simply a piece of morally rich historical literature, the biblical narrative describing the life of Job reveals a man who had to dig deep to find the strength that he sought.

Job recognized his *internal spirit voice* as that of *The Spirit*—a clear divine whispering of God that broke through to his conscience and consciousness. Even as his life crashed and burned all around him, he still chose to respond to that voice. He utterly refused to deny it— although many around him urged him to curse who he saw as the very source of that voice.

As the story goes, Job was wildly blessed and considered *"the greatest of all the children of the east."* (Job 1:3) He wanted for nothing and knew not hardship. And through it all, he retained a sense of faith-informed humility.

Yet Job's vast prosperity did not persist. In the narrative, God challenges Satan to test Job. He offered the challenge to prove that Job was not merely a fair-weather faithful servant who only held fast to following the Lord because of the ease of his life.

Satan accepted the challenge, and with God's complicit collaboration of allowance, Job was cursed in all imaginable earthly ways. He lost his vast livestock assets. All of his ten children were killed simultaneously by a terrible storm. And to top it all off, his very flesh became afflicted with the cruel satanic malignity of unbearable boils.

In the ashes of ruin, Job sat down and attempted to alleviate the deep stinging torture caused by his boils. He violently scraped his skin with a potshard. Observing all of this, his wife failed to see beyond the external reality of his affliction. In the limitation of her human sympathy, she cursed the circumstances of his pain as if they were simply accidental and something beyond the influence of purpose or Providence. She mockingly questioned the fortitude of his enduring faith by asking him why he still retained his integrity. She urged him to *"curse God and die"*—as if somehow that would help rid himself of the torture.

Job's wife wasn't seeking a deeper understanding of or lesson in her husband's suffering. She was just pissed that his suffering was affecting her happiness. She was pissed that Job's misfortune was indistinguishable from her misfortune. She was pissed that her life was hit with the shock and awe of extreme, unexpected tragedy—and she was sure her husband had somehow brought it upon them.

To be fair, her soul was ravaged to a degree that many of us could not even begin to comprehend. How might we respond if our marital estate was wiped out and all of our children were extinguished in a single calamity? For many of us, the answer may be *exactly the same way as Job's wife—or worse*. The lesson here is less in some focused condemnation of Job's wife's reaction and more in an examination of the contrast of her reaction with Job's response. The high lesson is found in Job's unique fidelity to his *internal spirit voice* and his steadfastness in decisively ignoring his wife's voice calling for faithlessness.

In her shallowness, Job's wife did not offer Job any sympathy at all. Instead, she frustrated his circumstances. Her voice sounded in direct opposition to the bold sound of his *internal spirit voice*. Her voice was a stumbling block lodged in the path of Job's difficult inner pursuit journey. It was a stumbling block he had to overcome in order to understand the potential meaning and purpose of his suffering.

Knowing that his wife was speaking *"as one of the foolish women speaketh,"* Job chose to disregard his wife's impression of God's purpose in their failure experience. Job knew that in life, we have to take the good with the bad. He questioned his wife accordingly, *"Shall we receive the good at the hand of God, and not receive the bad?"* (Job 2:10)

Job had unwavering fidelity to his *internal spirit voice* amid total devastation. He remained faithful in his belief that God was benevolent, in spite of his horrific suffering. And it was in his obedience to that voice, not the distracting voice of his wife, that Job found his deepest abiding strength.

Whether you recognize the source of your *internal spirit voice* to be that of God or not, *listen to it*. Align your decision-making with its whisperings. As you steamroll through devastating failure along your *calling journey* as an entrepreneur, anchor your fidelity to that voice. As you encounter loss while pursuing the application of your gifts as a creative, block out all but your *internal spirit voice's* definitive messaging. Or as you struggle with the failure feeling of meaning deficit as an employee living a life authentic, ignore the distractive voices of doubt around you as you work to shape an environment that more resembles a product of you.

Life will give you things, and it will also take them away. You are not your losses. You are not your suffering. Anchor **Failure Rule #5: *You Are Not Your Failures*** deep within your heart—but remember that you *are* how you decide to respond to the failures that unfold around you. Decide wisely. Decide to heed the calling of your *internal spirit voice* as you remain kind and good while ignoring the opinions of others. Chances are that your devastation won't be as total as Job's.

TATTOO FAILURE RULE #5 ON YOUR SOUL

YOU ARE NOT YOUR FAILURES

As you rise phoenix-like from the scorched ashes of your failures, live as if you have **Failure Rule #5:** *You Are Not Your Failures* tattooed on your soul. Approach impression management by being completely derelict—don't try to manage the impressions you leave on others at all. Instead, heed Leo Tolstoy's advice, and just be kind and good as you ignore the low-resolution impressions of others. Smile and take courage as you live each new day with a renewed understanding that your worth and your failures are not correlative. Decisively detach your self-opinion from the isolation—or even the accumulation—of your failure moments.

With **Failure Rule #5:** *You Are Not Your Failures* tattooed now indelibly on your soul, remember a young Dwayne "The Rock" Johnson who was not deterred by being in a failure state of having only seven dollars in his pocket. In his failure state, he was broke as hell but believed unequivocally that someday he wouldn't be. Knowing **Failure Rule #5** intuitively, The Rock wisely detached from the optics of his failures. And he was prophetically correct in his belief about his future. Remember also a younger J.K. Rowling, who detached from the optics of her failure of falling into state dependency following her divorce. Rowling used her rejection as fuel and made her rock bottom the foundation from which she built her new life on—starting with working on the manuscript for *Harry Potter* once again after not having touched it for three months.

Do not sit unnecessarily still under the positive pressure of entrepreneurial or creative ambition because you are waiting for some certainty of outcome or because you're paralyzed by a fear of failure. Know that when the inevitable failures punctuate your pursuits that *You Are Not Your Failures* anyway. Think of Jesse Itzler and his ability to stand ready and approximate his aim at multiple targets in parallel, only to fire with imperfection before refining his aims in flight amid his efforts to build an astoundingly robust *Portfolio of Pursuits*. If you operate like Itzler, chances are you will have to develop the discernment to know when to bypass permission. You will know this is necessary when your *internal spirit voice* is in clear opposition to the external feedback loops that surround you. In these times, remember what country star Toby Keith sings in his song "Get Got"—*ask forgiveness, not permission*.

Internalize the power of **Failure Rule #5:** *You Are Not Your Failures* and protect your idealism, while defiantly rejecting cynicism, no matter the magnitude of failure you're contending with. Remember what comedian Stephen Colbert observed about cynicism—*"Cynicism masquerades as wisdom, but it is the farthest thing from it...cynics always say no. But saying yes begins things."* Know that **Failure Rule #5** will allow you to say yes again after each failure. When you hit failure rocks in the stream of your *calling journey*, let your obstinate belief in idealism push you into adventurous new streams. Like pantyhose queen Sara Blakely did. Remember how she endured a low score on the Law School Admissions Test and a seemingly dead-end sales job before she discovered an adjacent possible that made her the youngest self-made female billionaire in the world.

Just because **Failure Rule #5** holds and *You Are Not Your Failures* doesn't mean that you ought not embrace the necessity of healthy shame amid your failures. If you find yourself in dependency, on the state or others, remember Benjamin Franklin's opinion that the best way out of such a dependency is to not be made easy in it. Remember the discomfort punk rocker Roger Miret felt in the welfare-supported poverty of his tumultuous youth. And remember the distinction he made as an adult between those who take handouts and those who embrace healthy shame as they accept a generous hand up with gratitude.

Prepare yourself for the times in life when you must choose between two terrible options. In such times of tragic moral choice, any choice you make feels like failure. But you must try to determine which option will suck less. Choose that option and then live with that decision with peace, remembering that **Failure Rule #5** is tattooed on your soul. Like Dr. Viki Kind did as she managed her father's end-of-life decisions.

It's not easy to anchor yourself to **Failure Rule #5: *You Are Not Your Failures*** if, like me and Ray Bradbury, you wake up each day feeling like you are a landmine. If this is the state of your Being each morning too, remember that you have the power to put the pieces together, after each explosion, with forward-enabling creativity every single day.

Be bold as you make your way as an *entrepreneur, a creative, or an authentic Being*. Because there will be times when you need to accept—even induce—division to forge forward with integrity as your authentic self. This takes boldness because you will fail to be all things to all people. Remember that this is a byproduct of greatness. Remember what legendary music producer Rick Rubin noted about divisiveness relative to art: *"The best art divides the audience: half love it and half hate it."* Don't be afraid to divide when it's necessary.

Part of separating your identity from your failures as you embrace **Failure Rule #5** being tattooed on your soul, is learning how to cultivate an insightful, playful, and self-deprecating sense of humor—*failure humor*. Sometimes you need to take yourself less seriously in order to seriously take steps to accomplishing your *Thing Two* dream. Like the iconic blue-collar failure comic Rodney Dangerfield did amid divorce, depression, and a dead-end job selling aluminum siding.

It becomes easier to wear **Failure Rule #5** tattooed on your soul when you fully grasp that you are the earthly CEO of your life. In this role, you get to decree that ***You Are Not Your Failures***. Like my old banking colleague who abandoned the predictability of his cubicle life and decided to chase radical discomfort by purchasing a one-way ticket to Syria so he could help fight alongside the Kurdish Christians who were at war with ISIS.

Never forget that every day you have the opportunity to re-sketch the story of the rest of your life—despite your failures—because **Failure Rule #5** is the truth: *You Are Not Your Failures*. Remember Glenn Beck's story of transforming from a broke, divorced, failing, alcoholic deejay to being inducted into the Radio Hall of Fame in 2020. As you begin to re-sketch your story after failure, remember that you don't need to come from wealth or have a stacked resume, a college degree, or substantial seed money to actualize your *Thing Two* dream. Sometimes bulldog tenacity and vision can often suffice, like it did for music entrepreneur Tony Brummel.

Because *You Are Not Your Failures*, you are also not your losses and your sufferings. *But you are how you decide to respond to your losses, sufferings, and failures.* As you strive to integrate this reality into your decisioning matrices, recall the biblical story of the life of Job. Remember how Job did not turn to bitterness, irrational finger-pointing, or infidelity to his God just because everything got taken away and his life was obliterated with the failure of total devastation. Instead, he found divine strength in the truth that *he was not his failures*. You might say **Failure Rule #5** was tattooed on his soul.

CONCLUSION

LIFE AFTER FAILURE

This book has largely been about dealing with failure in life that either enshrouds us by virtue of general circumstance or failure traceable to our own missteps and decision-making gaps. But sometimes failure strikes us because those we love or rely on fail us. This book has not really addressed how to think through this type of failure.

I am sitting comfortably on my leather couch in my bedroom right now as I type. It is Sunday. I am drinking black coffee and staring out the window, where lots of snow is beautifully making its way from the sky to the ground—including to my driveway. Later this afternoon, when the snow stops, if I haven't successfully commissioned some proper help, I will have to go out and shovel the driveway.

Pete Adeney, known by the twenty-three million readers of his blog as Mr. Money Mustache, expressed in an interview for Tim Ferriss's book *Tribe of Mentors* that shoveling enormous quantities of snow after a big storm is one of the absurd things in life that he loves. I like Mr. Money Mustache, but on this we part. I hate shoveling.

This is the second snowstorm to hit us within a week. The first one was a multiday storm. In preparation for that storm, I reached out to our guy who has been doing our landscaping and snow removal. My wife and I really like this guy. He's very funny, smart, and charismatic. One night after he finished cutting the lawn, he hung out on our porch, and we drank whiskey and got to know each other. He was beginning to feel like part of the family a bit.

But our guy has a complicated life. He's a divorced dad with several children from several different women. He's constantly dealing with some flavor of baby mama drama. I'm not sure if this is the root cause or not, but it seems like this has made him a bit unpredictable and, at times, unreliable. But I have a wide threshold of grace for these types of things, given that at the core of it, as Bob Ritchie (a.k.a. Kid Rock) sings, *"I ain't no G. I'm just a regular failure."*

Yet at some point even my threshold breaks and I must stop and decide how to handle it when someone fails me. Through multiple texts earlier this week when the first storm hit, our guy promised to remove our snow. Delay and revised estimated time of arrival (ETA) after revised ETA turned into no responses and complete ghosting. I was pissed, annoyed, and frustrated with the lack of respect and failure of communication. I hadn't budgeted in any time in my schedule to shovel. Had I known he was going to flake, I would have.

For some reason, my guy failing me on the snow removal chapped my ass and found me irrationally agitated for days. My reaction was disproportionate. I was not handling it well. I just couldn't believe that after the rapport we had built that he would flake like this and totally ghost me. And then I began to reflect on **The 5 Rules of Failure**, on my own relationship with failure, and on how I best needed to view my guy's failing me in this instance.

I will not be soliciting his services anymore, but I have jettisoned the bitterness I've been clinging to by remembering that failure is complicated. That life is complex. And that whatever is going on in his life is probably more tangled than I even suspect. I choose to believe that on the priority scale stacked against whatever chaos he's dealing with, smoothing things over with me around one day of failing to show up for snow removal is probably very low, if registering at all.

Because **Failure Rule #1:** *Failure Purifies* is true even in the smallest of things, I was stripped down to baseline self-reliance and had to shovel the first storm's mess myself.

Because **Failure Rule #2:** *Nothing Is Safe* is inescapable, my guy will have to navigate the impact of a lost customer due to his failure to properly mind his business—whatever the reason.

Because **Failure Rule #3:** *Money Is Spiritual* ubiquitously applies to all commerce and money is most fundamentally a thank-you note, I will be handsomely compensating any service provider who makes themselves available to help me remove the snow from today's storm.

Because **Failure Rule #4:** *Build Your Thing One and Thing Two Dependency* is a sound way to prevent unnecessary failure and eliminate future regret, I will continue to spend my day cultivating my *Thing Two* dream fully financed by the power of my primary *Thing One* enabler job.

Because **Failure Rule #5:** *You Are Not Your Failures* is critical to embrace, when I think of my snow removal guy, it is not his one act of failure that I will focus on. I will focus on all the characteristics of him that I have appreciated and enjoyed throughout my interactions with him.

Because I am not my failures.

You are not your failures.

And he is not his failure(s).

I hope you've enjoyed your time reading the diverse set of failure stories in this book. Now go forth and internalize **The 5 Rules of Failure.** And remember that after it sucks, if you know its rules, then eventually *Failure Rules!*

THE FAILURE RULES! SOUNDTRACK

All stories need soundtracks, including failure stories. Narratives find their animation when bolstered by guitars, bass, drums, vocals, beats, and melody. Attendant music amplifies the sensibilities of story, of colorful words, and of poignant lessons. Music makes words move more powerfully.

Music is also a powerful antidote to the harsh wounds of failure. Music strengthens you as you pick yourself off the floor and forge new ways forward. Music is a resurrecting tailwind that helps you sail through the headwinds of life's failures. Music helps catalyze the endorphins of your spirit that emerge to carry you through hard times. So you can let them make you.

As I've confronted each instance of failure that has struck me and labored to extract value from each one's distinct taste of pain, music was always there for me. There was always a critical set of songs undergirding my bootstrapped strength. Sometimes it was the song in its totality that represented the sonic strength I would harness to drive me forward. Other times it would be very specific lyrical phrases that precisely offered the visceral messages I needed to help me transcend circumstances and see the light of my next best step.

As you trigger failure, inadvertently fall into it, or slowly find yourself surrounded by it, remember the power of music. Remember the transformative energy of music's powerful poetry. Build a soundtrack to aid you in your triumph over and recovery from failure's thrashings.

I attached myself to many vital songs to help me metabolize and conquer failure over the years. The soundtrack below includes specific songs that augmented my writing of this book. Below I explain each one's unique meaning to me. Each one has come to represent different lessons learned, principles cemented, and experiences memorialized along my *calling journey*.

Below are explanations for most of the songs on the soundtrack playlist. **The playlist can be found on Spotify, Apple Music, and other streaming services listed under** *Failure Rules! Soundtrack.* There are other songs in the playlist that I don't fully explain below. The other songs are no less critically connected to the book.

Like the positive reboot messages in the song **"First Failure" by the Gorilla Biscuits.**

Like how **AC/DC's "Black Ice"** reminds me that when failure strikes, we need to sometimes submit to it in the same way we submit to hydroplaning through black ice by resisting the impulse to pump the breaks. Because sometimes our failures need to be accepted to help us find a better next path.

Like the lessons on rejecting envy found in **"The Grass is Always Greener" by Jake Owen with Kid Rock.**

Like how **Terror's "Always the Hard Way"** calls us to decisively choose the hard right over the easy wrong.

Like how when we are susceptible to the influence of an unloved mentality, **Sheer Terror's "Love Songs for the Unloved"** reminds us to reject such a temptation.

Like when we're stretched beyond capacity in maximizing our *calling journey* pursuits, **"The Way of the Road"** by **The Koffin Kats** reminds us that sometimes it's okay to burn the candle at both ends.

Like how **Flatfoot 56's "Odd Boat"** reminds me to always say farewell to shallow times and embrace meaning in all things.

And of course, like how **Black Flag's "Black Coffee"** fires me up each day to embrace a VUCA work environment with intensity and focus.

These are the sounds of failure. These are the sounds of hard times. These are the sounds of holding it down. These are the sounds of overcoming. These are the sounds that helped me rule.

Now go find your own failure songs so you can rule too.

1. MOTORHEAD: "ACE OF SPADES"

When I started the manuscript for *Failure Rules!* Motorhead, Lemmy Kilmister, and his mole, were still rocking. The man who had been practically gargling the words *"You win some, you lose some / it's all the same to me"* for decades had, by the time I wrapped up the first draft, sadly passed on to rock 'n' roll heaven.

If you've gotten this far in this book, you've already read the chapter devoted to Lemmy, so you know the importance of living to win, even when you feel you were born to lose. You also know the importance of remembering Lemmy's emphasis on **Failure Rule #2:** *Nothing Is Safe*.

Failure Rules! is about a lot of things, but ultimately it is about the essence of the entrepreneurial soul. "Ace of Spades" captures this essence succinctly when Lemmy sings that

"The pleasure is to play, makes no difference what you say
I don't share your greed, the only card I need is
The ace of spades."

2. THE KINGS OF NUTHIN': "FIGHT SONGS FOR FUCK UPS"

Full disclosure: I've released two records for **The Kings of Nuthin'** on my record label **Sailor's Grave Records**. But I didn't release the record that features this song. My friend Duane Peters (US Bombs) did on his label Disaster Records.

The iconic, swaggering, tattooed, greasy-haired poetic front man for the band, Torr Skoog, sadly passed away in 2013. But he has left content behind in the form of his music that will live on forever.

As I wrote *Failure Rules!* the song "Fight Songs for Fuck Ups" went through my head often. The song lingered when I thought of the sterility of many corporate environments and heard Torr singing words like: *"Cubicle confinement, waiting for retirement / We can't achieve, in what we don't believe"* in my head. The song bubbled up into my thoughts when I would excavate the failures of public figures that turned into tenacious successes, like comedian Rodney Dangerfield. In this reverie, I would hum the song's bold chorus that chants with a convicted cadence:

"This is a fight song for fuck ups
Keep on not givin' up
Fight song for fuck ups
When you've had enough
Fight song for fuck ups
Now everyone wants to be just like us."

Because an entrepreneur often keeps failing until they accidentally succeed. They keep on not giving up. They fight again and again, no matter how many times they fuck up. They can't achieve in what they don't believe, and they can't give up in what they do believe.

This is how *Failure Rules!* and hard times make us. By keeping on not giving up. And Torr Skoog and The Kings of Nuthin' capture this spirit immortally in this song.

3. CRO-MAGS: "HARD TIMES"

John Joseph "JJ" McGowan, the singer for the seminal New York Hardcore punk band the Cro-Mags, is a seeker of the truth—as you might have gathered from the foreword he wrote for this book. I've always been inspired by his life story, the guttural, urgent intensity of his music, and the visceral combativeness of his indomitable spirit.

I write about JJ in *Failure Rules!* because he is one of my hard times heroes. The Cro-Mags song "Hard Times" played a big part in the mix of inspiration that led to the writing of *Failure Rules!* It was this song that I was listening to as I walked along the beach back in 2013 when I was convicted to begin writing this book.

Because when "Hard Times" strike as an entrepreneur you have to *"Organize your life and figure it out / Or you'll go under without a doubt."* Sometimes, no matter how carefully you forecast, how closely you guard risk, and how diligent your work ethic, still, you look out and see that *"Hard times are coming through / But if you're hard they won't get to you."*

David Goggins, author of *Can't Hurt Me,* is a triathlete just like JJ. He urges his readers and followers to not stop when you're tired but stop when you're done. He urges them to stay hard, like John Joseph has done his whole life. Like you need to do if you're going to leverage failure's lessons for future success.

Take inventory of yourself. Listen to your *internal spirit voice.* Create an offroad path to improvise, overcome, and adapt. Hold fast, stay hard, and remember to *"never surrender, never go down! / Hard times! Hard times!"*

4. ROLLINS BAND: "SHINE"

"No such thing as spare time
No such thing as free time
No such thing as down time

All you got is life time"

When you have to find unique, rugged, and uncharted pathways out of an undesired life situation, there is no such thing as spare time. If your business is getting attacked from all fronts, all time is war time. Every thought boomerangs back to an analysis of the issue and a construction of the solution.

When you juggle a *Portfolio of Pursuits* and one is overwhelmingly extracting disproportionate time and energy yet is still crucial, there is no such thing as spare time, no such thing as free time. There is only hero time.

This is the case despite the optics. Despite the carrying on of normal routines.

A workout becomes a mental deep dive into the challenges at hand. Your endorphins assist in reaching those crystallized moments of revelation that lead to game-changing decisions.

A massage becomes a distillation of mind, body, and soul that recalibrates your direction and allows you to find the *peace of now* needed to march forward into the *reality of tomorrow*.

A session at the boxing gym becomes a metaphorical activity that motivates you to attack the tasks of tomorrow with a vigor and force otherwise unanimated.

A fine cigar becomes a relaxant that facilitates contemplative appreciation for the processes that fill the complex composite of everything you do.

No down time. All activities aid in the assimilation of high-octane living. All time is purposed toward an abundant, strident, full-throttle acquisition of deep gratitude, dream-driven planning, and hands-on TCB.

Hands-on TCB that makes you send three emails, while you're taking a three-minute toilet break, to move the needle for three different businesses.

Hands-on TCB that requires the planning of multiple business ideas in parallel.

Hands-on TCB that knows only how to bite off more than you can chew. And still integrates it all with an orchestral swagger to create a seemingly effortless well-balanced life.

In **Failure Rules!** I write about Henry Rollins's journey from ice cream scooper to front man of the seminal hardcore punk band Black Flag. To motivational speaker and author. To actor in movies such as *Johnny Mnemonic, The Chase, Heat,* and the TV series *Sons of Anarchy.*

Henry's journey was full of twists and turns. Hardships and doubts. As you've already learned, when he toured with Black Flag, there were times where he had to eat dog food to survive and get to the next show. But he kept going. He knew he was living his calling and he listened only to his *internal spirit voice.* He ignored the voices that would tell him to retreat. This is why in "Shine" he sings:

"If I'd listened to everything that they said to me, I wouldn't be here!
And if I took the time to bleed from all the tiny little
    arrows shot my way, I wouldn't be here!
The ones who don't do anything are always the
    ones who try to put you down."

It is always those who don't do anything that will put you down and tell you that you can't. They say this because they couldn't. Don't listen to them. Listen to those who succeeded despite having everyone around them tell them that they couldn't. Those who succeeded after having to eat dog food to survive.

There's no such thing as down time. Down time is bleed time. Bleed time acknowledges the arrows shot your way. Keep moving. Pay those arrows no mind.

5. DROPKICK MURPHYS: "MEMORIAL DAY"

Month to month for many months I was dealing with a P&L that was under water on one business and borrowing from another to float it. I hired consultants. I reshaped pricing. I restructured staff. I implemented a strong plan, and the fruits were beginning to take root. But it was clear that it would be a minimum of eighteen months before we would be in the black. And my burn rate was much shorter than that. So I closed the bleeding business to pivot full focus on the other. It was a difficult decision point. Leaving passion and regret behind. Among other things.

I remember listening to "Memorial Day" by Dropkick Murphys daily during this period. When I wanted a clear answer on next steps from a third-party consultant and realized it had to come from within, lyrics, such as *"You've gotta pick yourself up by the bootstraps / No one's gonna help you out when you fall"* reminded me that the decision was all mine and mine alone to make.

As I mentioned earlier, I knew I made the right decision in closing down the gym. It was a difficult tragic moral choice predicament. However, the profitable business ultimately lost its ground years later, and looking back, I know the gym would've worked with the right time and money. I had adjusted the business model to poise it for long-term success. Yet with the advantage of over a decade of hindsight, I still know shutting it down was the right decision. I could've found a way to hold on. The burn rate could've likely been extended somehow to match the turnaround plan. But it still would've never been profitable enough relative to the effort. My passions and efforts have since been appropriately placed with, and directed at, the appointed next pursuits of my *calling journey*. I heard my *internal spirit voice* clearly at that decision point. And I heeded it.

When you're in the heat of a difficult decision, sometimes you have to act on the pure signaling of your *internal spirit voice,* knowing no guarantees can be seen through any proverbial crystal ball. And accepting that good decisions do not always lead to good, linearly traceable results.

During this time of difficult decision years ago, Dropkick Murphys helped me by urging:

"You've gotta find a way out of your problems
When you're broke and you're backed up against the wall
If you sleep on your only chances
They'll never come around again
So dig deep and swing for the fences
You never know it might work out in the end."

In the end, I dug deep and hyper-focused on one business. And although that business didn't, in and of itself, prove to hold any staying power past three more years, had I not focused on it, I would have never discovered several other related businesses that blossomed out of that venture. Within the adjacent possible, I lurched into businesses with less risk, less work, and less expensive entry fees. The good outcomes from my good decision were not linearly connected.

Yeah, Dropkick Murphys were right. You never know, it might work out in the end.

6. EMINEM: "BEAUTIFUL PAIN"

I don't follow rap music. Or mainstream music. I am serious about this. I honestly would not recognize Taylor Swift in a picture. I'm in my own universe with music, and it's alien to most.

But I know who Eminem is. I know he's a little dated at this point, but I like his music. Moreover, I like his story and his attitude. His tenacity. His bootstrapping, ballsy mentality. His fearless approach to excavating his pain and turning it into powerful and brilliant art.

When I left my house after my ex-wife pushed for separation and an ex-business partner made a move to squeeze me out of our partnership, all in a month's period of time, my cousin texted me the lyrics to "Beautiful Pain."

I would normally not be inclined to download an Eminem record, but this day I did. And the song "Beautiful Pain" became an anthem of mine for the following two years as I went about *"setting fire to yesterday."*

And piece by piece. New opportunity after new opportunity. And eventually with a new marriage, I felt the beauty of the receding pain. And Eminem's words signified my ongoing transformation:

"As time passes, things change everyday
But wounds, wounds heal
But scars still remain the same
But tomorrow today's gone down in flames
Throw the match and set the past ablaze."

Failure Rules! is about throwing the match and setting ablaze the excess pain of yesterday's failure and utilizing the valuable pain to push you forward into your new tomorrow. It's about healing your wounds but cherishing your scars as critical milestones that mark your tumultuous *calling journey.*

I relished as I would *"feel the burn"* and *"watch the smoke as I turn."* And ultimately, with every emerging strength, I kept *"Rising, a phoenix from the flames,"* while also writing about the process in **Failure Rules!**

And it's because of that line in the song I decided to include a phoenix rising from flames in the book cover design.

Because failure in and of itself actually sucks. But when you learn the rules of failure, when you see the power you can harness from it, and when you learn to appropriate new discoveries from its ashes, then you learn that, in fact, **Failure Rules!**

7. BOB SEGER AND THE SILVER BULLET BAND: "AGAINST THE WIND"

From a genre perspective, this song is a bit of an outlier within the *Failure Rules!* soundtrack. But for some reason I was listening to a lot of Seger as I wrote *Failure Rules!*

I think it is something about the stripped-down, surface-breaking, soul-baring sensibility of Seger's classic American rock 'n' roll. There's no fancy aesthetic. No applicable subgenre application. All simple imagery. Love. Loss. Muscle Cars. Independence. Hometown pride.

It's this type of mindset that has to be the starting point in discovering your path. Strip away all the incidental slop that has accumulated on your life. Your work life. Your personal life. Your inner life. Your budget. All of it. Get down to bare-knuckled soul power, and take inventory of your why as you purge the extraneous whats that have entangled you.

Sometimes you have to shed, break down, strip out, and brush off to sufficiently rebuild, reshape, and pivot. Sometimes you need to do this often. Because life always throws stuff on you that you didn't plan, you don't want, and you don't need. You have to periodically stop, shed, and rebalance in accordance with your *internal spirit voice*.

Failure sucks in and of itself. But sometimes when it strikes, it will strip you down and force you to really identify your why so you can clearly see who you are and what you need to do. It can clear the brush and give you proper visibility. It is a painful process, but if you take it well and use it wisely, you will realize the deep value of **Failure Rule #1: *Failure Purifies.***

8. DOWN TO NOTHING: "NO LEASH"

I released two records for Down to Nothing on my label Thorp Records. In a time of struggle about fifteen years ago, I made a decision I now regret. I sold the Down to Nothing contracts to another label. The band was good then, but they're better now. I don't know if it would've mattered much financially if I had retained the rights, but I would've liked to still have that formal connection with a band I still love.

Down to Nothing is a straight-edge hardcore band. This means that they abstain from any intake of drugs, alcohol, or tobacco. This means that they chart their own course. It means that they don't conform when they're surrounded by people like me who appreciate a fine cigar and a glass of bourbon at the end of the day. They cut the leashes that they feel entangle them. They disengage from what they feel impedes their ability to manifest their authentic Beings.

As an entrepreneur, you need to learn how to cut the restrictive leashes that develop all around you. Gatekeepers. Regulations. Office politics. Credit access. Being time poor.

Destroying these leashes is your job.

An entrepreneur's job is to eliminate risk by being diversified as much as possible. You can do this partly by leveraging technology, human capital, intellectual capital, and trusted relationships to the fullest extent.

This means that you must diversify what spaces you play in. You need to diversify what products and services you offer. And what investments you commit to. This means that you need to develop many disparate interests—or seemingly disparate interests. Because sometimes seemingly disparate interests can create something entirely new and valuable if you can combine them.

This is how an entrepreneur avoids leashes. At least being on the wrong end of them. When **Failure Rule #2:** *Nothing Is Safe* is apparent.

Because when you become an octopus and create multiple income sources—*and the average multimillionaire has between seven and fourteen of them*—you build a web of safety devoid of leashes. When you accomplish this, even on a small scale—*think hundred thousandaire*—you eliminate so many gatekeepers.

You cut the leashes.

As you cut leashes in your life, the amount of people who hold enough power over you—*with which they can make a singular decision that could bring degradation or catastrophe to you economically*—begins to shrink. Wouldn't it be nice to work that number down to zero?

And let's face it, economic disasters bring other disasters. Sure, as I write about in **Failure Rules!** there can be amazing blessings in those disasters. Yet make no mistake, avoiding them is *always* the goal.

Think about your life right now. How many people have power over you right now that if for some reason—legitimate or not—you fell out of favor with them or their interests shifted, they could make a decision that could crush you?

If that number isn't moving toward zero, then you ought to think about what you can do to begin moving toward zero as soon as possible.

Hearing the boys in Down to Nothing sing,

"Like a one-way road
A formula to society
Carved in stone
Fit the mold
I can't do it
I will make my own"

reminds me to keep on not giving up as I work to get that number down to zero.

Build your tentacles. Become an Octopus with a *Portfolio of Pursuits*. Cut the leashes.

9. EVERLAST: "I GET BY"

I'm a sucker for everything Everlast has ever done. I still listen to old House of Pain material, and I love his solo stuff. There's something about the beats, the acoustic guitars, and his trademark gruff voice that just puts me in a zone to handle life well.

The song "I Get By" typifies this. This song and the rest of the *Songs of the Ungrateful Living* album have been a constant background soundtrack that has augmented my pursuits over the past few years. Years in which I had to rest in the "I Get By" mindset while I strived to build pathways to thrive. Years when risk and opportunity often intersected wildly, at varying intensities, until clarity would emerge.

Everlast has often been the equalizing voice that has helped me manage the urges of necessary impatience in times as I hear him sing, *"When I finally get home I can't relax / Cause I've been over worked and I've been overtaxed."* He's been that echoing voice of frustration in times of lean struggle, amid multipronged entrepreneurial juggling, when temporarily I'd have *"my bank accounts empty / All my cards are maxed."*

And because the true entrepreneur doesn't project external blame but recognizes truly identifiable root causes, I can somewhat relate when Everlast sings:

*"And I ain't looking for no pity, I'm just stating the facts
I voted for some change and it's kinda strange
Now it's all I got in my pocket."*

Through it all, I always echo a spirit of gratitude and can easily sing along as Everlast chants the chorus, *"I ain't gonna lie (got it good)."*

Because I know that I do—got it good, that is.

And the PMA drives me forward every day as I enjoy the rugged ride.

10. BLOOD FOR BLOOD: "LIVIN' IN EXILE"

I don't embrace every attitude, message, or ideology that emits from the powerful white-trash, hardcore rock 'n' roll of Boston's Blood for Blood. Even though I released their album *Serenity* on my record label Thorp Records. And even as I wear a Blood for Blood tattoo on my arm.

I don't support class warfare rhetoric. I don't believe in defeatism. But I do appreciate the pure, unadulterated angst that exists when one finds themselves cemented at rock bottom. I appreciate the empathy that this sensibility can create for others in similar circumstances. Falling into a rock-bottom experience can be an ego-leveling event that anchors one in humility. This humility is useful and instructive as one lifts themselves off from the bottom and scrapes their way back to a place of stability. Or upward into a flourishing trajectory.

The song "Livin' in Exile" captures that feeling of being on the run, being hunted down, and feeling exhausted by a downward spiral of circumstances that hovers around someone who can't seem to get traction on any positive movement in life. Or in a diehard entrepreneur's case, can't get sustainable traction in business.

This song has comforted me and breathed a fighting spirit in me on many occasions along my *calling journey*.

When I battled a convergence of losses with my record labels and was forced to put a moratorium on taking a salary—so I could honorably pay vendors and save the companies—I found myself in an exiled state. When I had to make the difficult decision to shut down my fitness center, severing the memberships of hundreds of customers, I found myself in a type of exile. When I was simultaneously confronting lawsuit threats by three different multimillionaires while undergoing a federal investigation, I found myself in the grips of exile's isolation.

In spaces of exile, my soul connected to this song as a mechanism to ingest pain and harness it to move forward. Lyrics from the chorus carried the most weight:

"I'm on the outside lookin' in
I hold the burnin' tears inside my heart
I been runnin', I been runnin' with the hunted
I been runnin' for my whole life. I'm in exile."

Sometimes failure yields a state of exile. When you become estranged from business partners. When you lose assets. Lose customers. Lose the support of loved ones.

But in this exile, there is a unique strength to be had that can allow you to see things differently when all is unraveled. It is a strength that sees the adjacent possible. It sees the new opportunities in an otherwise clouded field of vision. It is a strength that knows that it's often in the chaotic reshaping that exile forces in which the best paths are revealed.

11. H2O "BLACK SHEEP"

It's usually pretty easy to tell the difference between someone who tries to be different to be something they're not and someone who is authentically different as a natural extension of listening to and following the dictates of their *internal spirit voice*.

H2O's charismatic front man and motivational speaker Toby Morse is clearly the latter. Through his nonprofit organization One Life, One Chance, Toby speaks at elementary, middle. and high schools on the topics of breaking stereotypes, making healthy life choices, avoiding peer pressure, and maintaining a PMA.

Son of a single mom with three kids, he found his own way as a teenager. Football and high school keg parties didn't appeal to him. Skateboarding and punk rock did. Back then, neither of these things was cool, accepted, or ubiquitous in Disney shows and malls. Skate punks didn't win dates with the prom queen. They usually attracted a beatdown from the football team. If you had a board under your feet and punk rock on the turntable you were bound to get picked on and ostracized in school.

Toby sings about this in "Black Sheep:"

"Never fit in
I never wanted to
Picked on in school for my identity
Cos I chose to skate all day
Not go to keg parties
This path was my fate and I'll
Never find my place in a 9 to 5 world
I appreciate it all now
This path my fate
No 9-to-5 world."

As an *entrepreneur, a creative,* or an *authentic,* you may feel alienated often. Most people can't relate. You may often have to deliberately reach beyond the expectations set by friends, family, and the education system to carve your own path. And sometimes you have to categorically ignore their expectations.

But it's the silent acceptance of the not fitting in that yields the most strength. The ability to quietly deviate as you see fit to seize opportunities that others don't see and wouldn't believe in if they did.

This is very tough if you're living in a nine-to-five world. But if you're a true authentic, you will navigate through it. You'll emerge quickly from failures and false starts like a jack-in-the-box that pops up swiftly after being punched repeatedly. And with a smile on its face.

When listening to "Black Sheep" while writing the *Failure Rules!* manuscript, I was pleasantly reminded of the need to constantly draw on the strength that is produced from not fitting in. From seeing through, beyond, and out of the nine-to-five world.

If this is your path also, try to be like Toby and "appreciate it all now."

12. MACHINE GUN KELLY: "ALL NIGHT LONG"

My son introduced me to Machine Gun Kelly (MGK) around the time I began writing *Failure Rules!* I don't know much about rap, or whatever genre MGK is considered to play in, and hadn't heard of him yet at the time, but as I listened to him, this song struck me.

Machine Gun Kelly seems to have gotten where he is by eschewing the seduction of an ever-increasing envy culture. A culture that hates success and demonizes wealth. A culture that wants to take from people who have succeeded instead of learning from them. A culture that wants to punish the successful by confiscating their wealth instead of inspiring them to give freely. In "All Night Long" MGK raps:

"Success got everybody hating
Success to me is inspiration
Cause how we supposed to know that what we dream is possible
If don't nobody that looks like us makes it?"

Being an entrepreneur means getting all envy out of your heart and filling it only with inspiration, determination, and the grit of staying forever hungry for the wonderment of what might be possible. It means money is a byproduct and you're after it—whatever your "it" pursuit is—for it. Not for what it can bring to you materially. Financial rewards are just a positive after-effect.

Finding mentors is key. Even if they are virtual mentors who you only read about. Sometimes they are the best. Either way, find someone who looks like you do that has made it. Then you'll know that what you dream is possible. As a rapper, rocker, and creative, MGK knows the value in this.

In the interim, pay no attention to how you may or may not be perceived. If you think you may be a target of placism, ignore it. Know that self-doubt is often just in between your ears. I am covered in tattoos and have never let the fear that others may judge me stop me from moving forward on all my pursuits. As Jim Young (played by Ben Affleck) in the film *Boiler Room* advised, you must always act "as if." That means you constantly present yourself as if whatever you're pursuing is the most natural and appropriate pursuit for you. Despite whatever gaps and doubts may truly exist or be lingering in your head. **Don't fake it until you make it. Believe it until you become it. Fuck imposter syndrome.**

And while you're traversing from believing to becoming, know that many others have done the same. Which means that many who have made it are not as judgmental as you think. Some are. But many aren't. And the ones who aren't will look for your heart and ambition and not judge you by your clothes and your car. Or your ethnicity, religion, or politics. Or whether you have ink on your skin.

Don't get stuck in assuming you're surrounded by an attitude of placism. Most people will not judge you based on your temporary circumstances, or the place those circumstances have forced you into at any given point along your *calling journey*. I am reminded of this when I hear Machine Gun Kelly rap:

"And that is how to keep it real
How to never judge somebody by their steering wheel
Cause you know that motherfucker in that Ford Taurus
Could be the next motherfucker in that new Porsche."

Eschew envy. Pay no mind to your self-doubts. Assume everyone only sees your heart and your ambition. Live and work "as if." Keep believing it, no matter how many times you fail, until it becomes you. Whatever "it" is to you. If making it has a byproduct of money, then always recognize it as such and not the purpose.

13. HATEBREED: "THE DIVINITY OF PURPOSE"

My business partner had made moves to squeeze me out. My wife had made it clear she had changed her mind about working on our marriage. She still wanted a divorce. I made them both happy and honored their wishes.

No office to go to by day. No home to go to at night.

It was me, my laptop, and a hotel room.

And one of my most trusted, reliable friends...*The Divinity of Purpose*.

When I stepped outside of my circumstances, peered at them from the outside and took inventory of my life, it didn't look good. The optics were bad. The resources were stretched and unpredictable. I found myself firmly seeing that the *"odds were stacked against me."*

I felt alone, anchorless.

It seemed as if *"the world left no place for me."* I listened to my favorite Hatebreed song and felt aligned with Jamey Jasta as he sang, *"And when the skies crashed down upon me / I looked for someone by my side."*

Like him—whatever it was specifically that was going on in his life when he wrote the song—I needed someone by my side.

And like him, it was the loud, howling scream funneled from my *internal spirit voice* that showed me how to move forward.

That voice screamed with *The Divinity of Purpose*.

The Divinity of Purpose was *"there, when no one else was"* and it showed me that *"what's born doesn't always die."*

While fear attempted to thwart my focus, my drive, my faith, and my footing, I discovered that it was *The Divinity of Purpose* that *"found me with feet to edge and helped me step away."*

I had several deals on the table. Game-changers. Must-haves if I was going to pivot and reorganize my life in a strong and meaningful fashion. I had to harness *The Divinity of Purpose* daily to keep going, knowing that the *"pain of discipline was less than that of regret."*

Every day, pushing each step as I deliberately *"Lifted one foot from the grave when the purpose showed its face."* Forward. Advancement. Pushing. Every. Day. Against my emotions.

What exactly is *The Divinity of Purpose*? (see Definition of Terms)

You know it when it takes hold of you.

You know its supernatural momentum when it propels you—like an endorphin through intense pain—to a higher level of functioning amid adversity. To an advanced level of gratitude amid deep sorrow.

All three deals bore fruit and served to give me an entirely new and amazing life within six months. Because I listened to the *internal spirit voice*, ignored the impressions of others, and harnessed *The Divinity of Purpose* to its fullest. Because *"even on my weakest days,"* *The Divinity of Purpose* *"helped me find the strength."*

And it will for you too.

14. JOHNNY CASH: "SATISFIED MIND"

As I explained in the "Reject Both Envy and Greed" chapter, being an entrepreneur is not about greed. Pure greed rarely pays off.

Being an entrepreneur is about much more than just making money. It's about homing in on a purpose and a passion that screams from within. One that you must follow, or you will regret not doing so forever. This doesn't mean you march on without proper due diligence and realistic milestones. Or that you charge hard with reckless risk taking. Instead, you control and steer that purpose and passion to find those reachable, affordable next steps. You piece together your dream path one move at a time. Or several affordable steps in parallel.

To juggle the competing motivations that can fight for airtime in your brain as an entrepreneur, you have to make mindfulness, solitude, proper rest, and prayer—if you're of the persuasion—an absolute priority. Else you move too fast in too many directions, and you risk needless failure. Or, worse, you become susceptible to the seduction of greed. I've flirted with this line at times. And it's only through setting aside regular times of mindfulness and solitude that I have been able to remain guarded and grounded.

One song that has kept me anchored in the rumbling soul fire of authentic living has been Johnny Cash's version of "Satisfied Mind" (originally written by Joe "Red" Hayes and Jack Rhodes).

I'm blessed to constantly be reminded, as Johnny sings in the song, that *"the wealthiest person is a pauper at times / Compared to the person with a satisfied mind."* Because you must find the value and joy in the pursuits themselves. You must balance your pursuits with an enjoyment of the ongoing fruits of solid time with friends and family. You must stop and marvel at the power of the art that drips all around you in your daily life. Because life is art and art is life.

In **Failure Rules!** I write about Johnny Cash and his decision to not pursue a job working for his first wife's father. He ignored the safe route and instead pursued the rumbling soul fire burning inside. He turned off the external voices and turned up the *internal spirit voice*. And his recordings now live immortally to bless us for that decision.

But it's not just a thoughtless pursuit of money that can spoil you. As an entrepreneur, it can also be the thoughtless decisions you make when you have easy access to money that can cripple you.

Whether in the music industry, the online lending space, or the fitness business, there have been times where easy access to capital has led me to make decisions that I otherwise wouldn't, and couldn't, have made.

Sometimes it's better to have your back against the wall and only have access to just what you really need at the moment so that your next move is disciplined, meticulously calculated, and maximized to the hilt.

Daymond John, the creator of the FUBU clothing line and star of the TV show *Shark Tank*, puts it this way in his book *The Power of Broke*:

> I am suggesting that being broke can actually be an advantage for you in business—being broke forces you to be aggressive, creative, resourceful...all those good things. It forces you to be realistic about your pace of growth and keeps you from letting your hopes and dreams run away from you.

This is a tough line to walk, but I find it to be true. It's tough to be too concerned with what's realistic when you're seeking ways to make your fantasies real. But you must learn to walk that tightrope.

It's tough to get traction with no access to capital, but it can be done. Moreover, I've found that the best decisions I've made have been when I have access to just enough capital to make the lean, decisive next step to move the needle. When access has been too abundant, bad things sometimes happen.

I'm not suggesting that you be overly patient as you fold into your *calling journey*. Strong, but principled, impatience can be the greatest attribute of an entrepreneur or a creative carving out a path as a *solopreneur*. Just be careful how you use your impatience. Especially if you have your fingers on access to too much money.

Because in the end, what really matters is that you can always be able to know that *"there's one thing for certain when it comes to my time / I'll leave this old world with a satisfied mind."*

15. RANCID: "HONOR IS ALL WE KNOW"

It's hard to know honor in failure. It's hard to exhibit honor in pain. It's hard to maintain honor when you're worried about yourself but people you care about need you. But if honor is within you, and honor is all you know, you will find a way to maintain it. No matter what.

I was estranged for a time from my friend and former business partner. He'd been ousted from the business by an investor. I had promised to not let that happen, but the reality was that I was powerless to stop it. My friend had issues from a previous business. Legal issues. He was in prison for white-collar crimes. He was on his road to correction, redemption, and reinvention. He understandably had no interest in talking with me after I failed him. Including failing to help him keep an income going to support his family while he was away.

I had my own demons to battle. My own business challenges to confront. But my *internal spirit voice* wouldn't let me ignore calls to honor.

So I refused to stop reaching out to my friend. I got creative and found multiple ways to help support him and his family. I never disregarded his anger or the alienation he felt. I instead focused on making it clear that I was there for him no matter how he felt.

Honor is all I know.

Time might not heal all wounds, but often it will heal most of them. Over time, my friend's heart softened. He eventually understood my position. We forgave each other. From that point on, our friendship has endured and been fully strengthened.

Sometimes when *"the night has come and we no longer see / Better days around the corner, for you and me,"* we need to open our hearts, access our honor, and *"receive the horizon dawn's golden glow"* and *"don't forget, but forgive every man."*

Many people think that being an entrepreneur is anathema to honor and loyalty. The bad actors of unethical capitalism have left the imprint that business is all about greed, backstabbing, and gratuitous opportunism. But that road leads to emptiness. Capitalism pursued with ethics reaps abundant rewards.

Some of the best rewards that I have received from my entrepreneurial pursuits have been intangible. They were the abiding partnerships, deep friendships, and impenetrable bonds that have been created by going hand in hand with someone into caverns of risk and seeking out nuggets of reward.

When your focus is on the things that really last—*the spiritual, the intangible, honor*—then you can get to a place where you can sing along with Rancid and see that *"prosperity's river it will forever flow / Honor is among us, honor is all we know."*

ACKNOWLEDGMENTS

TWO ROCKERS, TWO WRITERS, AND A WWII ICON

If I were to try to trace the original inspiration points that converged to convict me to write this book, they would be distilled down to two rockers, two writers, and a WWII icon. And it would be focused on one walk on a Jersey shore beach and several reading sessions over lunch in a corporate break room.

I'll start with the WWII icon—Churchill, of course. While my most raw attraction to his legacy lies in an admiration of his decisiveness and an emulation of his cigar-smoking habits, it was his famous quote on failure that stimulated the idea to begin the journey of crafting this book.

As I walked up and down the Brigantine beach in the summer of 2013, my heart and mind swirled with an angst and tumult that seemed untamable. Marital and business chaos were coming at me quickly, and I knew it was going to get a lot worse before I would ever imagine it might get better. But the longer I walked, internalized the hardcore rock 'n' roll blaring from my earbuds, and ruminated on the following words of Churchill, the more peace settled into my soul:

> Success is the ability to go from one failure to another with no loss of enthusiasm.

I had already been conditioned by failure at this point in my life. And none of it, in the end, truly fazed me. My lust for life, challenge, adventure, and growth destroyed failure's pain each time and drove me into rebirth and reinvention time and time again. The core fuel of this strength was my unbroken enthusiasm. Reflecting on Churchill's vibrant quote reminded me of my strongest attribute. It was an attribute that I not only knew would continue to carry me and allow me to keep buggering on, but it was one I felt compelled to somehow amplify to the world.

This is when the ideas that now live in this book started to form. All animated, as you learned about in the introduction, by the songs "Hard Times" and "Ace of Spades," by the Cro-Mags and Motorhead, respectively.

That night I sketched out a page or two of very loose, disjointed notes of ideas for the book. Raw ingredients, if you will. Those ingredients would take just a lil' bit of time to evolve into a proper recipe before real writing began.

That real writing probably began sometime in 2014 after I had separated from my ex-wife and left my role as a full-time self-employed entrepreneur. I was living in a one-bedroom apartment, now single. I was setting my alarm clock each day, tucking in my shirt, covering up my tattoos, and working for someone else. Life had changed. I hadn't done any of those things for a long time.

As I would take my break each day on the job, I'd put on my headphones, head to the break room, open up a book to read and pray no one would try to talk to me. I needed introspection time. I needed soul time.

This is when I became immersed in, and inspired by, the two books I referenced in the introduction—James Altucher's *Choose Yourself* and Srinivas Rao's *The Art of Being Unmistakable*.

So thank you to two rockers, two writers, and a WWII icon: John Joseph, Lemmy Kilmister, James Altucher, Srinivas Rao, and Winston Churchill.

Thank you to my kids—Violet Faith, Chloe Hope, and Griffin Thorp. Whether you read this book while you're young or wait until I've given up the ghost, I hope you gain something actionable from it. I hope that you all hold fast to the dictates of your *internal spirit voices*. I urge you to wrestle with confirming the origin of that voice until you're convinced from whence it comes. I hope you eschew unreliable adherences to false notions of safety and instead take calculated risks to fall into the waterfall of your *calling journeys*. I implore you to deliberately build a thoughtful talent stack to enable a wide *Portfolio of Pursuits*. Grow your tentacles and become octopi.

I want to thank my wife, Laura, for her astute input toward and abiding enthusiasm for the development of this manuscript. Your support of the **Failure Rules!** vision and its value has been an immense encouragement. Your ability to think critically and dispassionately when it's called for, through complicated issues, is admirable. Thank you for being an encourager of big ideas and outside-the-box ambition. Thank you for being such a loving and dedicated partner. Your demonstrable fortitude, boldness, and pursuit of meaning in your own *calling journey* is a constant inspiration. And it is a reflection of the value inherent within the themes of this book.

To my best friend Rami Dakko, keep on giving up on giving up. Delco dirt forever. Your tenacity and undying fervor for giving your all in all you do is inspiring. Stay authentic and never give in to the noise of cowardly conformity. Never let your failure humor be muzzled. Long ashes.

Thanks to Danon Robinson for some key preliminary edits and feedback on the first shareable draft.

Cheers to Rich Downes for his helpful early readership.

Big thanks to my parents for always contributing to the wind in my sails even when my life may have seemed to not make logical sense. Thank you for respecting and understanding the value and importance of my individualism from the earliest of ages. Your discernment for when to be wisely hands-off gave me the freedom to clearly hear my *internal spirit voice* at every critical pivot point of my life.

To all of my past and present business partners, collaborators, and close colleagues, I hold sincere gratitude for each of you. To Matt Carberry, Duane Miller, John Hellman, Kurt Miller, Paul Cornish, Doug Steinhauser, and Joel Richardson. With each one of you, a unique intersection has existed that is meaningful regardless of the outcomes of any of the engaged pursuits. My respect for all of you runs deep and special amid all of the complexities that may have colored our partnerships.

Thank you to all of my virtual mentors, detailed in this book, whose stories have inspired me to keep on not giving up and to make all my failures rule.

High thanks and praise to the organized, talented team at Scribe Media for all of your guidance, feedback, effort, and competency in shaping this book to be market-ready—and then engaging the market to pay attention to it. Specifically, thank you to the publishing navigation help from both Vi La Bianca and Katie Villalobos. Special thanks to Nicole Jobe for the insights and ideas offered during editing. Huge thanks also to Anna Dorfman for nailing it on the cover design.

Thanks to my man Kevin Francis, the praying mantis and rhino of Wilmington, for taking the cover photo. Took a few tries, but we got it. Also, thanks for the tremendous creative input in the filming and editing of the *Failure Rules!* companion videos to this book. Check out @andrewthorpking on YouTube to experience the themes of the book in a different way.

Thanks to Pete "Swamp Yankee" MacPhee (Social Distortion, Dropkick Murphys) for the inside front cover art. Check out his work here: swampyankee.weebly.com

Thanks to Duke Cannon men's grooming products for keeping me smelling and feeling alternately like productivity, accomplishment, naval supremacy, and bourbon—all necessary forces for overcoming failure in the world.

Crucial thanks to each of the vices within my critical trinity of vices: *alcohol, nicotine, and caffeine.*

Many words herein found their form under the influence of *Woodford Reserve, Knob Creek, Maker's Mark, Bulleit, and Willett*, along with many other bourbons. All have helped me summon the muse.

Thanks also to *My Father, Padron, Partagas, San Lotano, and CAO* cigar companies for producing many fine sticks that accented the writing of this book with fragrant, aromatic, premium cigar smoke.

And credit to Death Wish Coffee Co. and Marley Coffee Co. for providing the perfect aggressive elixirs to drive my morning writing sessions.

Most sincere thanks to you, the reader, for taking a gamble on your time to test whether this book might bring you value. I hope these stories somehow empowered you, breathed fire into your own developing story in real time, and strengthened you to now smile maniacally each time life punches you in the face.

Lastly, high thanks to God and the mysterious impartation of creativity, perseverance, and reinvention that emanates from His spirit.

ABOUT THE AUTHOR

ANDREW THORP KING is an executive fintech banker, spy novelist, speaker, punk rocker, podcaster, ex-bodybuilder, cigar lover, and serial entrepreneur. He founded two independent record labels—Thorp Records and Sailor's Grave Records—and has invested in many spaces, including online lending, fitness, lead generation, and independent music.

Andrew Thorp King is also a serial failure. He has crashed and burned through bankruptcy, divorce, mortgage default, public assistance, and multiple business failures. But, like a jack-in-the-box after a punch, he pops back up every time, rebuilding his life—informed by failure—with a big smile on his face.

CONTINUE YOUR FAILURE RULES! JOURNEY

EMAIL

info@andrewthorpking.com

URLS

www.andrewthorpking.com
www.failurerules.com
www.soulonfiresupplyco.com

SOCIALS

YouTube: @andrewthorpking
Instagram: @andrewthorpking
LinkedIn: www.linkedin.com/in/andrewthorpking

AT SOUL ON FIRE SUPPLY CO., WE BELIEVE YOU NEED TO LIVE YOUR LIFE *HOT*...OR ELSE LIFE WILL SPIT YOU OUT LIKE LUKEWARM MILK.

Merch for the lonely artist. The underdog athlete. The genre-bending musician. The overlooked entrepreneur. The canceled comedian. The corporate misfit. The rejected writer. The politically homeless. The spiritually independent. The blue-collar outlaw. The college dropout with a different idea. The recovered addict whose hope is powered by pain. And the serial failure who always gives up on giving up.

Always be on fire.
Because a *soul on fire* is a *soul alive*.

SOULONFIRESUPPLYCO.COM

andrewthorpking.com

More designs and styles available at
SOULONFIRESUPPLYCO.COM

ALSO BY ANDREW THORP KING

When America's unsung, Mick-hero, Blaze McIntyre—retired CIA assassin and spy—becomes fatigued with the monotony of civilian life and decides to re-enter the world of espionage, he finds himself engaged in a mission he senses could be entangled in the vines of a twenty-five-hundred-year-old prophecy (War of Gog and Magog).

In Russia, a new czar rises that seeks to resurrect the Soviet Empire. In Iran, a new president emerges whose brutality and cultish apocalyptic obsession with the return of the Islamic messiah, the Twelfth Imam, dwarfs that of his predecessor. As Russia and Iran work together to galvanize the Middle East, North Africa, and Central Asia, a new threat is produced that terrifies the Western World, particularly Israel and the United States.

The global economy has spiraled to new lows with an increasing complexity unforeseen by any of the experts. World leaders are seeking transnational solutions, while they simultaneously swallow up private industry without hesitation, in their effort to harmonize the world and consolidate power and control.

As the United States struggles to find its new position in the world, the last hope of a weak U.S. President is found in a handful of operatives led by an obstinate, cigar-smoking, tattooed Irish-American warrior: Blaze McIntyre.

Under the counsel of his spiritual advisor, an Irish preacher with a drinking problem, Blaze struggles with warnings of a prophesied war as he springs forward into one of the most consequential operations of his career. Driven by his inner demons, natural propensity toward aggression, and obsessive love of country, Blaze eagerly accepts his part in a three-pronged mission to decapitate the source of the looming nuclear threats overseas.

Recommended for fans of: Brad Thor, Daniel Silva, Jack Carr, and Dan Brown

AVAILABLE NOW AT AMAZON.COM